10/94

Issues in Psychobiology

Issues in Psychobiology

Charles R. Legg

ROUTLEDGE
London and New York

First published in 1989 by Routledge
11 New Fetter Lane, London EC4P 4EE
29 West 35th Street, New York, NY 10001

©1989 Charles R. Legg

Typeset by LaserScript Limited, Mitcham, Surrey
Printed and bound in Great Britain by
Mackays of Chatham PLC, Chatham, Kent

All rights reserved. No part of this book may be reprinted or reproduced or utilized in any form or by any electronic, mechanical, or other means, now known or hereafter invented, including photocopying and recording, or in any information storage or retrieval system, without permission in writing from the publishers.

British Library Cataloguing in Publication Data

Legg, C.R. (Charles Robert), *1949–*
  Issues in psychobiology
  1. Psychobiology
  I. Title
  156'2

Library of Congress Cataloging in Publication Data

Legg, C.R. (Charles R.), *1949–*
  Issues in psychobiology.
  Bibliography: p.
  Includes index.
  1. Psychobiology. I. Title. [DNLM: 1. Neurobiology. 2. Psychophysiology. WL 103 L513i]
QP360.L44 1989 152   88–32505

ISBN 0-415-01405-0
ISBN 0-415-01406-9 (Pbk)

To Margaret

Contents

List of figures and tables   viii

1 Introduction   1
2 Animal subjects in psychobiology   22
3 Methods in psychobiology   34
4 Perception   57
5 Motivation   82
6 Emotion   105
7 Memory   126
8 Plasticity   148
9 Consciousness   170
10 Concluding remarks   189

References   203
Index   216

Figures and tables

Figures

2.1 A simplified phylogenetic tree showing the relationships between the major mammalian groups	25
3.1 An example of a decision tree to be used to design behavioural experiments	39
3.2 A simple associative network	45
3.3 Training an associative network	46
4.1 An idealized Difference of Gaussians (DOG) function	61
4.2 An edge detector circuit	62
4.3 Idealized representation of the responses of X- and Y-cells to periodic stimuli	69
4.4 The aperture effect	72
5.1 Time-sharing behaviour	96
6.1 A radial arm maze	115
8.1 Distribution of ocular dominance in the normal cat	151
8.2 The relationship between the visual field of the two eyes and the lateral geniculate body	153
9.1 Samples of EEG characteristics of the five types of sleep	179

Tables

3.1 The double dissociation paradigm	44
4.1 Some of the main distinguishing characteristics of X-, Y-, and W-type ganglion cells in the cat retina	67

1
Introduction

In *The Hitch-hiker's Guide to the Galaxy* the author, Douglas Adams, describes a planet inhabited by a race of hyperintelligent pan-dimensional beings who build a hyperintelligent computer to help them come up with the answer to Life, the Universe and Everything. After many millions of years of deliberation this machine finally delivers its verdict: the answer is forty-two. Naturally the heirs to the computer-builders are somewhat disappointed about this. After all, one expects better value for money for one's computer time. In its defence the computer points out that the problem lies not in its answer but in the question it was asked in the first place. In order to understand the answer they first have to understand what the question really means, and that, they are told, will require an even more powerful computer! All of which is a roundabout way of saying that what matters in this world is asking the right questions, rather than knowing the right answers. It is in this spirit that this book is intended to add to your education in psychobiology. It is a book that focuses on the questions that psychobiologists ask, rather than on the answers that they give to them. It is concerned with telling you as much about what we don't yet know as about what we do know.

Psychobiology, the study of the biological bases of behaviour, is a broad area covering everything from the evolution of mating systems in the toad to the functions of subregions of the human cerebral cortex. In a book of this length it isn't possible to cover everything, so let me declare my hand right away: what interests me most is the brain. Specifically, what fascinates me is how the operations of the billions of nerve cells that cohabit inside our skulls to form our brains are capable of giving rise to our actions and our conscious experience. This problem, so easy to state, is undoubtedly the greatest scientific challenge of our time, which probably explains why some of our most able scientists are turning their attention to it. Psychobiology is particularly exciting at the moment because advances in instrumentation are bringing us new ways of studying the brain while areas like artificial intelligence are providing new ways of thinking about how it might work as the 'organ of behaviour'.

Introduction

One of the frustrations of learning about psychology and psychobiology is that the practitioners frequently behave in what appear to outsiders as totally illogical ways. This usually takes the form of obsessively pursuing the minutiae of experimental phenomena and theories that leave a subsequent generation cold. Someone reading the latest work on the control of food intake, for example, might be puzzled at the amount of effort that went into understanding the effects of hypothalamic lesions on eating and at the theories that were erected around those experiments. To appreciate why certain questions are currently preoccupying psychobiologists, why they favour the particular answers that are in vogue, and why they seem to have neglected, until recently, many of the issues that non-psychologists would consider central to under-standing the biological bases of behaviour, a short lesson on the history of psychobiology is relevant.

The history of psychobiology

Contemporary psychobiology is a blend of two traditions of research and theory. One starts from the question of mind and behaviour and asks: 'How is it possible for a physical system, the brain, to produce this?' In other words, the focus is on psychological issues. The other starts from the brain and asks: 'What does this organ do?' In other words, the focus is on neurological issues. For many years these traditions operated independently of each other but recently they have converged to give the field a much more integrated look.

The psychological tradition

Psychobiology literally means the 'biology of mind'. As such its history can be caricatured as having had three stages. In the first the academic community denied the possibility of a biological basis of mind at all, in the second it denied the existence of mind and in the third, into which we have now entered, we are coming to accept both the existence and physical basis of the mind. These changing attitudes in part reflect changes in attitudes in the world at large but they also stem from the evolution of our concepts of 'mind' and its possible physical bases. For example, the increasing secularization of the western world means that there is less pressure to accept dogma, based on prescientific thinking, about the status of the mind. The development of electronic devices like digital computers that can have mind-like properties means that a physical basis of mind is much less improbable to us.

All scientists work through analogies with other systems that they already understand. The problem for would-be physiological psychologists is that until relatively recently there have been no other natural phenomena or man-made devices that we understand better than human behaviour that could act as a model or analogy. Indeed, for most of human history we have tended to do the reverse, to use the analogy of the human mind to explain what happens in the physical world, an approach known as 'animism'. By the seventeenth century, however, engineers had become sufficiently skilled at making complex mechanical devices, powered by clockwork or water, to be able to make toys that moved in a fairly convincing approximation to the way that people and animals move. Some were constructed so that they would only move when a passing person activated a treadle of some sort so that the toy would suddenly spring into 'life'. The French mathematician Descartes remarked on the similarity between this sort of toy and the behaviour of animals, arguing that the latter were nothing more than automatons whose reactions were constantly triggered by events in the environment (Jeannerod 1985). Not knowing about electricity, but knowing about hydraulic systems, Descartes suggested that the control of these reactions in animals was mediated by movements of fluids, initiated in the sensory nerves by stimuli, being carried to the ventricular system of the brain where contact was made with the motor nerves. The movement of fluid in the motor nerve then caused the actual movement. Since there is a large number of nerves the number of possible combinations and sequences of stimuli is enormous so it is possible for a system like that, in principle, to produce a very large number of possible reactions. Descartes was reluctant to extend this model to human behaviour. In part this reflected religious scruples since mechanical explanations for our behaviour were incompatible with religious teaching. It also reflected philosophical scruples since it wasn't obvious how a mechanical device could be conscious and, as Descartes is famous for pointing out, the only thing of which we can be certain is that we are conscious.

Although Descartes was wrong to use a hydraulic analogy, his idea that animals come pre-equipped with a range of motor responses to sensory input, reflexes, proved correct. In the nineteenth and early twentieth centuries reflexes were studied with enthusiasm. This work demonstrated two things. The first is that reflexes are largely mediated by the lower parts of the brain, and the second is that they are less rigid than one might think. Both points can be illustrated by studies on frogs. If the brain is removed from a frog but its spinal cord left intact it will still display reflexes including defensive reactions. One of these involves using the hind leg to scratch an area of skin to which an irritant has been applied. Furthermore, if the animal is prevented from using one leg, it will scratch with the other. Thus a sophisticated reflex is mediated by the spinal cord and the 'reflex' appears to be goal-directed.

If sophisticated reflexes can be mediated by the spinal cord, what is the purpose of the brain? William James (1950) argued that it was there to elaborate on reflexes, a position largely adopted by the behaviourist school of the early to middle twentieth century. A Cartesian reflex model holds that behaviour will be constant in a constant environment or, if not constant, it will not change in a predictable way. Thorndike (1913) and Pavlov (1927) showed that that is not so. The behaviour of man and other animals does change lawfully, under the impact of reinforcement contingencies. It therefore seems reasonable to suppose that the function of the brain is to mediate these more flexible links between stimuli and responses.

Stimulus-response (S-R) psychology has largely gone out of fashion now, yet in its day it carried the field, and even now its influence is still felt. For example, when describing experiments psychologists still refer to the subjects' 'response' to the 'stimulus' materials. Neurobiologists too work within this framework. For example, workers like Kandel and his colleagues (Hawkins and Kandel 1984), who are interested in the cellular bases of memory, are actively studying 'associative' learning tasks like classical conditioning in the belief that this represents a fundamental mammalian learning process. The attraction of S-R psychology, in its most radical form, lies in two things. The first is its simplicity; it reduces the whole of psychology to the study of learning. The second is that it unites psychology and biology since, in the early formulations, 'responses' were contractions of muscle groups, stimuli were physical events occurring at sensory receptors, and 'learning' was a real event occurring in the brain. This then set the agenda for how we study the brain; we treat it as a large reflex arc and trace the circuit from the stimulus 'analysers' to the motor system. This attitude is especially apparent in Pavlov's writings. Indeed, Pavlov believed that the study of classical conditioning was the only way to study the functions of the cerebral cortex.

S-R psychology didn't have things all its own way. Even in its heyday it was challenged by the Gestalt school (Koffka 1935), mainly working in Germany, who pointed out that there were real perceptual phenomena that were quite incompatible with the more radical versions of S-R theory. What the psychologists showed was that stimulus elements in groups had properties not present in the individual elements. Moreover, those properties are often distortions of the true appearance of objects. That is to say, lines which are physically straight will appear bent, lines that are the same length will appear different, exposure to one stimulus will alter the appearance of one presented subsequently, and lines and edges that are not physically present will be seen by the subject. The consistency of these distortions and the immediacy with which they occur convinced the Gestalt psychologists that they were dealing with a fundamental property of the brain rather than something that we have learned. Using an analogy fashionable at the time the Gestalt psychologists maintained that these distortions were due to interactions between 'electric' fields induced in the visual cortex by the stimuli. As was the case with Descartes's hydraulic model, the electric field model has not been substantiated by more recent studies of the brain. Nevertheless, the insight that the neural representations of stimulus elements interact with each other in the brain to distort our perception of the world has been validated again and again by sensory physiologists. Clearly the brain is more than a passive relay from stimulus to response.

Gestalt psychology is really only a minor nuisance to S-R psychology. The real problems came from studies by people like Tolman (1932), Crespi (1942), and Lashley (1963), who showed that behavioural change can come about too rapidly for incremental learning to explain it and that what animals learn is not a set of reflexes but the location of desirable objects and events. During the 1930s the most commonly used piece of laboratory apparatus was the maze, often modelled on the one at Hampton Court. Rats were trained to negotiate these mazes to obtain food. It was assumed that the food reinforcement in some way strengthened the response tendencies that led to the food, at the expense of other response tendencies. Tolman showed that rats would learn to negotiate mazes without experiencing reinforcement at the goal-box, although the introduction of reinforcement was necessary to persuade them to display their knowledge. Learning of this sort was termed 'latent-learning'. Crespi showed some surprising effects when you alter the amount of reinforcement a rat is given to run down an alley way. If you increase the amount of reward the rats run faster than rats that have always received the large reward and if you decrease it the reverse happens; the rats run more slowly than those that have always had the small reward. Furthermore, the change in speed occurs within a couple of trials of changing the magnitude of reward, which is too fast for conventional learning mechanisms. Lashley, for his part, showed that surgical damage to parts of the brains of rats could alter the types of movements they would make to negotiate a maze without disrupting their ability to reach the goal. In some of his experiments the rats were rolling along to get to the food in the goal-box. Experiments like these provide a fairly conclusive demonstration that, even in simple learning tasks, animals are learning about the nature and location of biologically important events like food. Their behaviour is a very flexible result of the interaction between that knowledge and their needs, such as their need for food. They are not forming stimulus-response associations.

During his long and distinguished career Lashley (1950, 1951), in fact, carried out a fairly effective hatchet job on S-R psychology. In addition to demonstrating the ease with which rats substitute one movement for another in reaching their goal he also demonstrated that cutting the nerve fibres that join the visual to the motor cortex does not interfere with associative learning, as Pavlov had predicted it would. He presented a detailed theoretical analysis of skilled movement, showing that the sequencing of actions, the serial order of behaviour, could not be due to feedback stimuli from one movement triggering the next, as S-R theory argued, but had to be due to central programming of the sequence.

Unfortunately, Lashley's achievements were largely negative. Along with people like Tolman and Crespi he showed the inadequacy of the S-R model without really replacing it with anything of use to the psychobiologist. As a consequence, psychobiologists turned away from these sorts of issues and concentrated on supposedly simpler problems like emotion and motivation.

Even while the behaviourist debate had been raging, people had been studying emotion. Indeed, as William James implied in 1884, emotion is a serious challenge to reflex models of behaviour because it implies experience without action. James's solution to this problem was simplicity itself. He redefined emotions as sets of bodily reactions which could, in turn, effectively act as stimuli to control further behaviour. In other words, emotions are the product of behaviour. Even if it isn't true, James's position was an excellent stimulus for research as it forced people who would adopt an alternative position to consider very carefully how else emotions might come about. Cannon and his co-workers launched a fierce attack on James. More accurately, they launched an attack on the idea that activity in the autonomic nervous system was a sufficient condition for emotional experience. The attack was based on a number of strands of evidence, including the fact that activation of the sympathetic branch of the autonomic nervous system was too diffuse to underpin the range of subtle emotional experiences of which we are capable, and the observation that severing the spinal cord in dogs does not prevent them displaying facial signs of emotion when provoked in an appropriate way. As an alternative, Cannon proposed a centralist theory in which emotion was seen as the result of activating specific mechanisms in the central nervous system. However, his evidence didn't permit particularly precise localization within the brain. It wasn't until Papez (1939) published his theory of emotion that the field really moved again.

Papez set the agenda for how emotion would be studied for half a century. This is remarkable, given how little evidence he really had for his theory and how much of the evidence he had was wrong! The basis of his argument is that emotional experience and emotional behaviour involve separate, although interlinked, parts of the brain. As Cannon and his colleagues had already shown, animals lacking cerebral cortex could still display emotional behaviour. Indeed, their emotional behaviour was often exaggerated. Papez therefore located the emotional behaviour mechanisms in the brainstem, especially in the mammillary bodies which, he believed, received sensory information via subcortical relay routes, and cognitive information from the cerebral cortex via the hippocampus and its subcortical projection system, the fornix. Emotional experience, on the other hand, he thought was the result of activating specific areas of the cerebral cortex in much the same way as activating other areas produced visual or auditory experience. On the basis of some remarkably weak clinical evidence he decided that the site of emotional experience was the cingulate gyrus, which lies on the medial surface of the hemispheres. All of the areas that Papez implicated in emotion are part of an anatomically identified system known as the limbic system. Many people, therefore, encoded his conclusion to be that the limbic system was the seat of emotion. As we shall see in a later chapter, the issues raised by Papez have yet to be resolved. There are still those who believe that the limbic system is the source of emotional experience, while others have implicated parts of the circuit in spatial ability (McNaughton and Morris 1987) or memory (Olton 1983).

The major developments in psychobiology to take place in the 1940s and 1950s concerned motivation. Motivation is inextricably linked with most S-R theories, explaining both why learning takes place and why animals engage in behaviour. Thorndike explained learning in terms of the action of reinforcement. Positive reinforcement was seen as being due to the presentation of 'satisfiers' but that is, of course, completely circular without being able to predict in advance what will satisfy an animal. This problem was largely solved by explaining reinforcement in terms of drive reduction, since drives could be readily manipulated by depriving animals of food or water and then using these items as reinforcement.

'Drive' was also called upon to explain variations in behaviour that could not be explained in terms of learning; but what is drive? Following on from Cannon (1947) most psychologists assumed that drive was simply bodily discomfort brought about by the deprivation state and that drive reduction was due to eliminating this discomfort. Again, this is brilliantly simple and probably wrong. It is wrong because you can eliminate all of the possible sensory mechanisms that might detect the tissue disturbance produced by a particular form of deprivation and motivation still persists. For example, cutting the nerve supply to the genitals does not interfere with sexual motivation in the short term; cutting the nerves to the stomach does not interfere with hunger. This led Morgan (1943) to argue that drive must be due to activating a central nervous system mechanism that represents the drive state, much in the same way as Papez was claiming that activation of the cingulate cortex represented emotion. Morgan did not know where to locate the source of this 'central motive state' in the nervous system. It was Stellar (1954) who put the finger on the hypothalamus as the seat of motivation, basing his arguments on a number of lesion studies that had shown quite specific disturbances of motivation after lesions in this region. It is a testimony to Stellar's insight that, even now, no discussion of the neural bases of motivation is complete without a discussion of the hypothalamus.

The 1950s were a watershed for mainstream psychology. They were the era when psychologists rediscovered mind, or, to be more accurate, mental processes like attention and memory. This was hardly accidental. In part it came about as a reaction to the inordinate complexity of S-R theory but, I believe, it had much more to do with S-R theory's failure to cope with real psychological problems like the performance of radar operators, and with the availability of machines, computers, with mind-like properties that made it respectable to think in mentalistic terms again. The rediscovery of mind had relatively little impact on the psychobiology of the time. If one looks back at the text-books and review papers written about psychobiology during this period one finds that they were largely preoccupied with topics like motivation and emotion. Some workers, like Hernandez-Peon (Hernandez-Peon, Scherrer, and Velasco 1956), began to explore the neural bases of attention, but their approach was tightly linked to the topic of motivation and emotion through the prevailing arousal theory that was gripping people at the time. It is true that a number of books were written that attempted to draw parallels between brains and computers but these largely served to remind us how different they really are. In fact it was largely people working outside the framework of experimental psychology who kept alive research into the physical bases of mental processes. It is to these people, who worked in the neurological tradition, we turn next.

The neurological tradition

Although our commonsense view of the world now tells us that the brain is the seat of mind and action, the idea is remarkably new. Even up to the end of the eighteenth century it was widely held that mind resided in the spaces within the brain, the ventricles, rather than in the neural tissue itself. To be fair to the scientists of the time the brain, as it appears when freshly removed from the skull, is hardly an appealing or inspiring sight! It looks like a sagging, browny-grey jelly that fairly rapidly decays into an unpleasant mush. Only when it is exposed to chemicals that harden the tissue and inhibit decay, a method known as fixation, is the brain easily studied and only then will it reveal the complexities of its organization. By the end of the eighteenth century a number of facts about the brain had emerged. The brain contained two sorts of tissue, grey and white matter. The outer mantle, the cerebral cortex, was folded into a pattern of sulci and gyri that was remarkably consistent from brain to brain and, within the cerebral cortex, some parts were anatomically distinct from others. This last point raised the interesting possibility that not only is the brain the seat of the mind but also, different parts of the brain might be involved in different aspects of mind. Nevertheless, none of the data really substantiated the imaginative *tour de force* of Gall and Spurzheim (in Kolb and Whishaw 1985) who, at the turn of the nineteenth century, argued that the human cerebral cortex is subdivided into functional areas, each responsible for a different mental faculty. Although the details of their theory are now seen to be clearly wrong, their insight, that different parts of the brain are responsible for different processes, has stood the test of time and research and informs much of our current understanding of the brain. The century and a half of research that followed was largely fixated on testing out this hypothesis of 'localization of function'.

In truth, Gall and Spurzheim's theory of localization was ahead of its time because there were no suitable methods available for testing it, although test it people did. For a start there were no agreed criteria for subdividing the cerebral cortex into regions, and criteria were not destined to be developed for about another century. Furthermore, there were no psychologists around to devise tests of mental faculties. Advocates of localization were in the same position as the explorers of the sixteenth century; they knew there was something out there but they didn't know where it was or what it might look like. Neurologists in the nineteenth century studied the effects of surgical removal of, or accidental damage to, the cerebral cortex in man and other animals without knowing the boundaries of the functional units they were proposing or their likely functions. Under the circumstances it is astounding that people managed to reach agreement so quickly.

While some of the clearest evidence for localization of function came from neurological studies on humans with damaged or disturbed brains, some of the best evidence against it came from experimental studies on animals. Broca (1961, in Kolb and Whishaw 1985) had reported that a series of patients with severe disturbances of speech had all suffered damage to the inferior part of the third frontal convolutions of their left hemispheres and Jackson (in Kolb and Whishaw 1985) had described cases of '*petit mal*' epilepsy which involved only a limited number of 'faculties'. On the other hand, Flourens (in Phillips, Zeki, and Barlow 1984) removed various parts of the forebrains of birds and found that the degree of disturbance of behaviour was very much more a function of how much brain was removed than which part was eliminated. Even in 1881 Goltz (in Phillips *et al.* 1984) was claiming that motor function invariably recovered from damage to the cerebral cortex.

It was not until the 1880s that there were consistent experimental findings to support localization. By then Fritz and Hitzig (in Phillips *et al.* 1984) had demonstrated the existence of 'electrically excitable motor cortex' in dogs and monkeys and Ferrier (in Phillips *et al.* 1984) had shown that a sufficiently extensive ablation of the appropriate areas of the cortex would produce complete and abiding paralysis in experimental animals. By the time of Fritz and Hitzig's work it had been known for nearly a century that electrical stimulation of nervous tissue would produce movements. The importance of Fritz and Hitzig's work lay in their demonstration that with brief, low-intensity electrical stimulation it was only possible to evoke movement from a restricted area of the cerebral cortex, hence the name 'electrically excitable motor cortex'. Ferrier showed that if the whole of this region was removed, then paralysis ensued, whereas sparing any of this region allowed the recovery of motor function. In a highly dramatic demonstration during a meeting on localization function held in London in 1881 Ferrier demonstrated that the recovery of movement described by Goltz in his studies was due to sparing part of this motor cortex.

Introduction

By the turn of the century it was accepted that certain parts of the brain were specialized for either sensation or movement but, as Brodmann (in Kolb and Whishaw 1985) demonstrated, there are large areas of the human cerebral cortex that are neither obviously motor nor sensory. Moreover, these 'association' regions consisted of a number of distinctive regions that could be identified on the basis of their internal cellular organization. By this time, clinical neurologists had begun to catalogue the effects of damage to association cortex, describing deficits in speech comprehension, object recognition, and spatial orientation, depending on which part of the brain turned out to be damaged.

Experimental studies on animals tended to lag behind the neurologists' at this time and for many years to come. In fact, it could be argued that the only significant finding on association cortex, made using non-human animals up to 1950, was the memory impairment in monkeys lacking frontal cortex described by Jacobson (in Gross and Weiskrantz 1964).

This is not totally surprising. Using animals in experiments requires us to make inferences about psychological processes from behaviour. This is virtually impossible from the day-to-day behaviour of animals in the laboratory, and the theoretical preoccupations of most psychologists distracted most of them from thinking about devising the sorts of formal test procedures we now use. Those, like Lashley, who were developing specialized test procedures for use with animals were either using them to explore general psychological capacities like 'intelligence' or were testing predictions from learning theories. It is only in the last thirty-five years that animals had been allowed to have 'mental' processes other than learning and so it is only in that time that psychologists have developed the behavioural tests to investigate them. Studies like those described by Dean (1982), in which he attempted to distinguish between deficits in visual memory and visual object categorization following damage to part of the visual association cortex in rhesus monkeys, would have been unthinkable forty years ago.

Neurologists expressed interest in the psychological consequences of brain damage long before psychologists got involved in this field. Indeed, clinical neurology predates the emergence of psychology as an independent discipline. They looked at psychological processes simply because they were the only way of monitoring what the brain might be doing. The deepening understanding of how brain cells work, that developed during the late nineteenth and early twentieth centuries, changed the situation dramatically. One significant development was the emergence of the neuron theory that held that the brain was composed of discrete cellular elements, the neurons, that were physically separated from each other by gaps called synapses. This opened the issue of how nerve cells might communicate with each other and eventually led to our now-sophisticated understanding of neurotransmitters.

A second crucial development was the discovery that nerve cells are spontaneously electrically active. Although electrical excitability in the nervous system had been demonstrated before the beginning of the nineteenth century, it was not until the late nineteenth century that it was shown that the brain was spontaneously electrically active (Jeannerod 1985), and it was only in the 1930s, after the invention of the valve amplifier, that it was possible to make meaningful records of this activity. Even then, these records were either the sum of the activity of many millions of nerve cells, as registered in the electroencephalogram (EEG), or the action potentials of single peripheral nerves. Recording the electrical activity of single brain cells in mammals only became a viable proposition in the 1950s. Many of the other facts of life that we now take for granted in psychobiology, like the identity of neurotransmitter substances, the actual structure of the synapse, and the availability of reliable methods for tracing connections in the central nervous system have a similar short history. Seen from this point of view, what is remarkable about neurobiology is how much we know about the brain, not, as you might think, how little.

The lessons of history?

People have been studying the behavioural functions of the brain for something less than two centuries and, for much of that time, their efforts have been hampered by a combination of inevitable ignorance and adherence to implausible psychological theories. The fact that any progress has been made is remarkable. What progress we have enjoyed has come about either as a result of skilled, painstaking experimental work or inspired guesses about how the brain works. Into the first category we can place the work of Ferrier and Fritz and Hitzig, who showed that previous ambiguous results in studies of experimental brain damage in animals were due to inadequately sized and placed lesions. Into the second category we can place Papez's theory of emotion.

A number of historical accidents have shaped contemporary psychobiology. Psychology's obsession with behaviourism owes far more to the fashion for logical positivism emerging from physicists in the 1930s than to any understanding of the needs of psychology. According to the logical positivists, the only permissible scientific concepts are those that can be tied directly to measurement. Anything that cannot be measured does not exist. Since the only things that psychologists can measure are stimuli and responses, these are the only things they can include in their theories. Undoubtedly behaviourism diverted people from thinking about fundamental issues, like the design of a brain that is capable of generating actions rather than reactions. It also gave us the belief, probably misguided, that there are two fundamental learning processes: classical and instrumental conditioning. The widespread belief that the limbic system is the substrate of emotion is also the result of an accident, in that Papez's theory of emotion was not justified by the evidence available at the time and there are other, equally acceptable, interpretations of the effects of limbic system damage. Historical accident is inevitable in science. It doesn't mean that the science is poor, but it does mean that we need to be sceptical of the assumptions that we receive. Often the most exciting work has come about precisely because those assumptions have been rejected.

Considerable progress has been made but a number of fundamental issues are still with us. For example, we are still concerned about localization of function and questions about the neural bases of consciousness are again being asked. Our measure of progress is that the way that we ask these questions has changed. No-one seriously questions that different parts of the cerebral cortex are specialized to carry out specific functions. They do question the likely degree of functional independence of these areas, given the amount of 'vertical integration' of cortical areas being demonstrated in recent anatomical studies. They also question the relationship between the processes occurring in discrete areas of the brain and the psychological processes that are the end-product of neural activity in the brain as a whole. Consciousness has, once again, been put on the agenda but the concept of 'consciousness' has been altered to fit in with ideas coming from fields like machine intelligence. It is no longer something mystical but is seen by some as an internal commentary on our own behaviour (Gazzaniga 1985).

The general issues

Many of the issues in psychobiology are specific to the topics concerned. Problems encountered in the study of perceptual mechanisms, for example, are distinct from those affecting the study of motivation. Nevertheless, there is a thread of general issues that runs through this book. They are: (1) the relationship between psychology and biology and the possibility of dispensing with psychology altogether once physiology has been developed sufficiently; (2) the value of studies on non-human species; (3) the degree of functional specialization in the sub-areas of the brain and the ways of analysing and describing those functions; (4) the way we are responding to the challenges of cognitive psychology; and (5) the importance of being able to explain what happens in the real world, rather than just the laboratory.

The relationship between psychology and biology

Psychologists often divide up their subject into 'hard' and 'soft' areas. Hard topics are supposed to have a large number of facts and a small amount of theory while soft topics have a large amount of theory and few facts. To many psychologists psychobiology is the epitome of a hard area, a reputation based on the belief that the psychology is underwritten by a solid body of biological fact. In reality biological knowledge is often no more secure than psychological knowledge but psychologists often feel a sense of inferiority in the face of biological data. This is exacerbated by the fact that there are some extremists who would argue that psychology is nothing but a crude way of approaching brain function that has been superseded by advances in physiological technique. On the other hand, there are others who take the opposing position, that biological evidence is irrelevant to understanding psychological processes. Neither view is tenable. A complete description of the workings of the brain must include a statement of its behavioural functions, and this is impossible without a proper idea of what those behavioural functions are. On the other hand, while it is true that it is rarely useful to explain behaviour in terms of neural events, our description of psychological processes must at least be compatible with what is known of their neural substrate.

Let me illustrate this point by introducing some recent work on the topic of visual perception. There is a long and distinguished history of studying the visual system using 'psychophysical' procedures in which variations in subjective visual experience with variations in visual input are studied. Perhaps the greatest achievement of this approach was the prediction by Young and by Helmholtz (in Mollon 1982), in the nineteenth century, of the existence of three classes of colour-sensitive receptor in the retina, each sensitive to a different wavelength of light, a prediction only confirmed by direct measurement in the last thirty years (Mollon 1982). You might think that Young and Helmholtz were wasting their time using psychophysical procedures when improvements in physiological techniques would allow direct measurements of this sort. To the extent that psychophysical measurements are indirect this appears to be a valid criticism but it does, in fact, ignore an important point about the psychophysical approach. The point is that the psychophysical approach forces you to develop a model of how the system, in this instance the mechanisms of colour discrimination, might work and it is this model that is used to guide the direct physiological measurements. In many ways the achievement of Young and Helmholtz was that they showed, in principle, that colour vision would be possible with only three receptors, providing those receptors were most sensitive to the right colours. The model told people what to look for both when doing psychophysical studies and when carrying out the direct measurements of receptor function all those years later.

The impact of psychological theory on physiological research is apparent in studies of the visual system using the single cell recording technique. Individual brain cells are electrically active, producing the characteristic impulses known as 'action potentials' which can be detected by fine probes placed near to the nerve cells or their axons. Cells in sensory pathways usually increase or decrease the rate at which they produce action potentials as a function of the type of stimuli presented. Many physiologists believe that an exhaustive study of the types of stimuli that increase or decrease the discharge rates of different types of sensory system cell will provide us with a description of how that system works. There are just two problems with this programme. The first is a simple logical point that without some model of how the system might work, there is no way of deciding which of the millions of possible stimuli available to use in testing a particular cell. The second is a historical observation, that during the thirty years or so since the first observations of single cell response properties in the visual systems of mammals, our understanding of how the visual system works has been driven as much by theoretical developments in the psychology of perception as the other way round.

For much of the 1950s physiologists probed the visual cortex using the single cell recording technique. At the time it was widely held that the early parts of the visual system acted like a closed-circuit television, with the eye acting as the camera and the visual cortex acting as the TV monitor. Activity in the visual cortex would, therefore, be a point-by-point replica of what happened at the retina, with cells at all points registering the intensity of the image at that location. A pessimistic interpretation of the findings based on this approach was that the visual cortex had nothing to do with vision, since few, if any, cells in that part of the brain showed any interest in spots of light they were presenting them with. In 1959 Hubel and Wiesel demonstrated the reason for their failure. Cells in the visual cortex responded very reliably to visual stimuli, providing they were bars or edges and providing they were properly oriented. By solving a physiological conundrum Hubel and Wiesel immediately created a psychological puzzle: how is visual perception possible in a system that only relays information about the location and orientation of edges? The psychological theory of 'feature detection' filled the gap, providing a context for interpreting these challenging findings on the visual cortex. According to this model we recognize objects by comparing a list of basic elements of the visual image, like lines, edges, and angles, with a list, stored in memory, of the attributes associated with a particular object. Thus the upper-case letter 'A' can be identified by the presence of two tilted uprights, an acute angle at the top, a horizontal bar, and two 'T' junctions between the uprights and the bar. One of the significant properties of this sort of model is that 'features' are very much an all-or-none attribute. Either they are there or they are not. This sort of theoretical framework encouraged people to study the responses of cells in the visual cortex by looking for 'trigger-features', using single stimulus elements and classifying their responses into 'present' or 'absent'.

Feature analysis is an attractively simple way of explaining visual perception but, it turns out, 'features' are much more complex than we first thought. In fact a 'feature' is an interpretation of part of the retinal image rather than an entity with its own physical reality. Recognition of the problems inherent in identifying features led to new ways of thinking about vision and to new ways of analysing the ways cells in the visual cortex respond to visual events. One such development was 'spatial frequency analysis', which is a complex mathematical way of representing visual images without reference to features. This approach led to a new series of studies in which visual cells were studied quantitatively using 'grating' stimuli instead of bars and edges. A grating is a set of light and dark stripes, usually of equal width. Gratings can differ both in terms of how many stripes there are to the centimetre and the differences between the brightness of the light and dark parts. Studies using these stimuli demonstrated further properties of visual system cells that had not been previously identified (Enroth-Cugell and Robson 1966).

In short, how we think about the way in which psychological processes, like visual perception, are carried out determines how we study the visual parts of the brain. Analysis of psychological processes is not a second rate substitute for studying the brain directly but a necessary adjunct to guiding our explorations of that organ. It is possible for outstanding physiologists to describe properties of the brain without reference to psychological theories, of course, but it is surprising how far the acceptance of physiological results depends on the availability of a psychological context in which to place them.

Animal models of man

Psychobiology is based largely on studies of behavioural and physiological processes in non-human animals. Most people study psychology because they want to understand human behaviour and question the relevance of work on animals to their overall goal. The time when scruples about extrapolating from studies on animals to humans would have seemed absurd, because it was widely held that basic behavioural processes were common to all species and that the complexity of behaviour was simply a function of the capacity of the organism to learn, is long since past. The resurgence of interest in cognitive processes makes it impossible to hold such a simple view any longer and nowadays most psychologists recognize that there are psychological processes, like verbal communication and the symbolic representation of future events, that can only reliably be demonstrated in other people. Since we believe that all variations in behavioural capacity reflect underlying variations in the nervous system, we have to accept that the human brain is, in some way, different from that of other species. Psychological processes unique to humans are a serious problem for committed psychobiologists. We can respond to this in two ways, either by abandoning studies on non-human animals and thus losing a major source of evidence, or by finding ways of making legitimate cross-species extrapolations. The problems of making extrapolations arise at both the behavioural and the neurological level.

We are reasonably certain there are psychological processes unique to our own species. There is a grey area of uncertainty about others. This is especially true in applied areas, such as the study of psychopathology, where we are uncertain whether animals experience the same problems as humans and, if they do, we are uncertain about identifying which disturbances in animals correspond to particular disturbances in humans. For example, we don't know whether non-human species get depressed and even if we were sure that they did there would still be a lot of doubt about which behaviours signified depression in an animal. The usual solution to this problem is to develop animal models of the human problem, in which animals are constrained to exhibit the sorts of disturbances that a particular scientist believes to be the salient feature of the human disorder. For example, one scientist might think that the most crucial feature of depression is a failure to escape from noxious stimuli, in which case the 'learned helplessness' model would seem the most appropriate. Another might think that it is a failure to respond to rewards, in which drug treatments that make animals insensitive to reinforcement would be the best model. Needless to say, there is a continuous and lively debate about whose model is the best.

How can we justify studies on other species in terms of their relevance to man? Our response to this problem is determined very much by our view of the evolutionary relationships between man and other animals. A widely held view is that animals can be ranked on a scale, a 'phylogenetic' scale, based on their degree of similarity to humans. This leads us to study animals that are most like humans and to restrict our studies to these animals, like the chimpanzee. Here we run into three problems. The first is a moral one, that if chimpanzees are really like man they may have the same capacity to understand what is happening to them and imagine their futures, which would make laboratory studies, especially physiological interventions, unacceptable. The second is an evolutionary one, that the biggest difference between man and other apes lies in the development of the human brain. The gulf between the human and the chimpanzee brain may be smaller than that between the human and the rat brain, but it is still large. The third is a logistical one. Chimpanzees are such an unsuccessful species that they are considerably outnumbered by neuroscientists. Research would be impossible if we restricted ourselves to this species.

Not only is it impractical, and possibly unethical, to restrict psychobiological studies to work on humans and great apes but it would also mean throwing out most of the work done to date, since most of that has involved the use of non-primates like cats, hamsters, and especially rats. Clearly we have to find some way of using these data without assuming that rats, for example, are just very small people. The degree to which this is possible depends very much on how the brain has evolved. The most pessimistic viewpoint is that the brains of different groups of mammals have very little in common because they evolved separately from a common ancestral form in which the brain was relatively formless, lacking the distinctive subdivisions that can be identified in the brains of modern mammals. If this is the case we can do very little unless we are dealing with large blocks of brain that correspond to units in the primitive ancestral brain. For example, since all mammals have a cerebral cortex we must assume that the ancestral form also had one. This means that we can legitimately ask questions about the functions of cerebral cortex and just as easily study hamsters as humans to get our answers. What we cannot do is ask questions about sub-areas of the cerebral cortex, for example the striate cortex of primates, and expect to get the same answers from studies on different groups. The most optimistic view is that evolution has involved a gradual accretion of new structures, added on to primitive ones common to all mammals. This means that there will be brain systems present in both rats and humans that can be just as easily studied in the former as in the latter.

In either event it is no longer safe to assume that non-human animals are just small versions of us, so direct extrapolations are going to be a risky business. Knowledge of how the brain evolved is likely to reduce that risk, but it can never eliminate it completely. Extrapolations are, therefore, best seen as working hypotheses requiring confirmation by studies made on people. Indeed, this is precisely how the more insightful psychobiologists, such as Weiskrantz (1968) and his collaborators, carry on. The point about studies on non-human animals is not that they replace studies on humans but that they provide us with pointers to what we should study in people and how we should study it.

The modular brain

It is now generally accepted that there is a division of labour within the brain, with different parts of the brain carrying out different functions. As you will discover in the remaining chapters, problems remain about specifying the actual functions of these modules, their degree of functional independence, and the consequences of functional independence for the integration of behaviour and consciousness.

Take what we know about the neural mechanisms of language, for example. Over a century ago Broca demonstrated that patients with damage involving part of the prefrontal cortex of the left hemisphere had severe speech deficits, although they could understand what was said to them. Damage to the corresponding part of the right hemisphere had no effect on speech. The immediate temptation was to identify this region of the left hemisphere, now known as Broca's area, as a speech centre, with the implication that this is all that is needed to generate speech. This view is, of course, too simplistic. Many other parts of the brain are important for normal speech. Furthermore, although it is smaller, there is an area that corresponds to Broca's area in the right hemisphere that doesn't seem to have anything to do with speech but which seems to have many of the same connections. This suggests that there is nothing inherent in Broca's area by itself that makes it crucial for speech. Rather, its importance results from where it lies in the circuits of the left hemisphere and the way that it processes the inputs it receives. To understand why damage to Broca's area impairs speech we need to know both where it gets its input from and what it does to that input. What it does to that input may not be susceptible to description in psychological terms.

Although the lesions that produce the speech loss are localized it would be a mistake to assume that their effects are similarly restricted. Broca's area is part of a larger brain circuit and has connections with many other brain areas. It is, therefore, possible that some or all of the effects of damaging this area are due to disruptive effects on these other regions. Since the effects of the damage are largely restricted to language, the disruption cannot affect the whole brain, so in that sense we are justified in thinking of the brain as consisting of functionally independent modules. Nevertheless, the disruptive effects of damage may spread to other structures intimately linked to Broca's area. As a consequence, the functional modules of the brain may well be bigger than the individual areas of the cortex or subcortical nuclei that are the conventional units of analysis.

Since speech takes place in the wider context of non-verbal behaviour, we also need to understand the relationship between the speech mechanisms and the other mechanisms in the brain. For example, we need to know how the speech system gets information from the systems that programme other movements so that we are capable of commenting on our own actions. While driving my car I am able to say to my passengers that I am about to turn right before I have actually done so. This requires integration between the systems that are programming my driving behaviour and those programming my speech. One of the challenges of psychobiology is to explain how this integration is achieved (Gazzaniga 1985).

The cognitive challenge

Psychobiologists have reacted to the rediscovery of cognitive processes in two ways. One has been to include cognitive processes in the list of functions that they are trying to relate to particular brain regions or systems. The other, much more recent development, has been to pay serious attention to modelling how cognitive functions might be carried out by the brain.

The first point can be illustrated by looking at the history of thought about the hippocampus. Few scientists paid any attention to this part of the limbic system until Papez published his theory of emotion in the late 1930s, whereupon considerable effort was put into identifying its role in emotion. When the results of lesion studies proved incompatible with this simple model scientists in the 1960s shifted to response modulation models (McCleary 1966). The 1970s saw a major shift in focus and suddenly people were describing the hippocampus as a 'cognitive map' (O'Keefe and Nadel 1978) or as the repository of 'working memory' (Olton 1983).

What most people wisely avoided was specifying how a 'working memory' could be constructed, or how 'temporal context' could be encoded in the nervous system. Recent developments in modelling cognitive processes on computers have changed the situation quite dramatically and there is now a realistic chance of being able to produce models of the way cognitive processes are carried out that are sufficiently precise and detailed for them to be tested properly against what happens in the brain (McNaughton and Morris 1987). However, these developments are in the early stages so there is very little concrete to report at the moment.

Laboratory models of the real world

Psychologists, like all other scientists, cope with the complexity of the real world by making models of it and working with those instead. We call these models theories. A theory is essentially a model of the world that draws an analogy between the process we are trying to understand and one we already know about. For example, we often talk about 'stress', which is a term that has a very precise meaning to an engineer. In psychology we use the analogy of mechanical stress, and its consequences, to describe and explain what happens to people when they are subjected to excessive psychological demands. Theories are not optional extras in science. They serve two useful functions. The first is to provide simple descriptions of complex data so that we can understand what is going on in our experiments. The second is to lay down the ground-rules for generalizing from one set of conditions to another; for example, from the laboratory to the real world.

Psychologists have a fairly negative attitude to theories, having been badly scarred by the experience of the grand theories of behaviour published in the 1930s and 1940s. They argue that we do not know enough to develop meaningful theories of psychological processes and relegate theories to the level of intellectual devices for stimulating experimentation. Many of the theories that are published are not really theories of psychological processes at all, but are theories of experimental phenomena. For example, in 1940 Hetherington and Ranson observed that rats with lesions involving the ventromedial hypothalamus ate excessively and became obese. In 1954 Stellar incorporated this finding in his 'two-centre' theory of motivation. Since then there have been a number of theories published on the experimental phenomenon of hypothalamic obesity (Powley 1977). While these theories address the problem of hunger, they do so only indirectly.

The other aspect of theories is that they enable us to make generalizations. By itself an experiment allows us to draw conclusions about the particular conditions in that experiment, and nothing else. A theory tells us that a set of experimental conditions is a particular embodiment of a general process. For example, there are theories of memory that tell us that the recall of recently presented items reflects the operation of short-term storage. We can therefore generalize from one experiment in which short-term storage is believed to operate to another in which we also believe it to be present. Generalization from one set of experimental conditions is daunting enough, but the real aim of a theory is to allow us to generalize to what happens in the real world. For example, we want to be able to take knowledge gained from studying the free recall of nonsense syllables and make predictions about our ability to remember things like telephone numbers, or the names of people we have just been introduced to at parties. Many of us escape from that problem by redefining our experimental paradigms and phenomena as things worthy of study in their own right, so we have a psychological literature that abounds in studies of 'classical conditioning', the 'serial position effect', the 'lateral hypothalamic syndrome', and 'risky-shift'.

The problem of generalization is a serious one in most of psychology but is particularly poignant in psychobiology because of the damaging consequences of getting it wrong. Realistic generalization is only possible, however, when there are good theories of the phenomena that occur in the real world. Fortunately more and more psychobiology is being done in this way.

Overview

For much of its history psychobiology has been a subject ahead of its time, often asking questions for which it had no meaningful answers. Part of our reaction to that situation has been negative, especially the behaviourist interlude that sought to define out of existence many of the issues that confront us, but for the most part the approach has been a steady accumulation of experimental data in anticipation of the day when meaningful theories could be developed. This work, it is true, was largely conducted in the belief that simply gathering information alone would eventually lead to an understanding of the brain, but the fact remains that we now have an impressive body of evidence against which to evaluate the new theories that are emerging. Furthermore, while many of our questions about the relationship between mind and brain had to be held in abeyance, it was possible to make steady progress in answering certain fundamental questions about the organization of the brain. For example, most scientists are now convinced that the cerebral cortex is parcellated into specialized sub-areas rather than working as a fully integrated system.

By virtue of being interdisciplinary, psychobiology has some special problems not encountered in mainstream psychology. One of these is its uneasy relationship with biology. Psychologists are often made to feel the poor relations of biologists, because the latter have more facts at their disposal, and to put a lower value on psychological than on biological data and theories. In fact, psychology and biology have to be equal partners in our analysis of the brain. A second problem concerns the use of animals in psychobiological experiments. Apart from the ethical concerns some people feel on this matter there is the pressing issue of the degree to which it is possible to extrapolate from one species to another, especially from non-human species to ourselves. There can be no definite answer to this problem at the moment. Instead, all extrapolations should be, and indeed usually are, considered to be working hypotheses that guide the way we study our own brains.

Much of the work that appears in the literature is largely descriptive in nature. There is a dearth of good theories in psychobiology. This is not surprising, given the difficulties encountered in developing them, but it does limit the ease with which we can generalize from one experiment to another or from experiments to the real world. For the sake of form, experiments are presented as if they are serious tests of hypotheses or theories, but this reflects the conventions of scientific journals rather than the realities of science. In fact, most people publish in the hope that their findings will continue to be relevant long after the particular theory to which they have attached them has been finally laid to rest. Fortunately, the situation is beginning to change as allied disciplines like machine intelligence provide us with models that will allow us to construct theories that are both realistic and have heuristic power.

2
Animal subjects in psychobiology

There is a convention among psychologists and neuroscientists that leads us to refer to 'the' brain, no matter whether we are talking about hamsters or humans. In other words, we act as if the brain of one species is very much like that of another. This is a convenient fiction that allows us to carry out research on non-human species, but it is by no means clear that it is true. The degree of similarity between the brain of one species and that of another should not be taken for granted. It is an empirical matter that requires careful investigation. As things stand at present it seems more appropriate to talk about 'brains' than about 'the brain'. In this chapter I want, first of all, to outline some of the reasons for believing that different types of animal have different types of brain, and second, to discuss ways of getting round some of the difficulties created when we want to make extrapolations between species.

It is certainly necessary to be able to make cross-species extrapolations, for otherwise we should be deprived of our main source of data. There are some purists who would argue that this is no bad thing, and that those interested in the human brain and human behaviour should stick to studying humans. They point to the alarming consequences of over-enthusiastic extrapolation across species. For example, it is widely held that Egas Moniz was stimulated into developing the now largely abandoned technique of controlling psychological disorders by the use of psychosurgery after hearing about the 'beneficial' side-effects of frontal lobe removal in chimpanzees. This, however, is probably unfair on both Moniz and the man whose work he was supposed to be responding to, Jacobsen (Valenstein 1980). It is unfair to Moniz because he probably would have developed the technique of prefrontal leucotomy anyway and it is unfair on Jacobsen because the substance of Jacobsen's work was that frontal lobe removal produced a severe cognitive deficit which no-one would wish on another person. Whatever the rights and wrongs of this debate, the fact remains that we do not live in a perfect world and, like it or not, we have to rely on a large amount of data derived from animals.

Evolution and the brain

One of the reasons for believing that cross-species extrapolation is possible at all is that all living animals have evolved from common ancestors that existed at some time in the distant past. They might, therefore, reasonably be expected to share characteristics that were also possessed by those common ancestors, even if they have unique characteristics as well. This is especially likely since evolution is considered a very conservative process, 'advanced' species building on features that were present in their more 'primitive' ancestors. Since all mammals evolved from a common ancestral stock we would expect their brains and bodies to have large numbers of common features which could be the basis of a reasonable level of extrapolation (Sarnat and Netsky 1981). The real issues concern the number of common features that are likely to be shared by different species and the impact of features unique to a species on the functioning of structures or systems that they share in common with others.

Much depends upon how evolution took place. On reading many accounts of evolution one might be forgiven for thinking that its purpose was to produce us, the species *Homo sapiens sapiens*, in a rerun of the biblical account of creation with the agency of God replaced by the blind force of natural selection. Evolution is presented as a progression from simple to complex forms with us at the pinnacle of it all as the most complex. Other animals living today are, in some sense, failed evolutionary experiments that approximate to us but do not reach the right level. This belief is echoed by most texts on physiological psychology that show pictures of rat, cat, monkey, and human brains with the implication that rats are simple versions of cats, and cats simple versions of monkeys, and so on. There are two reasons for believing that this isn't true. One is that the history of evolution shows it to be a process of radiation rather than of progression. The second is that comparisons between the brains of living mammals show that many of them contain specializations that are not present in our own brains.

Making comparisons between brains is a very risky business because there are confounding variables to confuse the issue. One of the most obvious is the size of the animal possessing the brain. All things being equal, small animals need less brain than larger ones and large brains might be different from small ones simply by virtue of their size (Russell 1978). For example, the folding of the neocortex of large mammals is largely a response to the need to cram more cortex into a small space in the cranium. Folding does not, by itself, indicate neural complexity. Were one to create a mouse the size of a moose, that mouse would probably have a folded neocortex if its cortex had increased in proportion to the increase in its body size. Increasing the size of the brain is likely to have other effects. For one thing, increasing the number of cells increases the amount of space that will be taken up by axons and their terminals, and this will alter the appearance of the tissue, so that regions of the brain will not always look the same in different species. For another, with a large brain the boundaries between areas will take up a smaller proportion of those areas than in small brains. As a consequence, the boundaries will be more distinct and it may be possible to identify more sub-areas.

What this means is that if we want to make realistic comparisons between species we have to make allowance for differences in the sizes of the animals concerned. Fortunately there are some very straightforward ways of making such allowances. They rely on the fact that brain weight will increase in proportion to body area, which is, in turn, related to body weight. It is therefore possible to calculate how much brain a mammal should have for its size and, by taking the ratio between the actual and the expected brain size, obtain a measure of how much 'extra' brain a species possesses. If you do this sort of calculation and compare mice and monkeys you find that monkeys have much more brain than would a mouse of equivalent size (Russell 1978). This indicates that there is something that distinguishes monkey from mouse brains other than the relative sizes of the two species.

Humans belong to the group of animals known as mammals, which are characterized by the presence of hair, mammary glands and sweat glands, tooth specialization, and the regulation of a constant body temperature. Mammal-like animals have been around for some 200 million years but didn't become particularly numerous until about 70 million years ago, around the time the dinosaurs became extinct. It is generally agreed that the primitive mammals existing at that time were shrew-like creatures that lived by eating insects, and that the various groups of mammals that we see today, such as cats, rats, monkeys, whales, and horses, all evolved from this unpromising ancestor.

We also know that the specialization took place very early in the evolution of mammals and that the ancestors of the main groups that are alive today all appeared around the same time, give or take a few million years. Since then those lines have been undergoing separate evolution, giving rise to yet further, more recent branches. For example, the primates, to which we belong, date back to around that time but our own branch of the primate line, *Homo sapiens*, dates back to less than a million years ago. Historically, evolution has been a process of radiation, with a considerable amount of time for lines to have diverged having elapsed since the first mammals appeared (Figure 2.1). The net result is that there is no more reason to believe that our brains are like a cat's than there is to believe that they are like a rat's.

Nevertheless, since evolution is a conservative process our brains are likely to contain some components in common with other mammals in so far as they contain features that were characteristic of the common ancestor. All we have to do is to find out what the brains of our common ancestors looked like to find out how similar we might expect the brains of mammals to be. There is just one problem: brains are part of the soft tissue of the body and so do not survive fossilization. Consequently, no-one has ever seen the brain of one of those early mammals. Can we reconstruct one on the basis of what we currently

Animal subjects in psychobiology

Figure 2.1 A simplified phylogenetic tree showing the relationships between the major mammalian groups

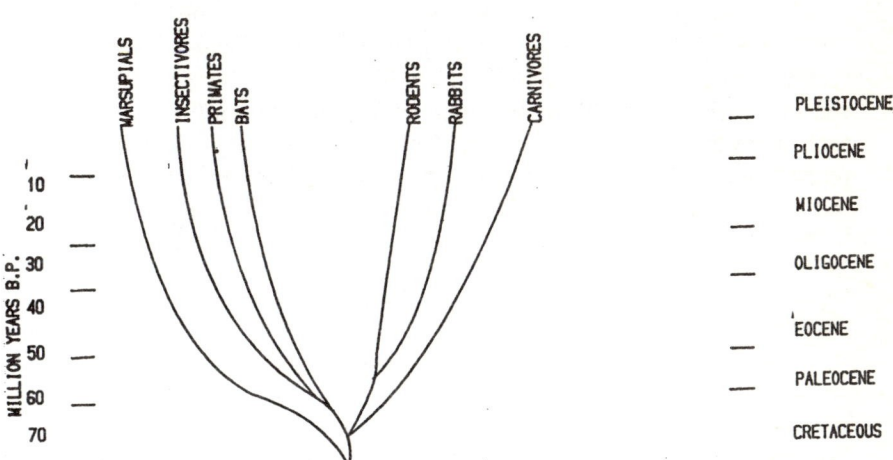

Note the early divergence of lineages (B.P. – Before Present).

know? Palaeontologists have applied two approaches. One, which could be seen as a little circular, is to look at the brains of mammals alive today and determine what they have in common. These common features then become the features that they share by virtue of having a common ancestor. Of course, it is more complex than that because allowance has to be made for convergent evolution, which is the acquisition of common characteristics by virtue of having been subjected to the same selection pressures, rather than because of sharing a common ancestor. Nevertheless, if you could identify common features it would be a good starting point for reconstructing the brain of the common ancestor. The other strategy has been to look for a species that is alive today that has physical characteristics similar to those of our common ancestor, and has the same lifestyle, and to use its brain as a model for the primitive brain. Neither procedure is satisfactory, but the combination might produce something of interest.

Making comparisons between species involves identifying what are known as homologous structures. Homology is identified on the basis of a number of criteria, including the form of the tissue, its embryonic origins, its connections with other parts of the brain or body, and, to a lesser extent, its function. It is assumed that homologous structures are there as a consequence of evolution from a common ancestor, so homologous structures common to all mammals would be presumed to have been present in our common ancestor. It is important to note that homologous structures don't have to look the same, and that structures that look the same don't have to be homologous. For example, a seal's flipper is homologous with the human arm, even though they look very different, while the wings of bats and birds are not homologous, even though they look similar. Similarity of appearance and function that is not based on homology is known as analogy. In the case of hard tissue, like teeth and bones, the identification of homology is relatively straightforward because it is possible to compare present forms with the common ancestor and this can be used as an additional criterion for homology. In the case of soft tissue, like the brain, we are on less certain ground.

Despite the problems we are inclined to accept some homologies in the nervous system, although there is disagreement about how far one should take it. Most people are happy with the idea of homologies at low levels in the nervous system. Few would dispute the fact that the brainstem of the rat, below the level of the thalamus, is largely homologous with that of primates. Structures with similar appearances, in comparable locations, that differentiate from the same embryonic tissue at the same stage in development, can be identified relatively easily and, in general, their connections tend to be similar. This isn't particularly surprising because the brainstem structure was probably inherited by the mammals from their common ancestor in the reptile stock. These homologies would provide considerable scope for direct extrapolation providing the functions of these brainstem regions are not modified by forebrain structures that differ from group to group.

Neuroscientists may amuse themselves by thinking up objections to homologies between brainstem structures, but this isn't pursued that seriously. The real conflicts arise when people get on to the cerebral cortex. Again, most of us are happy to accept that the cortices of all mammals are, as units, homologous with each other. The problems arise when people seek to draw homologies between specific cortical areas.

Anybody who has ever looked at sections of a rat's brain and then at sections of a monkey's brain will tell you that they look completely different. For one thing, in the monkey brain it is possible to identify quite sharp boundaries between areas that can be distinguished in terms of the shapes, sizes, numbers, and laminar distributions of their cells. In the rat brain there are regional differences in the structure of the cortex, but the areas that can be identified tend to blur into each other. For another thing, areas that one would expect to be homologous on the basis of their connections appear totally different in other ways. For example, the area of the primate cortex that receives the direct visual projection from the thalamus is distinguished by a dense band of white matter in layer four. This stripe, which gives rise to the alternative name for this area, the striate cortex, is visible to the naked eye in sections of the human brain. It is completely absent in the rat. Indeed, it is extremely difficult to distinguish between the primary visual cortex and surrounding areas in this species. Nevertheless, some optimists continue to refer to the primary visual area in the rat as 'striate' cortex.

Other procedures reveal other differences between these areas. If the visual cortex of a monkey is exposed to a stain that highlights the enzyme cytochrome oxidase it is possible to identify densely labelled blobs, which indicate high concentrations of the enzyme, in the upper layers of the visual cortex (Livingstone and Hubel 1984). Exposing rat cortex to the same stain produces uniform, moderately dense, labelling in the primary visual area. In many ways it looks like one big cytochrome oxidase blob! The extra detail visible in the monkey's brain might just be a consequence of it being bigger than the rat's, but a comparison between the somatosensory cortices of the two animals shows that this isn't so, for this time it is in the rat that the extra detail is visible. If the cytochrome oxidase stain is used on the rat somatosensory cortex, the cortex contains a large number of patches shaped like barrels (Land and Simons 1985). No such barrels are present in the monkey. We therefore have to face the fact that there are structural differences between rat and monkey cortex that cannot be simply attributed to differences in size.

None of this actually precludes the visual or somatosensory areas in the two species being homologous, but it does mean that we need evidence other than appearance to support the case. Embryology isn't a good guide because it isn't sufficiently precise. We can tell that the primary visual areas in rats and monkeys come from the same primordial tissue in the embryonic nervous system, but this isn't surprising since all of the cortex arises from this same region. Consequently, all that embryology tells us is that both areas are part of the neocortex. The connections of cortical areas may give some clues about homology. It is encouraging that the primary visual areas of both rats and monkeys receive input from the lateral geniculate nucleus of the thalamus but we should be aware of some circularity here since one of the criteria used for saying that the lateral geniculate nuclei in the two groups are homologous is that they both project to primary visual cortex! Certainly the lateral geniculate nucleus in rats looks nothing like the lateral geniculate nucleus in monkeys. On the output side the similarity is less clear-cut. In the monkey the primary visual cortex projects into a band of specialized cortical areas surrounding it (Maunsell and Newsome 1987). There are many such areas, each containing a full or partial representation of the visual field, some of which receive a direct input from the primary area and some of which rely on indirect projections for their inputs. Higher-order visual areas are also present in the rat, but it is unclear whether their organization is the same as in the monkey (Espinoza and Thomas 1983). In the rat the primary visual cortex has a sizable projection to the pontine nuclei in the brainstem (Legg and Glickstein 1984), while this projection is extremely sparse in the monkey (Glickstein, May, and Mercier 1985). In monkeys the lateral geniculate nucleus projects almost exclusively to the primary visual cortex, with only a few axons straying into the surrounding secondary cortical visual areas. In the cat, in contrast, the lateral geniculate nucleus projects to two distinct, but adjacent, cortical zones (areas 17 and 18), each containing a representation of the entire visual field. Clearly we shouldn't expect too many functional similarities between the visual cortices of rats, cats, and monkeys.

Once we move beyond the primary sensory receiving areas the situation gets even more tenuous. One widely used criterion for dividing up the cerebral cortex is the organization of inputs from the thalamus. For example, Leonard (1969) used this approach to identify the 'homologue' of primate prefrontal cortex in rats. In monkeys the dorsomedial nucleus of the thalamus projects exclusively to the prefrontal cortex so it seems reasonable that the dorsomedial nucleus projection zone would correspond to prefrontal cortex in rats. Accordingly, Leonard investigated the connections of the dorsomedial thalamus in rats and showed that it projects to two cortical areas, one lying on the medial edge of the anterior cortex and the other on the lateral edge, in the rhinal fissure. The problem with using thalamic nuclei as a guide to cortical organization is that primates have a thalamic nucleus, with extensive cortical projections, for which there is no clearly identifiable homologue in other species. That nucleus is the pulvinar, which projects throughout occipital, parietal, temporal and frontal cortex. We can be fairly certain that the pulvinar is not homologous with anything in the rat, or indeed in any other group, because its embryonic origins are so distinct (Rakic 1974). This means that the cortical areas to which the pulvinar projects are not strictly comparable with anything seen in non-primate species.

Comparative analysis suggests that there has been a considerable amount of divergence of evolution in the cortices of different mammalian lines. This level of divergence is compatible with the results of attempts to identify a living mammal that is comparable to the mammalian common ancestor. The favoured candidate at the moment is the humble hedgehog, a nocturnal insect-eater which possesses a remarkably undifferentiated cortex (Diamond and Hall 1969). In this species there is no clear distinction between primary visual cortex and the secondary visual areas that are present in most other species, ranging from rats to monkeys, and there is almost total overlap between the motor cortex, defined in terms of the area of cortex from which movements can be evoked by electrical stimulation, and the somatosensory cortex, defined in terms of the area from which electrical activity can be evoked by stimulation of the body surface (Kaas 1982). We are left with the rather worrying conclusion that cerebral cortex, as a whole, is homologous in all mammalian species but we should be very, very cautious about accepting homologies between specific cortical areas.

The implications of differences in cortical organization go beyond our understanding of the cerebral cortex. They are also likely to lead to differences in the way brainstem structures work, since the cerebral cortex of mammals is one of the major sources of input to these areas. This point is of more than academic interest since there are, in fact, quite significant differences in the functional organization of apparently homologous structures in different species. For example, the superior colliculus, a visual structure lying on the dorsal surface of the midbrain, has subtly different properties in different species (Goldberg and Robinson 1978). Electrical stimulation deep within the colliculus produces eye movements, even when very low-level currents are used, but the characteristics of the movements vary between species. In monkeys, stimulation produces rapid movements, called saccades, of an amplitude and direction predictable from the site of the stimulation in the colliculus alone. The effects of stimulation are 'all-or-none': either a saccade is elicited or it isn't, and its size and direction are not related to the intensity or frequency of stimulation in the colliculus. In cats, superior colliculus stimulation also produces saccades, but the effect is not all-or-none. Instead, the amplitude of the saccades increases with the intensity of the stimulation, up to a plateau that is characteristic of a particular stimulation site. McHaffie and Stein (1982) have also reported eye movements after colliculus stimulation in rats, although it is not clear that they are true saccades. In some ways the control is similar to that observed in the cat, in that eye-movement amplitude varied with stimulus intensity. In other ways the results were curious. First, the largest excursions of the eyes were only around 10 degrees. Second, the stimulation thresholds were much higher than in cats and monkeys. Finally, stimulation tended to cause the eyes to protrude from their sockets before moving. It may turn out that the differences are an artefact of the methods used in different laboratories, but it is difficult to see what the relevant differences may be.

Identifying homologies at the level of brain structures is fraught with difficulties. Fortunately, there are some issues that do not depend on such a level of specificity. One concerns the cellular mechanisms underlying processes like learning and memory, since we might reasonably expect that the basic properties of nerve cells are the same in all species. This is probably acceptable so long as we restrict ourselves to a single group, like mammals, but there is some dissent when people seek to extrapolate mechanisms from non-vertebrate species, like molluscs, to the mammalian brain (e.g. Hawkins and Kandel 1984). It would certainly be naïve just to assume that nerve cells are the same in molluscs as in people, but fortunately it is possible to rely on more than assumption. The advantage of this sort of work is that the descriptions of cellular mechanisms are very detailed and this provides a good basis for determining whether the same cellular mechanisms are available in mammals. For example, plasticity seems to depend on identifiable ion channels and catalytic molecules that activate or inhibit these channels. It is possible to use advanced biochemical techniques to look for comparable ion channels and catalytic units in the mammalian brain, without directly studying the role of cells in learning. The problem with this approach is that it doesn't allow for the possibility that there are additional cellular mechanisms of plasticity in mammals, that have evolved to underpin our greater learning abilities.

Extrapolation rules

Do these problems with identifying homologies rule out extrapolations between species? The optimistic consensus is that they don't but that one has to be very careful about making them, and the level of detail one can achieve may not be as great as one may like. There are a number of reasons for this optimism. The first is that the amount of evolutionary divergence in the organization of primate brains has not been anywhere near as great as the divergence between primates and other groups. Providing one sticks to primates there is much scope for successful extrapolation. The second is that homology probably doesn't matter that much. What matters from the functional point of view is analogy: carrying out comparable functions. Brains may carry out tasks in the same way even if the tissues involved are not strictly homologous. One might expect this because convergent evolution would lead to similar mechanisms to carry out similar functions. Finally, we can probably take advantage of variations in brain organization to understand the relationships between structure and function. The differences between the brains of different species are not accidental but reflect differences in the abilities and lifestyles of the species concerned. We might then be able to work back from lifestyle and abilities to predict what the brain of a particular species should be like (Legg 1983).

Comparative anatomists tell us that there are remarkably few differences between our brains and those of monkeys and apes, other than that ours are bigger. Since we are quite different in our behavioural capacities, notably in our possessing language, this may reflect a lack of subtlety on the part of the anatomists but it is probably reasonable to assume that the input and output ends of the system are pretty much the same in monkeys as in people. For example, it wouldn't stretch the truth too much to assume that the organization of the visual system is the same in rhesus monkeys as it is in humans.

As we shall see in a subsequent chapter there is good evidence for this optimism. Although no-one has explored the human visual cortex in the fine detail that the anatomists and electrophysiologists have studied the visual cortex of monkeys, there are a number of indirect sources of evidence to support this position. First of all, brain damage in people has been found to cause inability to perceive particular attributes of visual scenes without causing total blindness (Maunsell and Newsome 1987), and the single cell recording data on monkeys show that those attributes are processed by distinct parts of the cortex. For example, area V4 in monkeys is specialized for processing colour information but doesn't encode other attributes like motion or position. We would therefore expect to find patients who had lost colour vision without losing other attributes of vision, like motion detection. Such patients have been reported (Heywood and Cowey 1985). Second, the independence of processing of attributes like colour and motion suggests that they should be found to operate independently in psychophysical studies, and this is what happens (Nakayama and Silverman 1986). Finally, studies of the metabolic activity of the human brain have shown that different areas of the occipital cortex become active when different attributes of stimuli are highlighted in visual displays (Raichle 1983).

Although visual system physiologists treat the monkey as the model system of their choice for studying the visual cortex, a surprising amount of useful data has been gathered using cats as subjects, despite the known anatomical differences between cats and monkeys. The obvious reason for this is convergent evolution: the visual systems of cats and monkeys are doing similar jobs and use similar mechanisms to do so. It is important to remember, for example, that our main concepts of the functional organization of primary visual cortex were developed in studies on cats rather than monkeys. These include the existence of orientation selectivity as the main receptive-field characteristic, columnar organization, ocular dominance, and the distinction between simple and complex cell characteristics. Nevertheless, it is dangerous to get too carried away with the similarities since they can blind even the best researchers to new observations. A case in point are the receptive-field properties observed in the cytochrome oxidase blobs that are present in the upper layers of primary visual cortex of monkeys but not of cats (Livingstone and Hubel 1984). These blob areas are curious in that the cells have only poor orientation selectivity but are tuned to the wavelength of light instead. Hubel and his colleagues had studied the visual cortex of the rhesus monkey for many years without observing these cells and it was only when the cytochrome oxidase blobs had been demonstrated consistently and they started to look for receptive-field properties within them that they obtained these surprising results. Since their work on cats had conditioned them to expect all parts of the visual cortex to contain orientation selective cells this oversight is, perhaps, understandable.

Differences in neural organization must reflect differences in function. We could, in principle, come to understand how the brain works by correlating neural differences with differences in the behaviour of species. If, for example, we knew what animals with neocortices could do that species lacking them couldn't do we would know something about the cortex without having to ablate it in a single animal. If we know what animals with cytochrome oxidase blobs in their visual cortices can see that those lacking them cannot we can learn something about the functions of the blob system.

Whitfield (1979) has used this correlational approach to analyse the functions of the auditory cortex. Most vertebrates, including those without forebrain auditory connections, with functioning auditory systems can detect sounds, discriminate between sound frequencies, and localize sounds by means of orienting movements, indicating that these abilities do not depend on neocortex. What these animals cannot do is localize sounds independently of their position relative to the animal's body. Interestingly, this is also true of mammals from which the auditory cortex has been removed.

When applied to the newly discovered cytochrome oxidase blobs in the visual cortex of primates the correlational approach is quite revealing. The single cell recording studies carried out on rhesus monkeys show a very good correlation between the blobs and wavelength tuning, suggesting a role in colour vision. However, there is one monkey, the owl monkey of South America, that has little useful colour vision, being a nocturnal animal, but which still possesses these blobs. This suggests that the blobs are involved in something much more fundamental, like the detection of very coarse stimulus features, rather than colour analysis as such.

This comparative approach can also be used to analyse brainstem areas, the functions of which have been modified by the evolution of neocortical areas. The approach involves identifying variations in the functioning of target areas and relating those variations to known differences in cortical function. Once allowance has been made for variations in cortical function it should then be possible to identify the function of the subcortical area. An excellent example is the work that has been done on the hippocampus. The most obvious consequence of removing the hippocampus in the rat is that the animals have an immense difficulty in refraining from responses that lead to punishment, a deficit in passive avoidance apparently due to an inability to inhibit inappropriate responses. In humans, in contrast, surgical removal of the hippocampus has been found to produce a profound and abiding loss of memory. How can the findings be reconciled? One approach was to argue that the human memory loss was secondary to the failure of a more fundamental process, like the ability to inhibit inappropriate responses. The other approach has been to argue that rats have difficulty with passive avoidance because they cannot remember recent events.

Although people with hippocampal lesions have appalling memories they are, nevertheless, capable of learning. In the early 1970s this led Weiskrantz and Warrington (see Parkin 1987) to argue that the human deficit was not a failure of memory as such but a deficit in retrieval brought about by undue interference from incorrect items at the time of recall. In other words, the fundamental deficit was the same in animals and people: a failure of response inhibition. This proved quite a successful theory for a number of years, in that it stimulated a lot of research and produced a corpus of compatible experimental results. There were, ultimately, some findings that were distinctly incompatible with the theory and it was abandoned by its originators.

More recently, people have reversed the logic applied by Weiskrantz and Warrington and have suggested that the deficits in rats are really due to a memory loss (Kesner and DiMattia 1987; Olton 1983). In other words, rats with hippocampal lesions have difficulty in refraining from punished responses because they cannot remember what happened to them the last time that they did whatever it was that led to the punishment. Rats are normally very good at remembering where they have received reinforcement but lose this ability after hippocampal damage. For example, Olton (1983) tested rats on a 'radial arm maze', which is an elevated star-shaped maze with a number of arms radiating from a central choice point. At the beginning of each trial food is placed at the end of each arm and the rat left to move from arm to arm, in whatever sequence it chooses, in order to retrieve the food. Normal rats learn rapidly to avoid arms from which they have taken food on that trial. Rats with hippocampal lesions re-enter arms quite regularly. This isn't a deficit in response inhibition as such because the animals never develop a history of being reinforced in one arm of the maze in preference to any other. It is therefore simplest to interpret these results in terms of an inability to remember that food has just been obtained from a particular arm. Other data, discussed in chapter 7, support this point.

We should be cautious about putting too much weight on the analogy between the memory losses observed in people and the deficit in 'working memory' observed in rats, simply because the humans concerned have a deficit in verbal memory, and the rats don't have language. It would be interesting to know whether humans with hippocampal damage are impaired on the equivalent of a radial arm maze. This may sound frivolous, but it emphasizes the point that it is often far from clear what constitutes equivalent behavioural tasks when making comparisons between species, and this uncertainty creates problems for the comparative approach to brain function.

Conclusions

Using animals as a substitute for humans is a far from straightforward business. There are difficulties in identifying areas common to the brains of people and other animals and, even when that can be done, it is unclear how far one can rely on the areas working in exactly the same way. Nevertheless, there are certain things that can be done. One is to study our closest relatives, the monkeys and great apes, a second is to study the way that particular functions, like the visual analysis of form, are done, irrespective of the species involved; and the third is to take advantage of differences between species and correlate structural with behavioural differences as means of analysing the functions of brain systems. Whichever strategy is adopted there are going to be problems and it is important to be tuned into them when trying to interpret research in psychobiology.

3
Methods in psychobiology

A science is only as good as its methods. Physiological psychology presents a range of major methodological challenges, and how well we meet these challenges affects the ease with which we can interpret the experiments that we carry out. Some of these challenges are entirely technical but others are conceptual, stemming from the fact that most methods only make sense if one makes certain assumptions about the brain which may, or may not, be valid. There is nothing alarming or unusual about methodological problems; all sciences have them and it is quite common for the questions that people ask to run ahead of the techniques available for answering them. It is also quite common for theoretical predictions to go untested for want of appropriate experimental methods. The important point is to recognize that these methodological difficulties exist and allow awareness of them to influence our interpretation of experimental results.

Psychobiologists want to explain behaviour in terms of physiological events occurring in the brain and the body. To achieve this they need to be able first to specify the functions of individual components of the nervous system and related mechanisms in the body that have behavioural significance, such as the digestive system, and second to explain how these components, working together in an integrated system, give rise to human behaviour and human consciousness. Much of their effort is devoted to determining the functions of anatomically distinguishable parts of the brain. In pursuit of this goal they have developed a number of specialized techniques. The most commonly used is the lesion method, in which part of the brain is injured or entirely removed and the resultant changes in behaviour studied. Others probe the functions of different areas by applying electrical stimulation and looking at the behaviours, if any, that are elicited by it. Finally, advances in instrumentation have encouraged the study of neural correlates of behaviour, either by monitoring the electrical activity of cells or, very recently, by analysing the metabolic activity of different brain areas. In the past decade there has been a resurgence of interest in the role of non-neural systems in the control of behaviour, especially in the control of eating and drinking. Techniques analogous to those used in the study of the brain have been applied to these systems and it can be quite instructive to compare the way in which people have approached these non-neural systems with these methods with the way they go about studying the central nervous system.

Methodological problems come in two varieties, technical and conceptual. Technical limitations are those that affect our ability to do what we set out to do. Conceptual factors are those which limit our ability to draw conclusions from experiments, even if they are technically perfect. Technical problems usually revolve around the degree to which we can isolate or manipulate a single target system in a consistent and reliable way (Bures, Buresova, and Huston 1976). For example, in practice it is extremely difficult to make a brain lesion that entirely removes one part of the brain while leaving the rest intact; they are either too large or too small. Often lesions damage the connections of other systems that happen to pass through the lesion site. Unless carefully monitored, stimulation of the brain leaves us with the problem of not knowing the extent of the area that has been affected by the stimulation. Recording studies are not entirely exempt from these problems. Measurement of the metabolic correlates of psychological processes can only be done with a limited degree of spatial resolution at the moment (Raichle 1983). The problem with other recording studies, notably single unit recording work, is often too much selectivity with a resultant bias towards a particular subset of cells in a particular region of the brain. Different groups, using slightly different recording techniques, can end up with quite different descriptions of the response properties of the cells in the same region because they are, in fact, recording from different cell populations (O'Keefe and Conway 1978; Olds, Disterhoft, Segal, Kornblith, and Hirsh 1972; Stryker and Sherk 1975).

As if technical problems were not enough, there are also a number of conceptual problems surrounding the application of these methods. The basic problem is that most methods make implicit assumptions about the way the brain is organized. Clearly, bits of the brain do not exist in isolation. The functions of any single region of the brain are going to be expressed through that region's connections with other parts of the nervous system and the effects of our experimental procedures are going to depend on the nature of those interconnections. Understanding the functions of one part of the brain is going to depend on understanding how these others work. This is coming dangerously close to saying that we cannot find out how the brain works until we know how the brain works! We escape from this vicious circle by using the 'bootstrapping' procedure of making simplifying assumptions about the functional organization of the brain and interpreting our experiments in the light of them. As long as our experiments produce results that make sense we continue with these assumptions. When our experiments stop making sense we should go back to these assumptions to see whether they need revision. To understand what is going on in physiological psychology one needs to know what these assumptions are.

Some of our assumptions are about how the brain is organized but others concern behaviour itself. Psychobiology is characterized by our attempts to study the brain by correlating neural factors with behaviour, and there is genuine disagreement amongst researchers about how to study the behaviour itself. For example, some focus on 'natural' units of behaviour, while others use inferential behavioural measures to tap underlying cognitive, sensory and motor processes. With the inferential approach it is clearly necessary to have a good understanding of the psychological processes involved in performing the test procedures we use and good theories of those processes themselves. Good psychobiology, using the inferential approach, requires good psychology. Using 'natural' units of behaviour is not without its problems as it begs the question as to what constitutes 'natural' as well as sidestepping the issue of why particular parts of the nervous system are important for particular behaviours.

Since behavioural methods are central to psychobiology they are tackled first in this chapter. We then turn to the main techniques for studying the physiological side of the equation, lesions, stimulation, and recording, looking at the sorts of problems that affect our interpretation of experiments. Relevant features of the main methods are outlined where necessary. For more detail the reader is referred elsewhere (Bures *et al.* 1976; Carlson 1986).

Behavioural testing

In principle it should be possible to describe the functional organization of the brain simply by studying its anatomical organization and the functions of its individual components, the neurons. In practice that is a recipe for disaster since, without knowing what the brain and its components do, we will never know whether we have a good description of how they work. Since the brain is the organ of behaviour we must approach its functions through behaviour. There are two issues we must consider here. The first is whether we should study behaviour as behaviour, in the way that ethologists do, or study behaviour as a reflection of underlying psychological processes, as cognitive psychologists tend to do. The second concerns the nature of the 'functions' we ascribe to neural regions as a result of our studies. Should we identify brain functions with components of psychological processes revealed in psychological studies or do we need a new set of concepts for describing brain function?

Neuroscience has two traditions, the psychological and the ethological. According to the psychological tradition, behavioural tests are tools to give us access to psychological processes (Dean 1982). According to the ethologists, behaviour is interesting in its own right (Ewert 1980). Those working in the psychological tradition devise tasks or tests that are believed to place varying levels of demand on the cognitive, sensory, or motor capacities we believe our subjects to possess. Performance on these tasks is then correlated with our physiological manipulations and, on the basis of these results, we ascribe functions to areas of the brain. For example, if we have three tests that are apparently identical except for the increasing 'memory' load they entail, and the electrical activity of part of the brain increases systematically across the three, we would be inclined to think that memory in some way involved that part of the brain. Ethologists, in contrast, work on 'natural' units of behaviour, such as prey catching or mating, correlating these with their physiological manipulations. For example, a region of the brain that showed increased electrical activity during sexual behaviour, but not during other motivational processes or comparable movements, would have a sexual function ascribed.

It would seem that the choice of approach is irrelevant because the ethologists are, eventually, going to have to start explaining why particular parts of the brain are involved in behaviours like sex or hunting and that will involve ascribing psychological subprocesses to them. In other words, the results of the two approaches should converge. However, that is only true if the psychological processes that operate during natural behaviour sequences are also accessible to our arbitrarily selected behavioural tasks (Rozin 1976). They may not be. To take a fairly dramatic example, honey-bees are capable of extremely sophisticated mathematical computations that enable them to navigate from their hives to sources of nectar, using the sun's position as a guide and compensating for its movement during the course of the day. It is unlikely that even the most devious psychologist could devise a behavioural test, other than navigation, that would harness that computational ability.

This point relates back to the issue of cross-species extrapolation raised in the preceding chapter. Those of us who use inferential methods to study underlying psychological processes are inclined to argue that these processes are available to all of the animals we study. For example, it is argued that both rats and humans have memory mechanisms and that you can, therefore, study memory in either species. In practice the situation is complicated by the fact that our ability to study psychological processes in a particular species is highly dependent on the behavioural methods used. With some methods a particular species will appear totally devoid of a particular capacity yet, with others, a startling level of ability can be revealed.

Let us take vision as an example. Rhesus monkeys readily discriminate between objects and scenes on the basis of their visual appearance. In contrast, the laboratory rat appears totally blind to the casual observer, using touch and feel, instead of sight, to negotiate its way around the environment. In formal testing situations, in which the animals are rewarded for approaching one visual stimulus in preference to a second, rats will regularly fail to learn to make the discrimination. Nevertheless, rats can be trained to carry out visual discrimination tasks and will use visual cues to guide their natural behaviour. The problem is to devise tests that will demonstrate this. As Cowey (1968) has pointed out, rats readily learn visual discrimination tasks when the contiguity between the stimulus, the response, and the reinforcement is high. Ideally, the animal should make its response by manipulating the visual stimulus itself and should receive its reward from very close by. Even small reductions in contiguity, such as getting the animal to make its response on a lever next to the stimulus or putting the reinforcement dispenser in a different location, will result in a staggering loss of performance. Under these circumstances, there are grounds to doubt the value of comparing the visual capacities, and underlying visual mechanisms, of the rat with those in rhesus monkeys and other primates, such as ourselves.

One of our goals is to describe the 'functions' of particular parts of the brain, but what is a 'function'? Is a function a psychological process or is it a neural process? There is a general consensus that psychological processes are a function of the whole brain, not of its constituent parts. It therefore makes no sense to say that 'memory' or 'perception' is the function of any part of the brain. One solution, widely endorsed, is to break down psychological processes into putative substages and assign these to different parts of the brain (Dean 1982; Luria 1973). However, these substages are still described in psychological terms. For example, in his review of the functions of the inferotemporal cortex in rhesus monkeys, Dean concludes that this area may be involved in 'stimulus categorization', rather than visual perception. Given our lack of knowledge of both how circuitry in the brain actually works and how visual perception may be mediated at the neural level, this state of affairs is scarcely surprising. Terms like 'stimulus categorization' have to be used, because we don't have any other language in which to describe what parts of the brain do, but a term like this should be taken as a shorthand for 'neural processes that could mediate stimulus categorization, whatever they may be', rather than a conclusive statement about what an area does.

Given our present level of ignorance there is a good case for muddling along as best we can until the theory catches up with the data. Indeed, our studies may actually stimulate psychological theories. There is just one problem, which is that the way in which we conceptualize the processes we are studying influences the way we study the brain. An inappropriate model of visual perception will lead us to ask the wrong questions about the parts of the brain we believe to be involved in it. This point is well illustrated by the 'decision tree' approach described by Dean (1982). He rightly argues that the best way to find out what part of the brain does is to start out with very general questions about the sorts of thing it might do and then work through to more specific questions. For example, start off by asking whether lesions produce sensory or non-sensory impairments before finding out whether the non-sensory deficits involve 'memory' or not. Figure 3.1 shows a decision tree for applying this sort of approach to analysing the functions of the monkey inferotemporal cortex. At each point the decisions are couched in terms of psychological processes or subprocesses. Were perception conceived of differently, it is quite likely that the decision tree would have had a different structure and led to different conclusions. Fortunately, there is a check in the system. If you are thinking about the brain properly you should get sensible answers to your

Figure 3.1 An example of a decision tree to be used to design behavioural experiments

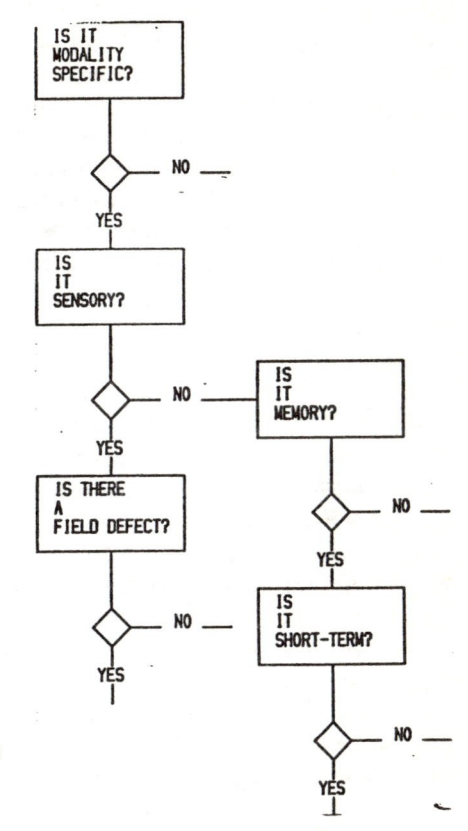

Note the progression through the tree from very general distinctions, in the upper left panel, to very specific distinctions, in the lower right.

questions. If, for example, you draw a distinction between two processes and your experiments keep on producing equivocal results, it is probably time to start thinking about the validity of the distinction.

Neural processes

The lesion method

Our goal is to make statements about the way different parts of the brain contribute to behaviour. It would seem that the simplest way of approaching this question is to remove part of the brain and assess the changes in behaviour that are produced. As might be expected, there are a number of problems with this approach. 'Removing' part of the brain is easier said than done. Brains are not designed like electronic circuits, with easily identified separate components that can be taken out independently. In fact, one never really removes a component cleanly in that sort of way; one has to damage the brain in order to eliminate a component. Consequently, we are always dealing with

39

the effects of brain injury, and those effects probably extend beyond the mere loss of a single component. For example, scar tissue may form or there may be a disturbance to the blood supply, both of which can affect the working of adjacent regions. The term 'lesion', meaning 'injury' or 'damage', reflects these problems. There are, therefore, technical problems about the lesion method. In addition there are conceptual worries. Even if the brain were designed so that components could be easily removed, there is the issue of what we can conclude about the functions of its components from knowing the effects of removing one of them. What are we entitled to conclude about the functions of an area we have removed from knowledge of how behaviour changes when it is eliminated?

Technical problems

To the naked eye the brain has a disturbingly homogeneous appearance. A small number of distinctive areas may be identified, but the functional sub-units that are the stuff of modern physiological psychology are nowhere to be seen. You cannot see prefrontal cortex, primary visual cortex, parietal association cortex, the ventromedial nucleus of the hypothalamus or most of the other structures that we are inclined to talk about. These can only be discriminated in thin sections viewed under the microscope after they have been exposed to appropriate dyes. Even then, adjacent areas often merge into each other so that the boundaries are blurred. Deep within the brain, in areas like the thalamus and hypothalamus, these problems are exacerbated by the presence of long fibre bundles that pass through interesting regions, carrying the connections of completely unrelated regions. As a consequence, attempts to remove one component often compromise the connections of others.

What are physiological psychologists to do in the face of these difficulties? They have three weapons in their armoury. The first is knowledge of the remarkable consistency in the organization of the brain, at least within individual species, the second, the availability of histological techniques which enable them to specify where a lesion has been made, after the event, even if it isn't completely possible before, and third, access to new chemical techniques for selectively destroying some components of the brain while leaving others intact (Kohler, Schwartz, and Fuxe 1979).

Much of our work concerns the mantle of the forebrain, the neocortex, which is now recognized by anatomists to be divided into a number of subfields or 'areas'. Within any species the topographical distribution of areas is constant (Zilles and Wree 1985). For example, you know that the visual cortex will lie towards the back of the brain, the motor cortex towards the front. Moreover, in animals with convoluted cortices, like cats, dogs, monkeys, and man, areas usually have a fixed relationship to the pattern of sulci and gyri on the cortical surface. For example, in the rhesus monkey, the primary visual cortex (area 17) always lies just behind the lunate and preoccipital sulci. This guidance is, of course, not available in smooth-brained animals like rats and mice, and in these it is extremely difficult to make accurate cortical removals. To reach structures deep within the brain it is not possible to use external landmarks, like folds in the cortex, directly. Nevertheless, it is possible to take advantage of the consistency of the three dimensional organization of the brain. Within any strain of a species, deep structures tend to be in a fixed position relative to certain landmarks on the skull, such as the joints between the bones that form its upper surface (Pellegrino, Pellegrino, and Cushman 1979). This enables us to use a stereotaxic instrument to guide probes like lesion-making electrodes into the brain at known distances in front of, to one side of, and below one of these landmarks and guarantee to get it into a selected subcortical area.

In most physiological psychology we take it for granted that lesions will centre on the structure selected by the experimenter. Most of the disagreement centres around how completely a structure has been eliminated, and what other structures have been damaged as well. This hinges on the quality of the histological information provided by the experimenter. Typically, at the end of an experiment the animals are killed, their brains removed and thin sections cut through the lesion sites. Exposure of these sections to dyes that are selectively taken up by either the bodies of neurons or by their axons enables us to see the structure of the lesion site. Often this is supplemented by other information. For example, the neocortex is connected to the thalamus in such a way that destruction of part of the cortex causes cells in a corresponding part of the thalamus to die, a process known as 'retrograde degeneration'. You can monitor the amount of cortical damage by looking at the extent of retrograde degeneration in the thalamus. All of these procedures are routine with animals, but are obviously the exception rather than the rule in studies of human neuropsychology, when all concerned fervently hope that the subjects will survive. To some extent we are able to get round the problems of localizing lesion sites by using modern imaging techniques like NMR (nuclear magnetic resonance) and CAT (computerized axial tomography) scanning (Carlson 1986). Nevertheless, as long as we continue to define the functional subcomponents of the brain in terms of features seen in stained microscope sections, these scanning techniques are of restricted utility. As a consequence there are, at present, serious obstacles to analysing directly the functional organization of the human brain.

Some of the problems of unintended damage to other systems could be eliminated if we could selectively destroy only certain parts of nerve cells, like their axons or their cell bodies. Recently the neurochemists have come up with a set of toxins which appear to be fairly effective in destroying only cell bodies, leaving axons intact (Kohler *et al.* 1979; Schwartz and Coyle 1977). These are not without their problems, however. Owing to the fact that some cells are more sensitive to these toxins than others it is possible for injections of the toxin in one site to result in lesions in a distant area to which the toxin has diffused, or been carried in the blood supply of the brain. This is known as the 'remote lesion effect'. Many areas of the brain are insensitive to the lesion making effects of the toxins currently available, so this approach has to be used quite selectively. A final problem is that these substances may be taken up into the blood supply as it passes through the brain and carried to other parts of the body where they may have toxic effects that confound their effects on the nervous system.

Conceptual problems

Despite these technical limitations, physiological psychologists take the lesion method very much for granted. If one were to suggest to an electronics engineer that he might want to study how a circuit works by pulling bits out and observing changes in function his reaction would probably be one of horror! His argument would be that most electronic circuits are organized interactively, by which we mean that the proper operation of one component depends on the normal operation of all of the others. Pull one part out and all of the others cease to function properly. As a consequence, the changes produced will tell you nothing about the normal functions of that part. Gregory (1961) illustrates this nicely. Imagine, he says, a radio set that works perfectly until you pull out a single component but then proceeds to emit a high-pitched whine. We would be unlikely to conclude that the function of that component was to inhibit the emission of high-pitched whines. Knowing how radio sets are typically organized we would be much more likely to conclude that the whole circuit was working incorrectly.

Interactively organized circuits are highly resistant to analysis by the elimination of single components so we can only really use the lesion method if we can convince ourselves that the brain is organized differently. Gregory was unable to do so and counselled us to abandon the lesion method altogether. Others, like Weiskrantz (1968) and Dean (1980; 1982), are much more sanguine and argue the brain is generally not interactive so that knowledge of what is lost after a lesion can be used to frame conclusions about the normal function of a region. Part of the case is anatomical in that some parts of the brain are scarcely connected to others. We must be careful with this argument because it is sometimes based on anatomical studies that have used insensitive methods or only a partial consideration of the data. In fact the brain has considerable anatomical scope for being interactive. The stronger argument is a functional one, that brains do not respond to damage like typical interactive systems. Interactively constructed devices are extremely sensitive to damage to their components. This is not surprising since damage to one part of the circuit affects how the rest of it behaves. In contrast, it is remarkable how little change in function there usually is when the brain is damaged.

The brain is highly resistant to damage. Engineers know that the way to make something that resists damage is to give it a modular structure. A modular structure is one in which groups of components are functionally isolated from each other so that, if one group is damaged, the rest continue to function normally. In fact, there are two ways of achieving this. One is to design functionally independent modules that all carry out different functions, the other is to have a number of identical modules, all capable of the same functions. I shall call the former a 'complementary' system, the latter a 'redundant' system. Complex electronic devices tend to involve both types of modular organization. For example, the central processor unit of a digital computer is usually a separate module from the memory and so they have complementary functions. Within the memory itself there will be a number of chips, each capable of working in the absence of the others, thus employing redundant modularity.

Neither Weiskrantz nor Dean argues that the whole brain is organized in modules, but they do maintain that there is sufficient evidence for modularity in enough systems for it to form a useful working hypothesis. Resistance to damage can be explained in terms of modular organization but is scarcely conclusive evidence for it. The apparent persistence of behavioural function after brain damage may equally reflect the insensitivity of our methods of assessing function. To continue with Gregory's example, his radio might emit a whine so high-pitched that it is undetectable to the human ear and can only be picked up by special test equipment. What makes the modularity argument more compelling is the fact that brain lesions usually do produce effects, but those effects are highly specific to the area that has been damaged. Damage to a particular part of the brain affects one function while leaving all others intact. Specificity means that not only is a function lost or impaired after damage to one part of the brain but that it survives damage to other parts of the brain that, in turn, produces other effects. This logic is embodied in the double dissociation paradigm (Teuber 1955), which is the most widely used experimental design in physiological psychology. The approach is summarized in Table 3.1. Two types of lesion are studied, both groups being given the same two behavioural tests. A double dissociation is said to occur when Lesion 1 produces a deficit on Task A, but not Task B, while Lesion 2 gives a deficit on Task B but not Task A. A good example of this approach is the work of Schneider (1967), who studied visually guided behaviour in hamsters. He found that destruction of the visual cortex (Lesion 1) produced impairments in visual discrimination learning (Task A) but not in visual orientation (Task B). Damage to a visual area in the brainstem, the superior colliculus, had the reverse effect. There was an impairment on visual orientation (Task B) but not visual discrimination learning (Task A). There is, therefore, a double dissociation between the effects of visual cortex and superior colliculus lesions, suggesting that they are functionally independent.

Double dissociations don't only favour modular organization, they suggest a particular type: complementary systems. Redundant systems won't provide such clear-cut results because all of the modules are capable of doing the same

Methods in psychobiology

Table 3.1 The double dissociation paradigm

	Lesion 1	Lesion 2
Task A	IMPAIRMENT	NO IMPAIRMENT
Task B	NO IMPAIRMENT	IMPAIRMENT

job. Such a system will be highly resistant to the effects of damage to individual modules and will only begin to show marked alterations in function when a large proportion of the modules has been damaged. Moreover, the effects of damage will be much more a function of how many modules have been damaged than of which modules have been eliminated.

Wood (1978, 1980) raises the interesting question of whether double dissociations are really a good sign of what I am calling complementary modular organization. Most physiological psychologists expect the brain to be made up of complementary modules and that lesions will produce double dissociations. Their experiments are designed accordingly and tasks selected and modified until the dissociations emerge. If the brain is genuinely composed of complementary modules this is a perfectly legitimate procedure since one is selecting the behavioural task that most closely reflects the functions of the system under study. If the brain isn't organized in this way then this approach is artificially biased towards finding double dissociations. In fact, the approach of modifying tasks until dissociations emerge is logically equivalent to what statisticians term 'optional stopping'. Optional stopping is the dubious procedure of adding subjects to the sample in one's experiment until a significant difference appears and then terminating the experiment. What Wood points out is that, if the system were not made of complementary modules but was redundantly organized with function distributed across all components, there are some conditions under which double dissociations would still arise. This conclusion is not based on studying real brains but on modelling a simple brain with known redundant organization. Consider a brain designed as in Figure 3.2. In this brain there are eight 'neurons' sending information into the brain and eight sending output, presumably to the muscles. Each of the input neurons connects to every output neuron. Output neurons can be activated in one of two ways, either by the 'output pattern generator' line, or by the input cells. The input cells are activated only by sensory input. The system is designed so that it will 'learn' to generate output patterns in response to input patterns. It can do this because the capacity of an input neuron to activate any of the output neurons increases every time the 'output pattern generator' activates the output neuron simultaneously with external activation of the input neuron. After a number of such pairings a particular pattern of input will come to evoke a selected output pattern, without the 'output pattern generator' being activated. Associative learning will have taken place. This system is, by

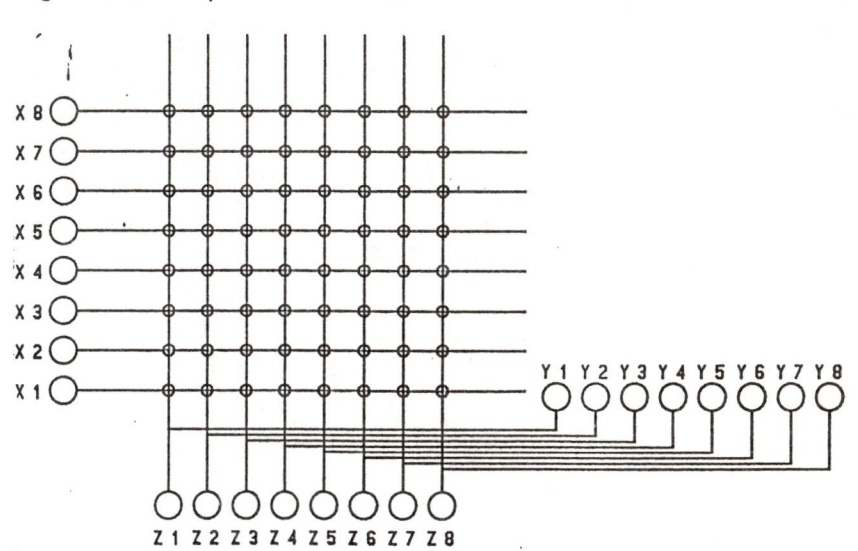

Figure 3.2 A simple associative network

There are three types of neurons, labelled X, Y, and Z. The X-neurons and Y-neurons are input cells, the Z-neurons, output cells. Each Y-neuron contacts only one output cell and is capable of activating that cell. Each X-neuron contacts all of the output cells. The activity of a Z-neuron is, therefore, the result of summing the effects of all of the X-neurons on that cell. The strength of the synaptic contact between an X-neuron and a Z-neuron is increased every time activity in the X-neuron coincides with activity in the Z-neuron induced by input via its Y-neuron.

definition, interactive since every input neuron can affect every output neuron. Using a mathematical model of this system, Wood has explored the consequences of 'lesions': removal of one or more neurons. For a wide range of input and output patterns this system responds to removal of neurons in a surprisingly robust fashion, showing little degradation of function until a large number of neurons have been removed. What is significant is that with some input patterns the picture is different. Under the conditions illustrated in Figure 3.3 this system gives a double dissociation.

Removing input neuron 1 produces difficulties with remembering output pattern A but not B. Removing input neuron 2 produces the reverse effect. Thus, by selecting the right 'task', we have constrained a system we know, because we designed it that way, to be organized redundantly to give a double dissociation. Under these circumstances the process we know to be distributed across all of the input/output cell connections appears to be localized in one neuron. Even with a simple system like this we cannot draw direct conclusions about the functions of a component from knowing what is lost when we destroy it.

Figure 3.3 Training an associative network

	Y1	Y2	Y3	Y4	Y5	Y6	Y7	Y8
G1	1	1	1	1	-1	-1	-1	-1
G2	-1	-1	1	1	-1	-1	1	1
G3	1	-1	1	-1	1	-1	1	-1
G4	-1	-1	1	1	1	1	-1	-1

	F1	F2	F3	F4
X1	-.196	-.229	.114	.912
X2	0	-.459	.912	.114
X3	-.196	.459	-.114	-.114
X4	.392	.229	.228	.228
X5	.558	-.459	.114	.114
X6	.558	0	-.114	-.114
X7	-.196	-.229	-.114	-.114
X8	-.196	.459	.228	.228

	Z1	Z2	Z3	Z4	Z5	Z6	Z7	Z8
X1	-.765	-.993	.6	.372	1.451	1.223	-.831	-1.059
X2	1.257	-.567	.567	-1.257	1.485	-.339	.339	-1.485
X3	-.655	-.427	.035	.263	-.491	-.263	.655	.883
X4	.162	-.293	1.077	.621	-.165	-.621	-.163	-.619
X5	1.016	.788	.327	.099	.128	-.1	-1.017	-1.245
X6	.558	.786	.33	.558	-.787	-.558	-.558	-.331
X7	.033	.261	-.654	-.425	.197	.425	-.034	.195
X8	-.655	-1.111	.719	.263	.192	-.263	.655	.198

	F'1	F'2	F'3	F'4
X1	0	0	0	0
X2	0	-.459	.912	.114
X3	-.196	.459	-.114	-.114
X4	.392	.229	.228	.228
X5	.558	-.459	.114	.114
X6	.558	0	-.114	-.114
X7	-.196	-.229	-.114	-.114
X8	-.196	.459	.228	.228

	Z1	Z2	Z3	Z4	Z5	Z6	Z7	Z8
Go1	1.34	1.2	.65	.51	-.7	-.84	-1.03	-1.17
Go2	-1.44	-.71	.19	.92	-1.3	-.56	1.07	1.8
Go3	1.06	-.94	1.06	-.94	1.66	-.34	.2	-1.8
Go4	-.55	-1.28	1.09	.36	1.63	.9	-.74	-1.46

	F'1	F'2	F'3	F'4
Go1	1.19	1.01	.76	.59	-.42	-.6	-1.2	-1.38
Go2	-1.62	-.94	.33	1.01	-.97	-.28	.88	1.56
Go3	1.15	-.82	.99	-.98	1.49	-.48	.29	-1.68
Go4	.15	-.37	.54	.02	.31	-.21	.02	-.5

Those of us who want to go on using the lesion method shouldn't be too despondent about Wood's results because the conditions under which a system like this will give double dissociations are likely to be very rare in nature. Close inspection of Figure 3.3, which is based on Wood's simulation, shows that two conditions have to be satisfied for this sort of result to emerge. The first is that the inputs in the two tasks are restricted to two different neurons. The second is that these neurons must not be involved in any other task. If they are, then the system simply won't learn the two tasks in the first place but will consistently generate inappropriate responses. If one task uses only one input neuron and the other uses the same neuron as part of a pattern of input, then the system responds to activity in that neuron as if it is a part of the larger pattern. This capacity to generate the same response to part of a pattern as to the whole of it is one of the merits of network systems (see chapter 7). In fact, the level of independence of inputs required for this sort of system to produce double dissociations is only likely to be achieved if it is composed of complementary modules.

Many studies stop at demonstrating double dissociations. This is unfortunate because there is a more stringent test of complementary modular organization; combining lesions to two modules should have effects that are the sum of those of the individual lesions. When lesions are studied in combination it is surprising how often this second test is failed. Returning to the visual system, it is known that simultaneous destruction of both visual cortex and superior colliculus produces complete insensitivity to brief light flashes in monkeys whereas destruction of either structure in isolation has no effect (Mohler and Wurtz 1977). This is compatible with the other version of modular organization, redundancy, but it is equally compatible with the system being

Figure 3.3 (continued)
Simulation of the effects of training a simple, eight-neuron, associative network with four combinations of input patterns and then removing one of the X-neurons. Columns F1 to F4 represent the four training patterns on the X-input cells and rows G1 to G4 represent four 'forcing' patterns on the Y-inputs. Columns Z1 to Z8 show the resulting strengths of synaptic contacts between each X-input neuron and each Z-output neuron. Rows Go1 to Go4 illustrate the magnitudes of the outputs produced at each of the output neurons (Z1 to Z8) by applying the four training patterns, F1 to F4. Go1 shows what is produced by applying F1, Go2 shows what is produced by applying F2, and so on. The right-hand side of the figure shows what happens if input neuron X1 is removed after training, represented by zeros in the X1 row, and the four training patterns applied again. The modified patterns are represented by F'1 to F'4. The resulting output patterns are shown in the bottom right-hand block. Again, row Go1 is associated with input pattern F'1, and so on. The output for training patterns F'1 to F'3 is little affected by removal of X1, but the response to F'4 is greatly distorted. Removing neuron X2 has a similar effect on response to training pattern F'3.

interactive, if we assume that removal of any one component has effects that are not detected by the behavioural task. This illustrates another problem, that the only effective difference between an interactive and a redundant modular system is the degree of disruption produced by damage to a single component. As yet we have no agreed criteria for how much disruption a single lesion needs to cause for the system to be deemed interactive, although common sense suggests that an interactive system would be much more vulnerable to disruption than the brain appears to be.

A further problem with the lesion method is how to move from the symptoms produced by the damage to a description of the normal functions of the brain area concerned. It isn't safe to assume that the normal functions of a system are equivalent to what is lost after a lesion because the effects of a lesion may be masked by positive symptoms. A positive symptom is something that happens in the brain-damaged animal that doesn't happen in the normal. A good example of a positive symptom is the spasticity that occurs after some forms of damage to the motor system. In spasticity, all of the muscles controlling a limb tend to be contracted at the same time, so that the limb locks into position. It is clearly circular, and not very helpful, to argue that the normal function of the structures concerned is to suppress spasticity.

Disconnection

Before leaving lesions in the central nervous system there is one variant that needs mention: disconnection. Instead of trying to eliminate neural centres the aim is to sever the pathways that connect them, leaving the centres themselves intact (Geschwind 1965). The aim here is to find out how much a system can do without the benefit of other forms of input. By concentrating on what survives after a lesion, rather than on what is lost, this approach seems more readily interpretable. The best example of the application of this approach is the work on the effects of cutting the corpus callosum in humans (Gazzaniga 1985).

Some thirty years ago an operation was introduced to control the spread of epilepsy from an affected cerebral hemisphere to the other, unaffected one. This operation involved cutting the main fibre tract that joins the two halves of the brain, the corpus callosum. This operation has little effect on day-to-day behaviour, although it is not completely without consequences. It has attracted the interest of physiological psychologists because it enables them to study the operations of one cerebral hemisphere, isolated from input from the other. Conclusions about the functions of one hemisphere that had previously been based on observations of the effects of injury could be confirmed by studies that showed that the self-same functions were retained by that hemisphere after section of the callosum, but were not available to the other. For example, many studies have shown that language is vulnerable to left, but not right, hemisphere damage in most people, suggesting that the left hemisphere has a special role in language. In split-brain patients it has been shown that the left hemisphere retains language function, the right does not. Not only is the left hemisphere normally necessary for language, it is also sufficient. That adds significantly to our knowledge of the role of the brain in language, and also confirms our faith in the conclusions that we can draw from lesions.

Analogous studies outside the central nervous system (CNS)

During the 1930s and 1940s physiologists were deeply concerned with the role of feedback from the digestive system in the control of hunger. Some authors argued that such feedback was the primary signal for hunger while others argued that the signal came from elsewhere. The issue seemed to be settled when a number of studies were carried out that showed that animals and humans still regulated their food intake even after the stomach had been removed, an experimental procedure analogous to ablation of part of the CNS. More recently, people have started to reinvestigate the role of the stomach in hunger and have found that, when the stomach is intact, feedback from it plays a vital part in controlling food intake (McHugh and Moran 1985; Rolls and Rolls 1982; Smith and Gibbs 1979). In this instance, when dealing with something as simple as the digestive system, the lesion method gave a false picture of the role of a particular component. This is because the method poses what may be a false question, 'is this structure necessary for the process I am studying?', when what we really want to know is 'what part does this structure play in the process I am studying?'

Stimulation

Many psychologists are very unhappy about lesions. They are much more at home with stimulation. Stimulation involves feeding a signal into some part of a circuit and measuring its consequences at some other point. Since you are not altering the brain in any other way, the way the brain is organized would not seem to affect the interpretation of stimulation studies. Stimulation will work as well for interactive as for modular systems. Nevertheless, in reality there are difficulties with this method that limit its use. One of these is technical, the other conceptual. The technical problem is that of ensuring that the stimulation is of a duration and intensity to be physiologically realistic. Ten minutes of stimulation at 100 volts in a system that operates on a millisecond timescale and deals in ion currents that generate a few thousandths of a volt is scarcely going to simulate what happens normally in the brain. The conceptual problem is that of interpreting the effects of localized stimulation in a system that probably deals with patterns of input.

Stimulation can either be electrical or chemical. Electrical stimulation is delivered via electrodes, often similar to those used in lesion-making studies. Chemical stimulation is delivered via fine tubes, cannulae, lowered into the intended stimulation site. Usually stimulation devices are positioned using a stereotaxic device. The main technical problems concern delivering stimulation at an intensity that mirrors the level of activity that occurs spontaneously in the brain, and determining which structures have been affected by it. Whether one uses electrical or chemical stimulation there is inevitably a gradient of intensity of stimulation as one moves away from the source. That means that in order to stimulate over a large area the intensity of stimulation at the input site is likely to be many orders of magnitudes in excess of normal levels of electrical or chemical activity. Not only are there likely to be unphysiological levels of stimulation, but it is frequently unclear, from published reports, how extensive the effective stimulation zone actually was.

Something can be learned from relatively crude techniques in which there is a large stimulation zone and high stimulation levels in the centre. They suggest the sorts of function an area might be involved in, and some degree of localization is possible by varying stimulation sites and finding the one that produces the largest response for the lowest level of stimulation. Nevertheless, by itself the traditional stimulation approach, using large sources of stimulation, is imprecise. Recognizing these problems, many people engaged in electrical stimulation work have moved to microstimulation. This involves stimulating through microelectrodes of the sort used in single unit recording studies (see below), with very low currents at a level calculated to affect a small population of adjacent cells or fibres. With this technique it is possible to restrict activation to a few cells and, by simultaneously monitoring single unit activity through a nearby recording electrode, establish the extent of spread of effective stimulation. What is remarkable is that, in some systems, such as the deep layers of the superior colliculus and the motor cortex, such stimulation still elicits reactions such as eye movements or muscle twitches (Donoghue and Wise 1982; Schiller and Stryker 1972). With these procedures it is possible to measure the extent of the effective stimulation zone, rather than assuming it.

Even if one has a stimulus of physiologically realistic intensity, that doesn't necessarily mean that one can readily interpret the effects of stimulation, because there are still two problems. The first is that the brain is organized with a considerable amount of parallel wiring, so that information about the same event may be encoded in the activity of a number of cells, not necessarily adjacent to each other. The second is that the electrical activity of the brain is temporally patterned: when a cell is active or inactive is as important as how much it is active. Unless one knows in advance how information is represented in part of a brain one can neither stimulate the right combination of elements, nor produce the correct temporal pattern of activity. Stimulation, therefore, only provides readily interpretable data when one either knows a lot about the brain, or the brain is organized in a simple way.

Stimulation provides readily interpretable data under two conditions. One is if local elements are arranged in parallel with independent access to the output mechanisms. The other is if a system is organized so that the amount of activity in its neurons is more important than their spatial or temporal pattern. The first condition is satisfied in parts of the motor system, in which cells in the brain project directly on to motor neurons in the spinal cord so that a small group of cells in the CNS have a 'direct line' to a small group of muscles, and perhaps in visuomotor centres in the brainstem (Donoghue and Wise 1982; Schiller and Stryker 1972). In both of these, microstimulation leads to discrete, repeatable movements. The second is probably satisfied in the ascending catecholaminergic pathways running through the hypothalamus (Stricker and Zigmond 1976; Stricker 1983). They are not obviously satisfied elsewhere and it is significant that these are the main areas that have proved susceptible to analysis by stimulation.

Analogous studies outside the CNS

Stimulation has been the method of choice for most researchers studying the peripheral mechanisms of eating and drinking. By producing precisely controlled changes in the concentrations of nutrients or salts in the blood it has been possible to explore the role of factors like blood glucose level or cellular dehydration in eating and drinking (LeMagnen 1985; Rolls and Rolls 1982). Within the last decade, analogous methods have been used to study the role of the gastro-intestinal tract in satiation. By loading specific parts of the system with food or water it has been possible to investigate, for example, the role of the stomach in the termination of eating and drinking. What emerges from this work is the complexity of the interactions between components of the system. For example, loading the stomach with food or water directly has some satiating effect, but not as great as when the substance is also allowed to pass into the intestine or has previously passed through the mouth. These findings raise another problem with stimulation methods, which is that the effects of stimulating at individual points in a system are only readily interpretable when the effects of activating separate parts of a system are additive. That is to say, the effects of activating two components together have to be the sum of the effects of activating either in isolation. If this doesn't occur with a relatively simple system like the peripheral mechanisms controlling appetite, there must be some doubt about how often this condition is satisfied in the central nervous system.

Recording

If part of the brain is especially important for a particular process, there should be some change in the activity of that area when that process is evoked. An area involved in memory should be more active during tasks that have a high memory component than during those that place few demands on memory. For many years 'activity' in the brain has been considered synonymous with electrical activity. That the brain is electrically active was established a century ago. Some fifty years ago the engineers came up with devices that could record the electrical activity of living brains and living nerve cells. Physiologists capitalized on this instrumentation to demonstrate that the electrical activity of the brain and its nerve cells was a function of what the individual was doing, or not doing, or how sensory receptors were stimulated. All along they were also aware that brains were composed of living cells that were active in non-electrical ways as well, but until recently the techniques for looking at this other activity were not available. The situation has changed and it is now possible to determine, for example, how much oxygen is being used by a particular area of the brain while a subject does a task like reading or memorizing a word list (Raichle 1983).

A wide range of electrical recording techniques are currently available, although not all are suitable for studying behavioural processes. The most important distinction is between those that register the activity of large numbers of cells and those that record action potentials from individual units. The simplest of the first type to record, but most difficult to interpret, is the electroencephalogram (EEG), in which the activity of the brain is monitored continuously through the scalp. This is used widely to determine the functional state of the brain, but is difficult to relate to the operations of different areas. More useful in this respect are 'event-related potentials', which are extracted from the EEG by signal-averaging techniques (Donchin 1984). They rely on the fact that although the EEG is very noisy there are, embedded within it, consistent changes in voltage that are time-locked to specific events like the presentation of stimuli or the performance of movements. By averaging the EEG across a large number of these events the noise cancels out and the signal emerges. Considerable localization is possible. Moreover, because the potentials have complex waveforms quite subtle analyses of the impact of experimental variables are possible. For example, it is possible to compare the effects of two experimental conditions on early or late components of the response, the former often being considered to represent 'sensory' events, the latter 'cognitive'.

Event-related potentials require many trials for the averaging procedure to work. They are, therefore, insensitive to trial-by-trial variations in performance or experimental conditions. They are also insensitive to the possibility that an area is, in some way, functionally heterogeneous. Recording from single units provides this additional information. Obviously it is rarely done in humans, but is routinely carried out in non-human subjects. Early work focused on single cell correlates of sensory stimulation in anaesthetized animals, but advances over the last twenty years have enabled us to monitor the single-cell correlates of behavioural activity in alert, freely moving animals (O'Keefe and Nadel 1978; Olds *et al.* 1972).

In some respects, action potentials are the tip of the neuronal iceberg. There is a lot of cellular activity, that may be relevant to behaviour, that does not get translated into action potentials. In anaesthetized, immobilized animals, this may be studied using intracellular recording techniques, in which very fine microelectrodes are passed into the cell, but these don't work well in freely moving animals. The more promising approach is to study the metabolic activity of the brain during behaviour. Two approaches have been developed. One, now widely used in animals, involves taking a 'snapshot' of the metabolic activity at a particular stage in an experiment (Sokoloff, Reivich, Kennedy, DesRosiers, Patlak, Pettigrew, Sakurada, and Shinohara 1977). The other allows for continuous monitoring (Raichle 1983). The snapshot technique involves injecting the animal with a radioactively labelled version of glucose, 2-deoxy-glucose (2DG), that 'sticks' in cells. The 2DG gets locked into cells in an amount proportional to that cell's metabolic activity (Sokoloff *et al.* 1977). If the animal is killed and its brain cut into thin microscope sections, the concentration of glucose in different parts may be determined by measuring the concentration of radiation. The need to kill the animal restricts the value of this method. Potentially more useful are the non-invasive monitoring techniques based on Positron Emission Tomography (PET) scanning (Raichle 1983). In this technique metabolically significant compounds, like glucose or oxygen, are given a very low-activity, short-lasting, radioactive label which decays in a highly characteristic way, giving off sub-atomic particles called positrons. By surrounding the subject's head with a detector array, connected to suitable computer hardware, it is possible to build up images of the brain, indicating the areas of different levels of radioactivity, and hence of metabolic activity. As yet this technique has limited spatial and temporal resolution but it does offer a means of looking at human brain activity in a fairly safe way. Apart from its limited spatial resolution the main disadvantage of this technique is that, for it to be safe, it has to be done with isotopes with extraordinarily short half-lives and that means that they have to be prepared on site. As a consequence, only laboratories with immediate access to particle accelerators can carry out this sort of work.

In some ways recording techniques offer the most 'direct' access to the brain and promise to provide objective indices of what part of the brain does. Nevertheless, there are still problems. Many of these are technical. For example, people who wish to record the activity of single cells in the brains of freely moving animals argue about whether to use very fine electrodes that can record from even the smallest cells but give very unstable recordings, or to use larger electrodes that bias the sample to larger cells but give more stable recordings (O'Keefe and Conway 1978; Olds *et al.* 1972). Since it may take many hours to establish what influences the activity of a single cell, this is a far from trivial issue. As many parts of the brain contain cells of varying size, which may not all be involved in the same functions, biases of this sort may determine which functions are most strongly associated with unit activity. With studies of metabolic activity there are still problems with calculating how much of the radioactivity in any part of the brain should be attributed to the utilization of metabolic fuels by the areas concerned, rather than simple uptake.

The difficulties with recording are not only technical, they are also conceptual. They relate to the issue of how information is represented in the nervous system. The basic question is this: is information represented in the brain at the level of individual cells or at the level of groups of cells? An analogy with what happens in digital computers illustrates this point. Computers are effectively large arrays of switches, which can be either 'on' or 'off'. The commands being executed are represented as a pattern of 'on' and 'off' switches in the central processor unit, so that a switch that is in the off state is carrying as much information as one that is on. In simple computers there are typically eight such switches, still allowing a large number of possible patterns. For example, having the first four on and the last four off may lead the computer to add together two numbers while the reverse may lead it to subtract them. It is clear that, in this example, any single switch in the Central Processor Unit (CPU) will be involved in all instructions. Nevertheless, in some instructions it will be 'on' but in others it will be 'off'. Finding the switch in the 'on' state would be good evidence that it was involved in an instruction. Finding it 'off' would be equivocal. Only by knowing how the processor was constructed could you say whether that state signified anything.

If representations depend on single units then changes in single cell electrical activity or overall metabolic activity can be fairly easily related to the function of the systems concerned (Barlow 1985). Any set of conditions that leads to an increase in the activity of an area does so because it is tapping its functions. Conditions that do not do so are irrelevant to its functions. If a process is distributed across a number of elements of a system then the situation is much more complex. Activity in any single unit can form part of many representations and the inactivity of a cell can be just as important for representing something as its activity. The same argument applies in principle to studies of metabolic activity. In a system that encodes information in terms of patterns of activity information processing could be going on without a net increase in metabolism. In practice this is unlikely, however, because changing the state of a cell is likely to involve energy consumption irrespective of whether the change involves an increase or decrease in activity.

When recording single cell activity there is an additional question: how do you know that the changes detected by an experimenter are detectable by other parts of the brain? In other words, how do you distinguish between those changes in neural activity that reflect the coding of information in the brain and those that are merely signs of activity with no functional significance? For most of us, some evidence of increased or decreased neural activity after the onset of some experimental condition seems sufficient evidence that something is being encoded, but as Burns and Lennie have pointed out (Burns 1968; Lennie 1981), the brain has no knowledge of these outside events. Its job is to decide whether some change in activity in a cell reflects the presence of such an event or is simply a spontaneous change unrelated to function. Both suggest that the brain does this by monitoring the statistical properties of activity. Information is then encoded as deviations from those statistical properties. In other words, it is not enough that a cell should be more or less active; the change must be sufficiently unusual statistically for it to function as a code. A further problem comes in deciding how to interpret differences in the amount of activity elicited by a set of conditions. Does the brain use all of this information, or does it work on a trigger basis so that, once a level of activity has been exceeded, the actual level is irrelevant? For example, if a cell doubles its discharge rate under one set of conditions but quadruples under another, does that difference affect how subsequent levels in the circuit respond so that one group of cells is excited by the first set of conditions but a second group is activated by the second set? These issues are far from resolved and affect our interpretation of some potentially significant findings.

Analogous studies outside the CNS

Numerous attempts have been made to correlate activities like eating and drinking with spontaneously occurring variations in the state of the body, like blood glucose level or salt concentration. In general these studies have tended to reinforce the conclusions based on stimulation studies and have yielded few surprises that affect the validity of the method.

Overview

Apart from the fairly depressing conclusion that it is very difficult to study neural mechanisms of behaviour, what else is there to learn from this summary of methodology? There are two main points that the reader needs to bear in mind when reading the rest of this book, or any other on physiological psychology. The first is that, although all methods have their shortcomings, they are not always the same. Consequently, although experiments conducted using a single methodology are open to many interpretations, studies of the same process using a variety of methods should be less equivocal. The second is that the experiments we do are only as good as the psychological theories that underlie them. If we don't understand the psychological processes that form the bases of performance on the tasks that we use in our behavioural studies our chances of understanding how the brain controls behaviour are limited.

A good example of convergence comes from studies of hemispheric asymmetry in man. It has been known for many years that damage to the left hemisphere is more likely to affect language ability than damage to the right, suggesting that the left hemisphere is very important for language. Disconnection studies in split-brain patients supported this conclusion, showing that the left hemisphere is sufficient for language. PET scan studies of metabolic activity during various forms of cognitive performance have further reinforced this point, showing that not only is the left hemisphere more active than the right during linguistic function but also that the sub-areas implicated in language by the lesion studies are more active than surrounding areas. Not only does this convergence substantiate our theories of specific psychological processes, it also enhances our faith in our methods, suggesting that the working assumptions we have made to justify their use may, in fact, be valid. Nevertheless, convergence isn't always forthcoming. For example, single unit recording studies suggest that the hippocampus is involved in classical conditioning (Thompson 1983) but lesion studies show that classical conditioning proceeds quite happily without a hippocampus.

Having shown that a part of the brain is involved in a process like language, for example, we are then faced with the question of specifying the nature of that involvement, which depends on having a serviceable psychological model of that process. Presumably the area is not responsible for the whole of language, only a component of linguistic performance, but what do these components look like? Psychological studies could provide some answers, but it is not obvious that the subprocesses of language, identified by the psychologist, will map on to individual brain areas, any more than the computational processes of a digital computer map on to individual parts of its hardware. Even if we can show that this mapping occurs, it is not a complete answer, since we then need a theory of how operations conducted at the neural level translate into behavioural subprocesses.

Methodological problems in psychobiology are not going to go away. Their existence should not be taken to mean that studying the neural bases of behaviour is beyond us, but they should be recognized when designing and interpreting experiments. Since all of our methods rely on making working hypotheses about the functional organization of the brain, these assumptions should be kept in mind all the time, and, if necessary, modified in the light of experimental evidence.

4
Perception

Perception is the basis of all action. Without perceptual systems to provide us with knowledge of the outside world we are impotent. The job of perceptual systems is to provide us with representations of what is happening in the outside world, representations based on information gathered from receptors based in different parts of the body that are tuned to specific classes of physical events. This process of building up internal representations turns out to be considerably more complicated than was initially thought. Our eyes are not cameras, our ears are not tape-recorders, faithfully but passively recording what is in the outside world. The physical events that activate our sense organs are already imperfect versions of the properties of objects that we wish to know about. For example, the perceived colours of objects are only loosely related to the wavelengths of light that they reflect into our eyes. Two objects may reflect the same wavelengths into our eyes yet be seen as having different colours. The same object may reflect different wavelengths at different times yet be seen as having the same colour. This is the stuff of colour constancy. Our sense organs are not passive relays, but encode the constantly fluctuating patterns of stimulation impinging on the receptors into fluctuating patterns of neural activity. These patterns are related to the patterns of input but already selective recoding has begun, since some aspects of the input will activate the nervous system more than others. For example, edges tend to activate the visual system more than areas of uniform brightness. Changes of pressure across the fingertips produce much more intense input from touch receptors than steady pressure. You can verify that for yourself by running your fingertips over a slightly rough surface and then stopping. The roughness that you feel while moving the fingers suddenly disappears. The job of perceptual systems is to take these fluctuating patterns of activity occurring at the receptors and interpret them in terms of what is going on in the outside world.

Many of the issues in the contemporary study of perceptual systems have come about because of our improved understanding of how the systems might work, based largely on people's attempts to build models of perceptual processes. One of the most exciting developments in recent years has been the degree of convergence between models of visual function built up by computer scientists trying to figure out how to build machines that can see and physiologists trying to work out what different parts of the visual system do. Other issues have derived directly from the study of perceptual systems. Two of the most challenging have been the demonstration of extensive parallel pathways conveying information about the same sensory modality into the brain and the demonstration that sensory systems contain multiple representations, or maps, of the outside world.

Some of the most interesting advances in perception have been made in the study of vision. The plan of this chapter is to review the main issues in the study of vision and then to consider how far what we have learned about the visual system can act as a model for understanding how other perceptual mechanisms work.

The visual system

The traditional view of the visual system is that it involves a cascade of processing stages running from the retina to the 'association' cortex. At each stage in the cascade information about the retinal location of the input is lost and is replaced with information about the properties of the stimulus object until, at the highest levels in the system, the identity of the object or objects is encoded. The system is supposed to be organized hierarchically, so that the properties of the information processing units, presumably single cells, at one stage are due to the convergence of inputs from a number of units at the previous level. Many anatomists identified three such stages of visual analysis in the cortex. In the first, primary visual cortex, V1 or area 17, as it is also known, there was considered to be a fairly faithful map of the retina with relatively little recoding of information having taken place between the eye and this part of the brain. In the second stage, usually identified with areas 18 and 19 (also known as prestriate cortex), information about where things are on the retina is lost and replaced with information about where they are in relation to each other. For example, Kolb and Wishaw (1985) claim that areas 18 and 19 contain cells that are maximally excited by the presence of corners. In the third stage, identified with areas 20 and 21 in the temporal lobe by Kolb and Wishaw (1985) and with the parietal cortex by Luria (1973), information about the retinal location of stimulus elements is largely lost and replaced with some form of representation of the object giving rise to the pattern of retinal stimulation.

This model, based initially on the fairly crude neuroanatomical data available a century ago, has stood the test of time remarkably well but data obtained over the last two decades have prompted modifications in the details. One of the most interesting findings to come out of recent research is that the visual system consists of a set of circuits arranged in parallel, rather than an hierarchically organized cascade. Parallel organization pervades the visual system at all levels. In most species there are at least three distinct classes of ganglion cells in the retina that conduct information through to the visual cortex in physiologically distinguishable streams. The optic tract projects to a number of anatomically distinct regions in the brainstem, each of which makes a unique contribution to visual function. Finally, at the level of the cortex, information is relayed in parallel streams to a set of cortical areas, each of which is devoted to analysing a particular attribute of the visual field, such as colour or stereoscopic depth. These developments have greatly enhanced our understanding of how the visual system functions. On the other hand, studies of the higher stages in the visual system, at the level at which information about the attributes of objects, such as colour or depth, is integrated into representations of objects, have been largely disappointing until recently. In part this has been due to a failure to look at the right parts of the higher order visual cortex, using the right stimuli. In part it has also been due to a lack of suitable models of how the combination of attributes could take place. Without such models it has been difficult to determine what the properties of these cortical areas should be.

Inevitably, much of the stimulus for our changing views of the visual system has come from empirical studies but, over the past decade especially, attitudes have also been changed by the development of detailed theoretical models of how visual information processing might take place. This computational approach has proved exceptionally useful in illuminating many of the findings emerging from the experimental literature.

The computational approach

There are two strategies for finding out how the visual system works. The first is to take visual systems apart, identify their components and characterize the way these components work. The second is to look at what visual systems do, build something that will do the same job, and then determine whether it works in the same way as a real visual system. The former strategy is the traditional experimental approach, the latter is the computational approach. In reality it is difficult to divorce them completely. Even the most hardened empiricists start off with some idea of how the system might work. They have to, in order to be able to decide what constitutes a sensible experiment. Computational modellers, for their part, usually have some idea of how the visual system is put together and let that guide their model building. Nevertheless, there are features peculiar to the computational approach that have important implications for physiological psychologists and these are the topic of this section.

Historically the computational approach has been most actively pursued by engineers eager to build machines that can do the same things as humans. They concentrate, in the first instance, on how things could, in principle, be done rather than focusing on whether humans do things in that particular way. Their approach is to go back to first principles, looking at the constraints that link objects and events in the real world to what happens in the retinal image and then looking for rules that can be used unambiguously to recode retinal events in terms of the outside world (Poggio, Torre, and Koch 1985; Ullman 1986).

Take, for example, the problem of an edge. To most of us the location of boundaries is self-evident but, surprisingly, boundaries of an object are far from obvious in the raw visual image which consists of a continuously varying distribution of light intensities across the retina. The location of edges has to be reconstructed by the visual system. Is there an invariant property that links edges in objects to the retinal image? Marr (1982) and others have argued that there is, and that it is the fact that edges are associated points in the image where the intensity is changing most rapidly. To locate edges in images all you need is some means of calculating the rate of change of intensity of the image and locating the points where that rate is maximal. This analysis corresponds to what Marr terms a 'computational theory' of edge detection, since it specifies the goal of the computation and the strategy by which it will be carried out. Needless to say, there are many possible ways of turning this rule into practice. The selection of the most appropriate way is the subject of the next stage, the stage of representation and algorithm, in which a set of decision criteria for identifying maximum rate of change is established. The mathematical principles of determining where the rate of change is maximal are, for mathematicians, very straightforward. They involve the process of double differentiation. If you knew the equation relating light intensity to position in an intensity profile it would be a relatively simple matter to apply double differentiation and extract the points of maximum change. Unfortunately, your visual system cannot do this. It can only work on local regions of the image and, moreover, in the real world the distribution of light intensity is two-dimensional rather than one-dimensional. As a consequence the mathematics become more complex. Nevertheless, there is a computation that can be carried out on local areas of the image that will do the same job. When this computation is carried out on local areas of the image, the product of the computation goes from positive to negative at the sites of maximal change. These transitions from positive to negative, known as 'zero-crossings', provide an indication of the location of edges.

From the point of view of an engineer wanting to make a machine that can 'see', these two stages are adequate. From the point of view of the physiologist or psychologist another stage is necessary, that of turning an algorithm into the hardware of the brain. It is unlikely that any component of the nervous system carries out exactly the same computation as the zero-crossing detector described in the previous paragraph but it is possible to make a simpler device that works very much like a zero-crossing detector. This device is a spatial filter with two antagonistic inputs, an excitatory input from a narrow central region and an inhibitory input from a broader region that covers the centre but extends beyond its boundaries. The filtering occurs because the effectiveness of a stimulus varies with its location, being normally distributed

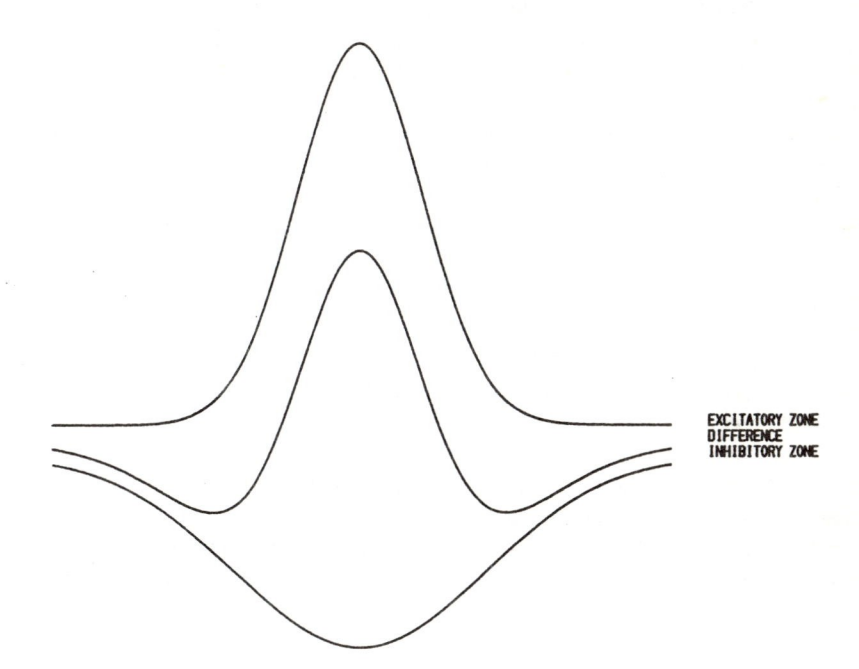

Figure 4.1 An idealized Difference of Gaussians (DOG) function

EXCITATORY ZONE
DIFFERENCE
INHIBITORY ZONE

This results from subtracting the effects of a broad, inhibitory surround from a narrow, excitatory receptive field centre.

around the centre of the receptive field of the device. Thus point stimuli located at the centre of the receptive field produce a large output while stimuli falling away from the centre produce a smaller output. The effect of the inhibitory zone is subtracted from the output from the excitatory region. Such a device is known as a Difference of Gaussians or DOG filter (Figure 4.1). The reason for this amount of detail is that DOG filters are not just a figment of the imagination, they are actually embodied in a class of retinal ganglion cells, the X-cells.

A DOG filter is not an edge detector. It needs another stage to interpret its output and locate the zero-crossing it may have encoded. The problem is that, because it is simply a filter, the output of a DOG will vary with both the location and the contrast of the edge that is present. Since it gives only a single output there will be no distinction between the zero in its output due to an edge being properly located in its receptive field and a zero due to the absence of an edge altogether. One solution to this problem is to sweep the image backwards and forwards across the retina so that edges modulate the output of the DOG filter. A subsequent stage could then monitor the change in output over time and locate edges at the points at which the cell's output changes from below to above background as the edge sweeps over the receptive field. In practice this wouldn't work because the detectors would need impossibly precise information about the speed of eye movements and the phase lag between the central movement commands and the actual movement of the image. Marr and his colleagues have come up with a simpler explanation which relies on the fact that there are two classes of ganglion cells, on-centre and off-centre. Both will fire more when an edge is placed slightly off-centre than when it is symmetrically placed, an on-centre cell when there is more light than dark edge in the field, and the off-centre cell when the conditions are reversed. If you take an on-centre and an off-centre cell with slightly overlapping receptive field and add their outputs this value will be greatest when an edge is positioned between the two. Thus unambiguous edge detection and localization can be achieved by feeding the outputs of two such cells into a subsequent level of the system in which cells will only respond when both of the input cells are active. This, Marr and his colleagues argue, is precisely what happens in the visual cortex (Figure 4.2).

I have spelled out the computational approach to edge detection for two reasons. The first is to show the level of attention to detail required to make

Figure 4.2 An edge detector circuit

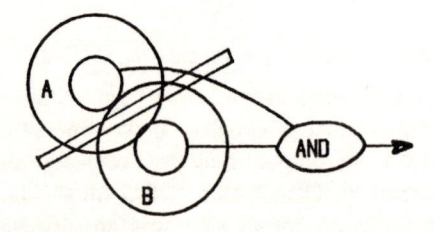

Circuitry that will convert the output from DOG filters into an unambiguous signal about the position of an edge. 'A' represents an 'on-centre' cell that is maximally excited by the onset of stimulation in its centre and 'B' represents an 'off-centre' cell that responds maximally to the offset of stimulation in its centre. Both cells will be most active when an edge is just off-centre of each, with the bright area over the 'on-centre' field and the dark area over the 'off-centre' field. The presence of an edge, signalled by simultaneous activity in the two cells, is detected by the AND-gate.

the approach work. It is not enough to say that the visual system must contain edge detectors, one also has to say how edge information could be reconstructed from the retinal image and how far the units in the CNS that appear to respond to edges do, in fact, operate according to these computational principles. For example, it is necessary to show mathematically that a DOG filter will act as a zero-crossing detector and that there are cells in the visual system that operate as DOG filters. The computational approach is, therefore, much more rigorous intellectually than that to which many psychologists have been accustomed. The second reason for spelling out the approach is to highlight the limitations in current attempts to relate computational models to the actual operations of the visual system.

At present computational models of the visual system are running ahead of our neurophysiological understanding. Marr (1982) describes many processes that have yet to be mapped on to the nervous system. Nevertheless, even if the level of precision demanded by the computational approach has not yet been realized in most instances, the approach does have other benefits. The main one has been to make us think more closely about how the visual system might be organized. One of the major points to emerge from computational theory is that the best way of achieving a representation of the environment is via a modular system that represents different properties of the environment in different parts of the system. Mathematically this is relatively straightforward. It means little more than that you can compute the direction and velocity of movement of an object independently of its colour or its depth. In terms of how the visual system is organized it raises the exciting possibility that different properties of objects are computed by anatomically distinct circuits. As we shall see, this prediction is being borne out by current work on the visual cortex.

The parallel visual system

Parallel pathways exist at a number of levels in the visual system. At the gross anatomical level the optic tract can be seen to terminate in a number of discrete relays in the brainstem. Of these the largest are the dorsal lateral geniculate body, in the thalamus, and the superior colliculus, in the midbrain, but there are a number of other sites which also receive direct retinal input. These include the pretectum, the ventral lateral geniculate body, the suprachiasmatic nucleus of the hypothalamus, and the three terminal nuclei of the accessory optic system in the midbrain. Initially it was believed that only one of these, the dorsal lateral geniculate nucleus, was involved in visual perception and that the rest were involved in visual reflexes like pupillary control (the pretectum), orientation movements (the superior colliculus), and stabilization of the visual field when the head moves (the accessory optic system). Since the late 1960s, however, a number of authorities have argued that some of these other pathways are also involved in visual perception. The issue is far from resolved.

One of the most provocative findings in recent years has been the degree of parallel organization hidden within individual anatomical regions. Enroth-Cugell and Robson (1966) started the ball rolling by showing that, in cats, there are two functional classes of ganglion (relay) cells in the retina. One class, the X-cells, responds in a sustained way to effective stimuli but only when an edge is located in the correct part of the receptive field. The other class, the Y-cells, responds transiently to steady stimuli but will respond to an edge no matter where it is located in the receptive field. Since 1966 our knowledge of ganglion cell classes has increased in leaps and bounds (Stone 1983). A new class, the W-cells, has been added, descriptions of the properties of the three classes have been extended, and it has been shown that this segregation into three classes extends to subsequent stages in the visual system, including the visual cortex. People like Sherman (1985) now argue that there are three separate streams or channels of information passing up from the retina and through the visual cortex. The great challenge is not so much describing the physiological and anatomical properties of the cells in these streams but understanding their functional significance.

Independently of the discovery of X-, Y-, and W-cells came the demonstration of multiple representations of the visual field in the secondary visual cortex. This is most clearly seen in studies of the primate visual cortex (Maunsell and Newsome 1987). Visual field representations are mapped by sampling successive locations in the visual cortex with a microelectrode and, at each location, determining where you have to place a stimulus in the visual field to activate single cells at that location. You find that cells in adjacent parts of the visual cortex are activated by stimulation in adjacent parts of the visual field. The cortex is said to be retinotopically mapped. It has been known since the turn of the century that the primary visual cortex must be retinotopically mapped. What came as a surprise was that the secondary visual cortex contained not one further map but a number of them, at least five. In some of them the retinotopic organization is quite loose but in others it is very precise. Why are there so many visual areas? What is their relationship to each other? What is their relationship to the visual cortex?

The subcortical visual system and visual perception

A distinction is often drawn between the relatively direct pathway from the retina to the visual cortex, by way of the dorsal lateral geniculate body, and the projection to other sites in the brainstem. These other sites are often referred to as the subcortical visual system. The question is whether this system contributes to visual perception in the normal brain.

The strongest evidence for such a contribution comes from studying the effects of removal of the primary visual cortex. In most mammals, apart from the cat, the dorsal lateral geniculate nucleus projects exclusively to area 17.

Ablation of area 17 leads to almost total loss of cells in the dorsal lateral geniculate body, a process known as retrograde degeneration. Nevertheless, mammals that have had the whole of area 17 removed surgically can still engage in non-reflex visually guided behaviour. They will readily learn to distinguish light from dark and there is some evidence that they can also distinguish patterns and colours, although it must be said that this capacity is extremely limited compared with the normal capacities of the animals concerned (Pasik and Pasik 1982). Some of the best evidence for sophisticated residual pattern vision after visual cortex ablation comes from work on tree shrews which can relearn some pattern discriminations after total removal of primary visual cortex (Killackey, Snyder, and Diamond 1971). However, the patterns used in these studies were extremely coarse and could probably be discriminated by developing tricks like scanning the eyes across the stimuli and judging how much the brightness changes during the course of the scan. It is significant that when the stimuli are modified to make that sort of strategy unworkable, for example by surrounding pairs of upright and inverted triangles with broad rings, tree shrews lacking visual cortex can no longer do the discriminations, whereas normal animals can. I have described these studies in detail because they are considered by many to be the best evidence for sophisticated residual pattern vision after visual cortex ablation. In nearly all of the other work residual pattern and colour vision was found to be extremely poor and only demonstrable after extensive training with special testing procedures.

When it comes to humans the issue is more clouded. For one thing it is rare for a human to suffer total loss of the visual cortex without extensive damage to the rest of the brain that confounds interpretation of the results. Most of our knowledge is based on studying regions of blindness in the visual field (scotomas) produced by partial damage to the visual cortex. This means that attempts to relate studies on animals to those on humans are not really comparing like with like. Furthermore, with subtotal damage you have no real way of knowing in advance exactly how large the scotoma should be. A major problem is that the results are so inconsistent. There is a small number of well reported cases of residual visual function within scotomas in people. For example, a number of groups have described patients who can point to the location of briefly flashed stimuli, even though they deny seeing them. Others have failed to replicate these findings (Barbur, Ruddock, and Waterfield 1980; Blythe, Bromley, Kennard, and Ruddock 1986; Campion, Latto, and Smith 1983; Weiskrantz 1980). Even within the positive results the details are often inconsistent. Most groups say that their patients are not conscious of the stimuli but some have reported that their patients are conscious of them (Barbur *et al.* 1980; Zihl 1980; Zihl and VonCramon 1985). The debate over what has become known as 'blindsight' has become very heated in recent years and it is difficult to see which side is correct. Two points do seem in order. The first is that, if it exists, blindsight, like residual vision in other mammals, is again rudimentary. The second is that it is unclear whether the findings on animals really predict what has been observed in humans.

One difference between the animal and human studies has already been mentioned, the fact that, in humans, residual vision is studied within scotomas. Some work has been done on monkeys with restricted visual cortex ablations (Mohler and Wurtz 1977; Weiskrantz and Cowey 1970) and, in these, it has been shown that the ability to detect light flashes and make saccadic eye movements to fixate stimuli within the blind field is retained. No-one has studied pattern discrimination or stimulus localization by reaching movements within the scotomas of monkeys. A second difference is that animals are tested using instrumental learning procedures to shape their choice behaviour. These have never been used in studies with humans. Finally, the most convincing evidence for residual function in animals comes from studies using very coarse stimuli that are presented for a long time. In contrast, residual vision in humans is usually tested with relatively fine stimuli presented for a hundred or so milliseconds.

What can we conclude from all this? Clearly, information from the subcortical visual system can, under some circumstances, be used for more than the control of visual reflexes. It can also influence learned and voluntary reactions to visual stimuli when the visual cortex is absent. However, it is a big jump from saying what a system can do in the absence of the visual cortex to describing its functions in the normal, intact brain. We need additional, converging, evidence to show that the subcortical visual system contributes to normal vision. The most convincing evidence would be that capacities that are retained after ablation of the visual cortex are lost after damage to subcortical systems. There is some evidence for this, but once again the situation is not clear-cut.

There is good evidence that visual reflexes retained after visual cortex ablation are lost after subcortical lesions. Destruction of the pretectum abolishes the pupillary light reflex, leaving the pupil permanently dilated. Ablation of the superior colliculus interferes with reflex orienting movements to stimuli in the peripheral visual field (Goldberg and Robinson 1978; Sprague, Berlucchi, and Rizzolatti 1973). The problems arise with visual discrimination performance. Deficits in visual function following subcortical visual system lesions have been reported many times but it is difficult to interpret them. Part of the problem is that they are often on tasks that are also severely impaired after destruction of primary visual cortex. Furthermore, the results are often inconsistent, especially when comparisons are made between different species. For example, superior colliculus lesions are reported to affect many forms of visual discrimination performance in tree shrews (Casagrande and Diamond 1974). In cats comparable lesions have some effect, but only when the animals are being trained on discriminations that are novel and with which they have had no preoperative experience, or if the lesions extend into the pretectum

(Sprague et al. 1973). In rats and monkeys superior colliculus lesions have no detectable effect on most forms of visual discrimination performance (Goldberg and Robinson 1978; Sprague et al. 1973).

Brightness discrimination performance usually survives destruction of primary visual cortex (Bauer and Cooper 1964). It is selectively impaired by lesions involving subcortical visual relays but detailed analysis of the deficit shows that it is probably due to a mild impairment in detecting contrast similar to that obtained with small cortical lesions (Legg 1988; Legg and Cowey 1977; Legg and Turkish 1983). Furthermore, a similar effect can be produced by applying a substance to the eyes that artificially dilates the pupils (Legg 1988). It is unlikely that these deficits are due to loss of a neural mechanism dedicated to brightness discrimination. There is also evidence that different mechanisms are involved in residual brightness discrimination. For example, lesions involving the pretectum can produce a deficit in normal brightness discrimination (Legg 1988) but other work suggests that it is the area rostral to the pretectum that is critical for residual brightness discrimination (Cooper, Battistella, and Rath 1981). In all, the search for visual relays working in parallel with the primary cortical visual mechanisms has been disappointing, even though there is good evidence that these areas must be capable of operating in the absence of the visual cortex. This suggests that the visual mechanisms involved in discrimination performance change after visual cortex ablation.

Table 4.1 Some of the main distinguishing characteristics of X-, Y-, and W-type ganglion cells in the cat retina

	X	Y	W
Percentage of ganglion cells	5%	45%	50%
Concentration in retina	Area centralis	Area centralis	Uniform
Latency to optic tract stimulation	Short	Moderate	Long
Receptive field diameter	Large	Small	Large
Contrast reversal test	No null position	Null position	No clear pattern
Response to drifting grating	Twice grating frequency	Grating frequency	No clear pattern
Response to steady contrast	Transient	Sustained	Mixed

The X-, Y-, W-cell debate

The idea of three separate channels running from the retina to the visual cortex via the dorsal lateral geniculate body is now well established. The criteria for distinguishing between the three are laid out in Table 4.1. Most of the criteria are electrophysiological but X-, Y-, and W-cells in the retina may also be distinguished on morphological grounds. Most of the electrophysiological properties are only apparent when appropriate testing procedures are used.

Conventional procedures for studying receptive fields involve presenting small spots of light or dark, or light/dark edges and moving them around until you find the point in the visual field where they affect the response of the cell. In more sophisticated tests two stimuli may be used, one probing the centre of the receptive field while the other explores the surrounding region to detect the presence of antagonistic effects from the surrounding region. This allows you to say where the receptive field lies and a little bit about its spatial organization but, unless you are very lucky, it would not allow classification into X-, Y-, and W-categories with any confidence. Most of the classificatory procedures involve studying response to periodic stimuli. Visual stimuli can vary periodically in space, time, or both. With periodic stimuli you can begin to ask questions about the optimal frequencies for generating responses and whether the response is linear. Temporal periodicity is fairly self-evident. It is the number of times part of the display cycles from light to dark to light again in each second. Spatial frequency is less intuitively obvious but is related to the number of times the display cycles from light to dark to light again as you go a fixed distance in a single direction across the display. For technical reasons spatial frequency is expressed in cycles per degree rather than cycles per centimetre. For most experimental purposes spatial variations occur in only one dimension so that the stimuli appear as light and dark stripes. Such patterns are known as gratings. Although it is not strictly necessary, most work is done with stimuli that vary sinusoidally in space or time. The luminance profile of a typical grating pattern is shown in Figure 4.3. Linearity is a complex concept that relates to the degree to which the output of a system mirrors its input. A system is linear if its output is an undistorted representation of its input. This may be assessed by moving a grating over the receptive field of the cell and measuring the output of the cell as a function of the position of the grating relative to the centre of the receptive field. A linear cell will give a response profile like that of the middle curve in Figure 4.3. A non-linear cell will give a response like that of the upper curve in Figure 4.3. Note that cells with linear response properties usually have a 'null position'. That is to say, there is a way of positioning the grating relative to the receptive field centre that results in no response. This means that absence of output from linear cells is ambiguous. It could mean that no stimulus is present or it could mean that it is in the wrong position. On the other hand, the presence of a response is highly informative since it not only indicates the presence of a stimulus but also gives

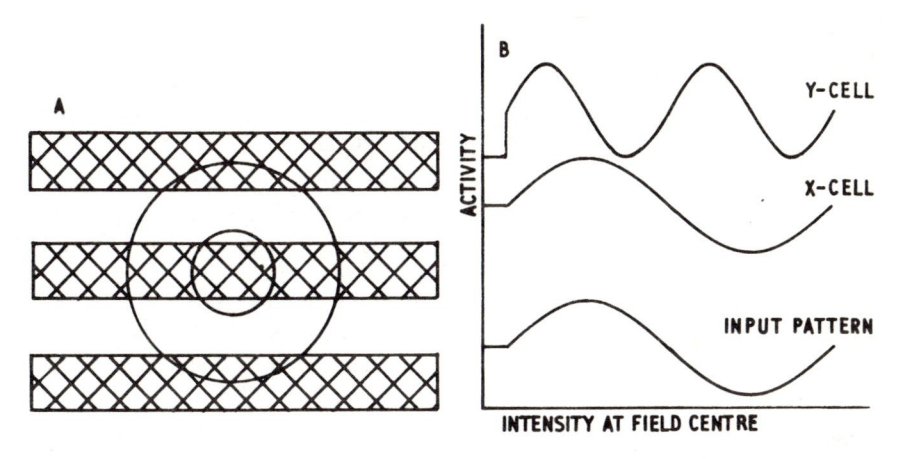

Figure 4.3 Idealized representation of the responses of X-and Y-cells to periodic stimuli

'A' indicates the experimental condition, with a grating (cross-hatched) placed across the receptive field (concentric circles). Usually, the grating is moved slowly across the field. 'B' indicates variations in the input and output over time. The lower curve shows the light intensity at the centre of the receptive field as a sinusoidal grating drifts across it. The middle curve shows the corresponding output of an idealized X-cell. Note the modulation of activity at the same frequency as the input intensity and the fact that the mean activity of the cell does not change. The upper curve shows the corresponding output of a Y-cell. Note the modulation at twice the input frequency and the elevation of mean activity level.

some information about the location of the stimulus relative to the centre of the receptive field. To complicate matters some cells behave linearly under some conditions and non-linearly under others.

We can now begin to make some sense of the differences between the three classes of ganglion cells. The first point to emerge is that W-cells are not a homogeneous class. Some are linear, others non-linear. Some have clear centre-surround organization, the others do not. The only things that unite this class are the slowly conducting axons, the large receptive field sizes, and their poor sensitivity and resolution. X-cells are fairly straightforward. Conduction velocity is average, spatial summation within the receptive field is linear (they have a null position usually), the receptive field has a centre-surround organization, and receptive fields are small. These cells respond quite vigorously when medium and high spatial frequency stimuli are used, but are less responsive when low spatial frequency stimuli are employed. Good spatial resolution means that they tend to respond to high spatial frequencies. Their temporal resolution, which is fair, refers to the highest temporal frequency with which the cell can follow reversals of stimulus intensity within the receptive field. Y-cells are possibly the most complicated of the lot. Their axons conduct very rapidly. However, as Lennie (1980) points out, that does not mean that these cells respond more rapidly to visual stimuli than the other classes, since the latency of response to visual input is determined largely by events in the retina. At low spatial frequencies they are linear but as the spatial frequency is increased non-linear properties emerge. This is believed to be due to the complex organization of their centre-surround mechanisms. Receptive fields are of medium size, i.e. larger than those of X-cells, smaller than those of W-cells. They respond well to low spatial frequencies. They will respond to high spatial frequencies but, as mentioned above, the response is non-linear. Their temporal resolution is better than that of X-cells. Under the conditions that usually obtain in receptive field plotting studies one further distinction has been reported. X-cells respond to standing contrast with a sustained response that persists as long as the stimulus is present, while Y-cells give a transient response that fades during the course of the stimulus presentation. This is not a good criterion, however, for three reasons. The first is that it says nothing about W-cells. The second, and more important, is that it depends on the test conditions. It is possible to make X-cells behave transiently and Y-cells to behave in a sustained manner if the stimulus intensity is altered. It is therefore unlikely that, under normal conditions, X- or Y-cells behave in a reliably sustained or transient manner. The third is that, in the real world, the eyes are moving all the time so that even cells that would behave transiently in electrophysiological studies in which the eyes are routinely immobilized, would generate a continuous output as the stimulus sweeps backwards and forwards across the receptive field. The distinctions between the three cell types are quite subtle and may only be obvious after quite extensive testing. What then is their functional significance?

The first point to note is that no-one has a convincing explanation for the existence of W-cells. Most of the debate centres on the X-/Y-cell distinction. Given that the number of W-cells in the retina probably exceeds the number of Y-cells, this is unsatisfactory. For many years the favoured explanation for the X-/Y-cell distinction was that Y-cells are involved in the analysis of stimulus change, especially movement, while X-cells are involved in spatial vision and the localization of features (Lennie 1980). This argument is based on the fact that X-cells have better spatial resolution than Y-cells while the latter have better temporal resolution, plus the fact that Y-cells tend to respond only transiently to sustained contrast. In fact, this hypothesis makes much of what are fairly small differences in the functions of these cell types and, more importantly, ignores the fact that under most normal conditions visual perception operates well within the limits of resolution of the visual system. We can still identify objects when they are blurred, which removes the higher spatial frequencies, and most of the time moving objects are moving neither very fast nor very slowly. A hypothesis that stresses how these cell types work at their limits is unsatisfactory (Sherman 1985).

Lennie (1980) has come up with a more challenging suggestion. He argues that Y-cells are so rare in the retina they cannot possibly contribute to visual perception because their resolution, by themselves, is inadequate to convey any useful information. Instead, he argues, they provide a tonic input to the cortical units that are processing input relayed by X-cells, modulating the activity of these units to improve the efficiency of visual processing. Sherman (1985) objects to the idea that Y-cells are irrelevant to spatial vision on the grounds that spatial vision persists after removal of the X-cell system. The evidence for this comes from work on cats, a species in which the X-cells terminate almost entirely in area 17 of the cortex while the Y-cells project additionally to adjacent areas of the visual cortex. In cats, ablation of area 17 alone does not abolish form vision but additional removal of adjacent parts of the visual cortex does. On the basis of these studies Sherman argues that it is the Y-cell system that is responsible for form vision while the X-cell system is responsible for visual functions that require very high acuity, like hyperacuity tasks and stereoscopic fusion. While the evidence he cites shows that Y-cells may be capable of sustaining some form of pattern vision it does not show that they are responsible for it in the normal brain. For a start, the visual tests used in these experiments are simple in the extreme and place few demands on the discriminative capacity of the system. Second, it has yet to be shown that the reverse experiment, removing the immediately adjacent areas of the cortex while leaving area 17 intact, has the devastating effects on visual perception that would be expected. A simpler interpretation is that the experimenters have rediscovered what Lashley (1950) showed many years ago, that partial removal of the cortical area to which the dorsal lateral geniculate body projects, has remarkably little effect on simple form discrimination tasks and that it is only when the entire cortical projection zone is removed that severe deficits, detectable in the simple behavioural paradigms we use, emerge.

Undoubtedly the existence of three parallel visual channels running from the retina to the visual cortex is one of the most important findings in visual physiology in the past two decades. Any workable theory of visual perception must incorporate this discovery. At present, however, we lack an entirely satisfactory theory to explain the existence of the three mechanisms. Lennie's (1980) proposal makes the most sense of the relative number of the cell types in the retina but is difficult to reconcile with the lesion data. Since these behavioural data are so crucial to interpreting the physiological findings they will repay careful scrutiny.

Multiple visual areas

One of the major discoveries of the last two decades has been the mosaic of visual field representations that bounds the primary visual cortex in all of the mammals that have been studied so far. When these representations are studied in detail it turns out that they differ from each other in a number of important ways (Maunsell and Newsome 1987). The amount of cortex given over to the central as opposed to the peripheral visual field can differ, as can the size of receptive fields of cells within the area. Receptive field properties also differ from area to area. For example, V4 in rhesus monkeys contains a very high density of colour coding cells that are unresponsive to white stimuli. Such cells are rare in the other visual areas. Area MT is rich in movement-sensitive cells and V2 contains cells tuned to 'retinal disparity', the cue that is the basis of depth perception.

One of the puzzling features of these areas is that the receptive field properties of their cells appear to repeat properties already present in primary visual cortex. For example, V1 has colour-coding cells that do not respond to white light. It also has movement-sensitive cells and cells tuned to particular retinal disparities. Why are these properties repeated in secondary visual cortex?

To answer this question we need to know what is and is not being done in the primary visual cortex and here our understanding has been greatly advanced by the computational approach to vision. One of the paradoxical achievements of the computational approach is that it makes even very elementary processes seem complex while, at the same time, actually simplifying problems that were once thought complex. A good example of a simple problem made complex is movement discrimination. To understand the problem we need to look at a moving object from the point of view of a single cell in the visual cortex. What does that cell see? It sees a tiny patch of the visual field measuring a few degrees of visual angle across. The object that it is looking at will be many times larger than a single receptive field. Under these conditions the 'aperture effect' operates, which is that no matter what the true direction of movement of the object through the visual field what you see through the aperture is movement at right angles to the orientation of the

Figure 4.4 The aperture effect

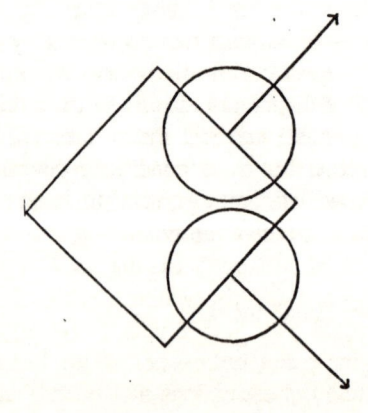

A diamond moving from left to right, but viewed through one of the two small apertures, will appear to move either to the lower right or the upper left.

edge that is passing across the aperture. The problems that this will create can be seen from Figure 4.4, which shows a diamond moving across two receptive fields, one located above the other. As the leading edge of the diamond crosses the upper cell, that cell will 'see' movement up and to the right. The lower cell will see movement down and to the right. When the trailing edge crosses the reverse will happen. The upper cell will see movement down and to the right and the lower cell will see movement up and to the right. Both cells will see movement to the right but the direction seen will vary by 90 degrees. The brain's problem is to convert this ambiguous information about the movement of edges through the visual field into an unambiguous representation of the movement of an object, in this case a diamond moving from left to right.

Movshon and his colleagues (in Maunsell and Newsome 1987) have shown that this translation from the movement of edges to the movement of objects probably takes place in area MT. The experimental demonstration is quite ingenious. If you present someone with a set of stripes on a TV screen and make them move at right angles to their long axis, that is the direction in which the person will see them move. If you add a second set of stripes, at right angles to the first but also moving at right angles to their axis, the person will not see two sets of stripes but a set of chevrons moving at 45 degrees to the true directions of movement. This is because the aperture problem has been overcome at some level in their visual system. Movshon took stimuli like these to test the responses of movement-sensitive cells in V1 and MT of rhesus monkeys. Initially he tested preferred direction of movement for each cell using a simple stimulus and then tested again using the double grating patterns. Cells in both V1 and MT responded to the double grating stimuli but with one important difference. In V1 the cells would only respond to the double grating if one of the two moved in the preferred direction of the cell as tested with simple stimuli. They did not respond if the perceived direction of movement of the chevron was in the preferred direction. In contrast, cells in MT only responded when the perceived direction of movement of the chevron matched the preferred direction assessed with simple stimuli. The cells did not respond if one of the gratings moved in the preferred direction. In a more complex version of the same test the stimuli were three gratings moving in different directions. Under these conditions the human observer sees a chevron, made up of two of the gratings, moving against a background made up of the third. Which two gratings are combined into the chevron depends on a number of factors. What is important is that cells in area MT of monkey always responded according to the illusory direction of movement of the chevron perceived by a human observer rather than to the physical direction of movement of the component gratings. Cells in V1, in contrast, always responded according to the direction of movement of the component gratings. These findings explain why movement is represented twice in the visual cortex. In the first representation it is movement of features across the retina that is represented.

In the second it is the movement of objects. How the computation of object motion from image motion is carried out is currently the subject of intense research (Hildreth and Koch 1987).

It is well established that objects are perceived to have the same colour despite quite extensive variations in the colour of the light with which they are illuminated and hence the wavelength of the light they reflect back to the retina. Colour constancy, as this is known, proved a problem in visual perception for many years. It was usually solved by arguing that our visual systems use our knowledge of the identity of objects we are looking at to dictate the colours we attribute to them, independently of the wavelength information available at the retina. This theory makes the unlikely prediction that you will not experience colour constancy with objects you cannot identify. Nevertheless, we do not have difficulties judging the colours of unfamiliar objects. Pieces of abstract art do not suddenly change colour because we have moved them from artificial light to daylight. The theory also has difficulty in coping with colour perception when a particular object may come in a number of colours. For example, apples can be red, green, yellow, or brown, depending on their type. Even oranges can be green! It makes much more sense to assume that our colour experience is linked to the properties of the retinal image rather than to our knowledge of objects. How is this to be achieved?

Land has come up with a credible answer in his Retinex theory of colour perception (Land 1974). His starting point is the fact that we have three classes of receptors in our eyes, each tuned to respond to a different wavelength of light, one to 'red', one to 'green', and one to 'blue'. This has, of course, been recognized for over a century. Where Land's theory differs from previous models of colour vision is that, instead of relating colour directly to wavelength, he argues that colour experience is related to the relative outputs of these three classes of receptor in different parts of the visual field. If the wavelength composition of the light falling on a scene changes then the wavelengths reflected by, say, a red area will change accordingly but so will the wavelengths reflected by an adjacent green area. As a consequence, although the amount of, say, blue light reflected by the red area may have gone up, so will the amount of blue light reflected by the green area. As a consequence, the ratio of blue light in the two areas will remain the same, as will the ratio of green light in the two areas and the ratio of red light. If the system is set up to compare the amounts of each wavelength coming from different parts of the scene the problem of colour constancy is solved immediately.

Recent work by Zeki (1983a, b) shows that Land's theory is of more than theoretical interest because cells in area V4 have properties compatible with it whereas cells in V1 do not. There are many wavelength selective cells in area V1. These cells are tuned to a particular wavelength and will only respond when that wavelength alone is present. If their receptive fields are illuminated with spectrally pure light, say red, these cells respond vigorously, even though the stimulus may not look particularly red to a human observer. If the stimulus conditions start with a spectrally pure red light shining on to a red area, the cell will fire even though the area looks like a washed-out red to a human observer. If the stimulation conditions are altered so that a red coloured area is presented, illuminated by red, green, and blue light, that area will look strongly red to the observer but the cell won't fire! In contrast, cells in V4 respond relatively sluggishly when spectrally pure colours are used to illuminate scenes, especially when the scene looks washed-out to a human observer. These cells respond most vigorously when a combination of wavelengths is used for the illumination, and the area of the stimulus is seen as strongly coloured by human observers. These properties of V4 cells only appear, however, as long as a large part of the scene is illuminated and the scene contains more than one coloured area, which Zeki achieves using a multicoloured stimulus array he calls a Mondrian. If the area visible to the cell is reduced to its classically defined receptive field the cell is less likely to respond to coloured objects. Interestingly, the loss of responsiveness in the cells is correlated with a change in appearance to human observers looking at the stimuli through a similarly sized aperture. The work of Land and Zeki is important for two reasons. The first is that Land's theory of colour perception makes sense of there being two cortical stages in colour vision. The second is that it is only when people think about what the visual system does in the real world that they begin to study it appropriately. Zeki's results would never have been obtained if he had continued to study V4 cells using spectrally pure light sources that are the tradition in visual system physiology, rather than coloured objects which are the normal source of our colour perception. Theoretical analysis of the function of the visual system helped the experimental analysis. This work has, in turn, had an impact on behavioural research. Two recent reports have described colour specific impairments following prestriate damage in monkeys (Wild, Butler, Carden, and Kulikowski 1985) and humans (Heywood and Cowey 1985).

Zeki's data show that colour is represented in V4 while only wavelength information is prominent in V1 but, while these data go some way towards answering some important questions about colour vision, they don't solve all the problems. The main outstanding issue is that we don't know how colour-coding receptive fields are constructed out of wavelength-coding receptive fields at other stages in the system.

Are the colour-coding receptive fields created by the internal circuitry of V4 or is the relevant processing carried out in V1? Analysis of this problem is greatly facilitated by the fact that we can identify anatomically the subregions of the visual cortex most likely to be involved in colour vision. V4 receives input from V2 which in turn receives input from V1. It is now known that information flow from V1 to V4 is segregated in an anatomically discrete channel so that V4 receives input from identifiable subfields of V2 which receive their input from similarly identifiable zones in V1. What identifies these zones is that they contain a high concentration of the enzyme, cytochrome oxidase (CO). Brain tissue can be stained so that CO is visible, areas with a high CO concentration having a dense brown colour. In V1, CO-rich regions appear as regularly spaced blobs in the upper layers of the cerebral cortex while, in V2, they appear as stripes. The neural pathways involved in converting wavelength to colour information are restricted to these regions so, in order to understand colour coding, we need to restrict our attention to them (Maunsell and Newsome 1987).

The nub of the issue is that colour analysis of the sort proposed in the Retinex theory requires analysis of the wavelength output of different parts of the visual field. Put into operational terms this means that, at some point, there are likely to be cells that respond in one way to one wavelength at one point in the receptive field and differently to the same wavelength in a different part of the field. For example, we would expect to find cells that give an excitatory response to long wavelength light shone on one part of the retina and an inhibitory response to long wavelength light shone on to an adjacent part. Such cells have never been described in V1 (Livingstone and Hubel 1984). However, cells with a more complex form of spatially inhibitory organization have been identified. These are the double opponent cells of V1 (Livingstone and Hubel 1984; Maunsell and Newsome 1987). These cells give a large excitatory response to the onset of a small spot of one wavelength shone on to their receptive field centres and a much smaller response to a much larger spot. This indicates the presence of an inhibitory surround. When a complementary wavelength is used the response to the small spot only occurs at the offset of the stimulus. Again, there is no response to a large spot. These cells will convey information about wavelength boundaries that could be used to compute true colour. The colour-coding cells in V4 probably depend on input from these cells. However, as Livingstone and Hubel (1984) point out, they cannot be computing colour according to the algorithm derived by Land.

The significant point to emerge from Zeki's work is that a perceptual phenomenon once believed to be the result of high level cognitive processing now turns out to have a single cell correlate at an early stage in the visual pathways. Other constancies may turn out to have similarly straightforward explanations. Indeed, perceptual constancies are only a puzzle if it is assumed that the visual system acts like a camera. Once it is recognized that the job of the visual system is to recode the retinal image in terms of a representation of the outside world, and that much of this encoding can be done by comparing the properties of the retinal image in different parts of the visual field using fairly straightforward rules, constancies present no problem. However, it is important for us to remember that we still don't really understand how this recoding is done by the brain.

Visual association cortex and the recognition of objects

We have seen that the visual areas of the prestriate cortex recode image properties into properties of the object that gave rise to the image. At no point in this system is the object itself represented. According to traditional views this takes place in the next tier of visual areas. Immediately we have a problem: what form would the respresentation of an object take? The simplest, in principle, would be that individual cells in these higher order areas would respond whenever a particular object was presented. They would do so because they receive convergent input from cells at the lower levels of the system that represent the defining properties of that object. The model is referred to as the 'grandmother cell' theory because it predicts that we should have populations of cells in our brains that fire only when we see our grandmothers. Barlow (1985) has argued very strongly for just such a model.

The model is simple to test. All we need to do is to push microelectrodes into the regions to which the prestriate cortex projects and look for the cells that only respond to particular objects. There are two main areas that receive input from the prestriate cortex. One is the inferior temporal cortex and the other the inferior parietal lobe. In general the results of single cell recording studies on these areas have been disappointing. What is usually found is cells with massive receptive fields with very non-specific receptive field properties. Virtually anything waved around in the receptive fields of these cells will evoke a response under the right conditions. In other words, these areas are visual but the degree of stimulus specificity demanded by the theory is generally absent.

There are some notable exceptions that have attracted attention. Gross and his colleagues have reported that cells in the inferior temporal gyrus sometimes had very specific stimulus requirements before they would respond (Gross 1973). For example, one cell would only respond when a hand was moved in front of the animal's eyes. However, these cells were embedded in a much larger population of cells that were non-specific in their requirements. More impressive are the recent reports from Perrett and Rolls (Perrett, Rolls, and Caan 1982; Perrett, Smith, Potter, Mistlin, Head, Milner, and Jeeves 1985) that cells in the superior temporal sulcus, which forms the upper margin of the inferior temporal lobe, are often only responsive to faces or parts of faces. Even here there is debate about whether the activity of any single cell could be used to identify a particular face. Usually the cells fire strongly to one face and less strongly to others. However, in nearly all instances there is some response to any face. Furthermore, the response is dependent on the orientation of the face to the animal. A cell that will respond to somebody in full face will fail to respond to the same person in profile. It is fair to say that cells in this area are encoding the properties of faces but they cannot be encoding their identities.

In some ways Perrett's findings can be seen as an extension of the results on prestriate cortex in that higher order properties of objects are being encoded, using information from representations of lower order properties. Nevertheless, the identity of objects is still missing. This raises the question of whether it is necessary to represent objects at the single cell level. One good reason for not doing so is that 'grandmother cell' models have real difficulty in explaining how our visual systems cope with novel input. Clearly we would have to have a separate system for representing the presence of objects and their features that was not dependent on knowing their identity. This duplication would be wasteful. An alternative to the grandmother cell theory is network theory. Network theory has already been mentioned once in this book when we discussed methods. Network theory holds that information can be represented in a distributed form, in terms of the pattern of activity in a large number of elements. Associations can be formed by allowing two networks to intersect and interact so that patterns of activity in one network can evoke predictable patterns in the other. Network theory is proving very powerful in modelling a range of cognitive processes. It is too early to say whether this is the way the brain works but, as Rolls (1987) points out, it would make a lot of sense of a lot of uninterpretable data if it was; it also makes sense on logical grounds, since it gets round the problems associated with grandmother cells, like the problem of perceiving novel objects and the complexities of arranging the massive degree of convergence of input required for grandmother cells to work.

Of course, the question of how the identity of objects is coded is separate from the issue of whether object recognition is localized to these high levels of the visual system at all. The possibility that this sort of information is represented across an array of cells, rather than at the level of the single unit does, however, mean that single cell recording alone will not give us a useful answer. What about lesion evidence? Since 1954 it has been known that focal lesions of the inferotemporal cortex produce a severe and abiding impairment in visual discrimination performance in monkeys (see Dean 1982). Indeed, this was shown before it was demonstrated that the inferotemporal cortex was anatomically part of the visual system. Initially it was thought that there was an impairment in memory for visual stimuli but work carried out in the 1970s largely dispelled this notion. Instead, the factor that most influences the outcome of inferotemporal cortex lesions is not memory load but whether or not the animals are required to categorize the stimuli before making their choices (Dean 1982).

Given that object recognition is a categorical process, in that one doesn't recognize each individual chair one sees but identifies it as belonging to the same category as other chairs one has seen, this suggests that the inferotemporal cortex has a major role to play in object recognition. According to Cowey (1982) and Humphreys and Riddoch (1987) humans with damage to the temporal visual cortex, or the prestriate areas that feed into it, also suffer major impairments in object recognition, known as 'agnosias'. In this instance there has been a remarkable convergence of evidence, from a variety of sources, on the conclusion that temporal visual areas are involved in object recognition. As Rolls (1987) implies, the real question now concerns the identity of the coding processes going on there.

What of the parietal lobe areas identified by Luria (1973) as being so important for object recognition? Considerable progress has been made in analysing the functions of the visual areas in the parietal lobe, but little of the evidence favours a role in object recognition. Ungerleider and Mishkin (1982) argue, from behavioural evidence, that the parietal areas are involved in spatial vision, an argument that is supported by clinical evidence in humans. After parietal lobe lesions monkeys have difficulty with a landmark test in which they have to remember the location of a food reward relative to prominent stimulus on the test board and humans have difficulty recognizing objects when they are presented in unusual orientations (Warrington 1982).

Other sensory systems

We do the same types of things with our other sensory systems as we do with vision. For example, we identify the sources of stimuli on the basis of patterns of stimulation on the receptors. We might, therefore, expect them to work in the same sort of way as the visual system. Anatomically, the sensory systems with large cortical representations, the auditory and somatosensory systems, are very similar to the visual system. There are relatively direct, 'lemniscal' pathways from the receptors to the cortex and other, less direct, routes that involve largely subcortical relays. At the cortical level there are multiple representations of the receptor system. For example, even the hedgehog has two somatosensory representations in its cortex, while monkeys have up to seven (Merzenich and Kaas 1980).

Nevertheless, we shouldn't attach too much significance to the similarities because we either don't have the relevant evidence or the details are different. Clinical and some behavioural evidence from animals (Kolb and Whishaw 1985; Whitfield 1979) suggests that there must be auditory and somatosensory areas akin to the temporal lobe visual areas of the primate. On a priori grounds we would expect humans to have an auditory area corresponding to temporal visual cortex since speech requires the categorical perception of sounds. However, such areas have not been well characterized in physiological and anatomical studies. Most studies on these systems have concentrated on the topographically organized representations that probably correspond to striate and prestriate cortex in monkeys. Turning to differences in detail, in the primate visual system all visual submodalities are represented in the primary visual cortex. It is the second tier of visual cortex that specializes. In contrast, the data we have on the somatosensory cortex indicate that all of the areas specialize in some way and that there is no generalist area. It may turn out that the somatosensory and visual systems are not organized in exactly the same ways.

This wouldn't be surprising in some ways, since it is not clear that the visual system is organized in the same way in all species. For example, in primates the projection from LGd is almost exclusively to area V1 while in cats it projects to peristriate cortex as well. In rodents it is difficult to identify an area that corresponds to temporal visual cortex, there is debate about the existence of a parietal visual area, and the prestriate cortex has yet to be shown to be subdivided on the basis of submodality as in primates. If the same system can vary so much between species there is no good reason why different systems should be the same within a species. As things stand, the visual system is proving a good model to guide investigation of other sensory systems but we need to be cautious about interpreting data and to avoid forcing these other systems into a straitjacket defined by the visual system.

When it comes to other sensory systems, much of the problem is that we haven't the sort of clear ideas about how they might work that we have about the visual system. In recent years there have been some significant advances in studying the auditory system, especially in the analysis of computational maps that recode intensity and phase differences in the two ears into the representation of auditory space (Knudsen, DuLac, and Esterly 1987), but this work has focused on subcortical mechanisms. We know that the auditory cortex is involved in more complex processes like the categorical perception of sound, but at this point our lack of good theoretical models becomes apparent. A similar state of affairs affects our understanding of the somatosensory system. At this stage what would prove helpful is computational models of hearing and touch.

Overview

Although we cannot yet say conclusively how objects are recognized visually we are beginning to converge on an answer. The insights gained from computational models of visual perceptions are facilitating the interpretation of findings of physiological studies of the visual cortex and a picture is emerging of a modular system in which different attributes of the image are processed in different cortical areas before the information is passed on to higher order systems. Our understanding of hearing and touch tends to lag behind our understanding of vision. In these systems we have good descriptions of their anatomy and of the physiological properties of the major types of nerve cells but, at the cortical level, we don't have good explanations of what the systems do or the way they do it, except in the broadest terms.

The main outstanding issue in perception, including visual perception, concerns the processes that combine information about the attributes of a particular scene into a representation of the object that gave rise to the image, sound or pattern of touch. In the case of vision we can pinpoint the brain regions likely to be involved, but it remains to be seen how they actually work.

At present the most promising approaches are coming from network models, but they are in their very early stages and the day of a convincing object recognition network is still some way off.

5
Motivation

Motivation is one of the central concepts of psychology. As with most other psychological concepts we all have an intuitive grasp of what it means but find it difficult to give a precise and inclusive definition of it. When we talk about motivation we are usually concerned with the goals or purposes of somebody's actions. As psychologists we are concerned with understanding why people are pursuing particular goals at particular times and how the pursuit of those goals actually affects their behaviour. Implicit in most of our commonsense views of motivation is that it is something that arises 'spontaneously' within the individual, rather than being evoked by environmental circumstances. Naturally, this creates difficulties for those of us who want to study motivation within a biological framework since it is our job to specify the neural and bodily systems that generate these apparently 'spontaneous' events. The way we have solved this problem has been to relate motives back to needs, to argue that motivational states arise because the individual lacks something. We can then study motivational processes by controlling people's or animals' access to things that they need and observing the impact of these variations in need state. The easiest way of controlling motivation is to work through basic biological needs, like hunger and thirst, that are common to all animals and which can be shown to have a powerful effect on behaviour. It is therefore not surprising that much of the work that has been done on motivation this century has been biologically oriented.

Models of motivation have changed quite considerably during this century. One of the ironies about theories of motivation in the 1980s is that they now have as much in common with the theories of the 1920s as with the theories of the 1950s that superseded them. Up to about 1950 theories of motivation concentrated on the peripheral effects of deprivation and satiation on behaviour but, in 1954, Stellar published his influential two-centre theory that focused our attention on central mechanisms. To be fair to Stellar his model was far more complex than most text-books make out and included a major role for peripheral factors but it has only been in the past decade that there has emerged a serious renaissance of interest in their role in motivation. The task ahead is to synthesize what is being learned about peripheral factors with the established literature on central mechanisms.

Since the early 1950s research on the control of eating and drinking has focused on two broad issues: the variables that control the waxing and waning of motivational states, and the identity of the neural circuits controlling the response to those variables. Studies on controlling variables have proceeded apace and the catalogue of factors that can influence eating and drinking has expanded significantly since the middle of the century. There have been three major changes in approach in the past ten years. The first has been the realization that it isn't enough to itemize the possible controlling variables, it is also necessary to specify how they operate under normal conditions and how they interact with each other. The second has been the rehabilitation of 'peripheral' factors in the control of food and water intake. That is to say, it is now recognized that factors like the rate of flow of food through the mouth, or the volume of food in the stomach do affect food intake. The third has been the realization that it is necessary to distinguish between the variables that initiate food and water intake and those that terminate them. The position over the neural systems involved has become much less clear. In the mid 1950s it looked fairly clear that the ventromedial hypothalamic (VMH) and lateral hypothalamic (LH) areas had a major role in the control of eating. This view was epitomized in Stellar's (1954) two-centre theory of motivation. Since then the position has altered drastically in two ways. First, it rapidly became unclear whether lesions in the hypothalamus, which were the primary source of data for the two-centre theory, had such simple effects on food intake as was first thought. For example, although it is widely held that ventromedial hypothalamic lesions make animals overeat, it was shown fairly early on that this effect depended on the quality of the diet (Keesey and Powley 1986; LeMagnen 1985) and it was subsequently shown that animals with VMH lesions would become obese even when fed on the same diets as control animals (LeMagnen 1985; Powley 1977). Second, a number of studies carried out in the 1970s cast doubt on the assumption that the effects of hypothalamic lesions had anything to do with hypothalamic function as such since lesions outside of the hypothalamus, or lesions interrupting tracts running through the hypothalamus had the same effects as lesions destroying part of it (Grossman 1975).

It is important to know about the control of food and water intake as topics in their own right but much of the work that I am going to talk about was started in the hope that it would cast light on motivational processes in general. When a rat is food deprived and placed in a Skinner box, for example, that experiment is done on the assumption that the motivational state arising from the food deprivation will affect behaviour in exactly the same way that the desire to do well in an examination, or to be the driver of the first car away from the traffic lights, affects our own behaviour. How far are we really justified in generalizing from what happens in a single species in a single need state to motivational processes in general?

This chapter looks first at ingestive behaviours and discusses the role of peripheral factors in generating motivational states and the identity of the neural mechanisms that mediate the response to these factors. It then turns to the question of whether food and water intake are good model systems for studying the biological bases of motivation in general.

Ingestive behaviours: food and water intake

The initiation of motivated behaviour

Systemic factors

In the monotonous environments experienced by most laboratory animals the primary determinants of the initiation of eating and drinking are believed to be changes in the state of the internal environment. The evidence for this is well rehearsed in most text-books of physiological psychology and I do not intend to repeat it in detail here. Instead I want to focus on some of the outstanding difficulties associated with this conclusion. There are three requirements for something to act as a signal for the initiation of eating and drinking. The first is that it must vary to a measurable degree under normal conditions. Something that is rigidly regulated by internal physiological mechanisms is unlikely to act as a good stimulus for behaviour (Friedman and Stricker 1976). The second is that the probability of eating or drinking should correlate very tightly with changes in that variable, under normal conditions. The third is that experimental manipulations that produce variations within the normal, or physiological, range are effective in eliciting eating or drinking and that the effects are 'dose related' so that, the bigger the manipulation, the bigger the effect on behaviour. These conditions have been largely satisfied in studies of drinking but not in studies of eating.

It was argued for many years that the osmolarity of the blood was the major determinant of water intake but it was only about twenty years ago that good evidence for this position became available (Fitzsimons 1971; Rolls and Rolls 1982). The osmolarity of a liquid like blood plasma refers to its capacity to promote the movement of water across a semi-permeable membrane. A semi-permeable membrane is one across which water will move but which impedes or prevents the passage of other substances dissolved in the water. The osmolarity of the liquid is a measure of the concentration of these other substances. When the concentration is high, water moves readily across the membrane into the liquid, so the osmolarity of the liquid is high. When the concentration is low, which means low osmolarity, only a small amount of water moves. Although correlational studies, in which drinking is monitored simultaneously with the osmolarity of the blood, are conceptually simple they are technically difficult, especially in small mammals like rats. Consequently, experimental studies were carried out first. In these studies animals were given injections of concentrated salt solution to raise blood osmolarity. Up to around 1970 they had been carried out many times but with mixed results. In most instances the animals drank more than controls, but the expected dose-response curve, linking the amount drunk to the amount needed to redilute the blood back to its normal level, was not obtained. Fitzsimons (1971) recognized that there was a simple explanation for this: the animals were excreting excess sodium as well as drinking to dilute the blood. He therefore carried out studies on nephrectomized rats, which couldn't excrete the salt because their kidneys had been disconnected from the blood supply, and in these animals there was a perfect relationship between the amount drunk and the amount required to redilute the blood. These results were particularly impressive because the effects were obtained with very small injections of salt solution, reaching, at most, 4 or 5 ml of solution in a large rat, so that the changes in blood osmolarity were probably within the physiological range.

Measurement of blood osmolarity is a difficult matter that used to require large quantities of blood for any accuracy. With advances in analytical instruments it is now feasible to measure blood osmolarity in animals as small as rats (Rolls and Rolls 1982). Water deprivation raises blood osmolarity in all mammals as well as producing drinking, and the amount drunk correlates with the increase in osmolarity. Therefore, osmolarity fulfils another criterion for acting as an important stimulus for thirst. However, water deprivation is an extreme procedure. While it may occur from time to time in the natural environment, most animals probably start drinking long before they are seriously deprived. It would, therefore, be very interesting to see the result of experiments in which variations in blood osmolarity were related to drinking behaviour in non-deprived animals engaged in normal drinking.

Plasma osmolarity is not the whole story on drinking. For one thing it turns out that osmolarity itself is not the effective stimulus. What matters is whether the substances in the plasma raise osmotic pressure within the body and have the effect of pulling water out of the cells of the body, a process known as cellular dehydration. This distinction may appear nitpicking but it is quite significant. Many substances that increase the osmolarity of the blood, when that is assessed using standard laboratory tests, do not provoke drinking. One such substance is urea, which moves readily across cell walls. Furthermore, changes in plasma volume also influence thirst. This is apparent in cases of haemorrhage in which blood volume falls without any change in osmolarity. Haemorrhage patients who remain conscious usually have a raging thirst. A similar effect can be produced experimentally by injecting substances like polyethylene glycol into the body cavity. Polyethylene glycol has the unusual property of absorbing water to produce what is known as a 'colloid', which is a solution of water in another liquid. When blood plasma enters the colloid it takes with it the substances dissolved in it so that the osmolarity of the surviving fluids remains constant. Nevertheless, a powerful thirst-provoking effect is obtained. In this case it has been shown that one of the main signals for what is known as extracellular thirst is the release of renin by the kidneys, in response to a fall in the amount of blood passing through them. Renin promotes the production of a second messenger substance, the hormone angiotensin, in the blood stream. Angiotensin acts as a powerful thirst-provoking agent (Fitzsimons 1971; Rolls and Rolls 1982).

Although it is complicated, the general story about the internal stimuli controlling drinking is remarkably consistent. When it comes to eating, the position is less satisfactory. The most obvious candidate for a controlling variable is blood glucose level, which has to be maintained within close limits for the body and brain to function normally, but the evidence for control of eating by this variable is inconsistent. There are two problems. The first is that correlational studies on the relationship between blood glucose level and eating or subjective reports of hunger in individuals not deprived of food often produce negative results. The second is that there are experimental manipulations and pathological conditions in which high blood glucose levels are associated with hunger and low blood glucose levels with apparent satiety.

Most studies on blood glucose concentration and hunger have produced negative results. For example, in a study on humans Scott, Scott, and Luckhardt (1938) found no correlation between blood glucose level and subjective reports of hunger. In a study on rats, Steffens (1969) reported no association between eating and the concentration of glucose in either the jugular or the hepatic portal veins under conditions of *ad libitum* access to food. The one exception to this trend is the work of LeMagnen and his colleagues (LeMagnen 1985), who found a small, but highly consistent drop in glucose concentration in the jugular veins of rats just prior to their taking a meal under *ad libitum* feeding conditions. LeMagnen attributes their findings to the improved sensitivity of their measurement procedures and one is inclined to believe him, given that the drop tended to be in the order of 6–8 per cent starting some 6 to 7 minutes before the onset of the meal. However, if this is the explanation, it is puzzling that the much larger falls reported in previous studies were not associated with hunger.

Although eating in rats is associated with a small drop in veinous glucose level that doesn't mean that the eating is triggered by that fall. There are a number of lines of evidence suggesting that the situation is more complex. The most widely discussed is that there are situations in which the expected relationship between blood glucose level and hunger may be reversed. Injections of insulin produce an immediate drop in blood glucose concentration that may be ten times as great as the drop reported by LeMagnen, yet insulin only induces eating after a 20- to 40-minute delay in rats (LeMagnen 1985). If blood glucose concentration is the controlling variable it is difficult to see why a 6 per cent drop produces eating within 6 minutes while a 50 per cent drop only has its effect after 20 or more minutes. The absence of insulin, as occurs in insulin-dependent diabetes mellitus, is associated with chronically elevated blood glucose levels. This is partly due to glucose not being able to enter cells and partly to the production of glucose from fats and proteins, triggered by the lack of glucose within cells. Paradoxically, the elevated blood glucose levels of untreated diabetes are associated with increased hunger.

Mayer (1955) recognized these difficulties and proposed the now widely accepted version of the glucose-level hypothesis which stresses glucose 'availability' within cells. Glucose availability is the rate at which glucose moves from the blood stream into the body's cells. It makes sense that this would be the more important variable because any receptors adapted to measure the level of glucose in circulation would only work if the glucose could enter them. In addition to the paradoxical findings with insulin injections and diabetes mellitus the other evidence for Mayer's position comes from measurement of the arterio-venous (A-V) difference in blood glucose concentration, which is considered to reflect the rate of utilization of glucose in the body. It is argued that high rates of utilization are a reflection of high rates of availability. Although absolute blood glucose level does not correlate with hunger or eating in humans the A-V difference does. High A-V differences are associated with subjective reports of low levels of hunger while low A-V differences are associated with reports of high levels of hunger. It looks as if the problem is solved.

Although experimental and pathological events can dissociate blood glucose level from glucose availability, under normal circumstances they are linked. Increasing blood glucose concentration leads to the secretion of insulin that promotes increased utilization, while decreasing blood glucose leads to reduction of insulin output with an attendant decline in utilization. Thus, as LeMagnen (1985) strongly implies, when it comes to the day-to-day control of food intake under *ad libitum* feeding conditions the variable that will have the most impact is blood glucose level. The question then arises as to where these variations in blood glucose level are going to be detected.

According to LeMagnen (1985), the receptors influenced by the small decline in blood glucose recorded in the jugular vein just before eating are to be found in the hypothalamus, but there are problems with this simple story. The main problem is that the uptake of glucose into brain cells is governed by the amount of activity in those cells, rather than the concentration of glucose in the blood stream or the amount of insulin in circulation, unless their levels lie well outside the normal physiological range (Friedman and Stricker 1976). The second problem is that LeMagnen has not demonstrated that there is any change in the glucose concentration in the blood being delivered to the brain anyway, since his data are from venous blood samples which reflect both circulating glucose levels and rate of utilization. The simplest explanation for the small decline in glucose concentration in the jugular vein recorded by

LeMagnen and his colleagues is increased neural activity just prior to eating. In other words, his data may reflect the neural response to the hunger signal rather than the signal itself. Finally, Friedman and Stricker (1976) report that, in rats, eating that has been induced by insulin injections can be inhibited by injections into the somatic blood supply of a sugar, fructose, that does not cross the blood-brain barrier and that will not, as a consequence, act on central glucose receptors.

According to Friedman and Stricker (1976) it is only in the somatic, that is non-neural, tissue that glucose utilization varies with glucose level, because it is only in these tissues that there is insulin-dependent glucose uptake. These sorts of consideration have led Russek (1970), Friedman and Stricker (1976), and Novin and VanderWeele (1977) to argue that detection of changes in glucose level or availability is mediated peripherally, in the liver. The liver plays a pivotal role in the control of the body's energy supplies and, therefore, has to have systems for detecting changes in glucose availability in order to compensate for them. It also has connections with the CNS via the vagus nerve.

Again, the evidence for a hepatic role in feeding is contradictory. In some studies infusion of glucose into the hepatic portal vein, which carries blood from the intestine to the liver, inhibited food intake, while in others it did not (Novin and VanderWeele 1977; LeMagnen 1985). The outcome depends, in part, on whether the animals are food deprived. Cutting the branch of the vagus nerve that serves the liver or reconnecting the hepatic blood vessels so that the liver is effectively bypassed also fails to affect normal patterns of food intake (LeMagnen 1985).

All of these observations suggest that, under conditions of normal food intake, even if variations in glucose availability occur, they are unlikely to affect the potential receptors in the CNS. On the other hand, while there are a priori grounds for believing that the liver is involved in detecting changes in glucose availability, it turns out to be redundant for normal control. Nevertheless, there is evidence that both the lateral hypothalamus and the liver are important for normal food intake. Cells in the lateral hypothalamus are sensitive to glucose, and injections of glucose into the hypothalamus can suppress insulin-induced feeding. On the other hand, hepatic portal vein injections of glucose have no impact on eating in free-feeding animals but suppress feeding in animals that are twenty-two hours food-deprived. One way of resolving these contradictions is to recognize that the control systems involved in day-to-day regulation of food intake in animals on *ad libitum* schedules are different from the control in animals that have been starved, or in which blood glucose levels have been seriously compromised.

Starvation induces a range of energy-conserving and pursuing actions that are different from normal feeding behaviour. For example, some animals respond to starvation by sleeping to conserve energy while others respond by increasing activity, presumably in the hope of finding food. Starvation is also associated with changes in the sources of energy used in the body. Under free-feeding conditions most of the energy used comes from glucose while starvation results in the breakdown of proteins and fats. Indeed, Friedman and Stricker (1976) argue that it is the transition from using glucose as the metabolic fuel to the use of fats that acts as the signal to eat.

If changes in glucose availability are the signal for starvation responses, what is the signal for initiating feeding under *ad libitum* conditions? It is not clear that there needs to be one. As we shall see in the next section, it is possible that the cue for eating under these conditions may simply be the absence of peripherally mediated satiety signals. One reason for believing this is that meal size does not correlate with the amount of time since the preceding meal, which one would expect if the stimulus to eat came from depletion of an energy store, but with the interval before the next meal. This is what would be expected if a simple cue like the amount of stomach distension was the main variable that affected whether we eat under *ad libitum* conditions.

Peripheral factors

Most work on the initiation of intake has focused on central factors like availability of glucose or other metabolic fuels, but the part that they play in controlling intake is very much determined by the sensory properties of the substances available to eat and drink. For example, when rats are tested on instrumental tasks it is normal to deprive them of food to make the food pellets we use an attractive reinforcer but other foods can be used as a reinforcer without the need to deprive the animals. One of the most reliable of these foods is corn oil. If standard food pellets are used in studies of eating there will probably be some relationship between intake and levels of deprivation or measures of the state of the internal environment whereas studies using corn oil as the food would probably not find such strong systematic relationships.

The observation that the presence of certain foods alone can elicit food intake, irrespective of physiological needs, appears to create problems for the central models of intake control. However, there is a way of rescuing these theories and it is known as the cephalic phase hypothesis. The sight, smell, taste, and feel of foods all elicit reflexes designed to facilitate its digestion. These are the cephalic phase reflexes. The most obvious of these is the production of saliva, in response to food being placed in the mouth. Saliva both moistens the food to make it easier to swallow and contains enzymes that begin the digestive processes. In addition to salivation there are a number of other reflex adjustments, one of which is the production of insulin. The amount of insulin produced is proportional to the perceived caloric density of the food (Geiselman 1987; Powley 1977). In other words, concentrated sugar solution produces more insulin than dilute sugar solution. Thus the very sight or taste of food will provoke insulin production which, in turn, will reduce glucose availability and thus provoke appetite. It is, therefore, possible to reconcile the peripheral induction of appetite with control by systemic factors like glucose level or availability.

There are some problems with this model, relating to the time course of the effects of insulin on food intake. For the cephalic phase hypothesis to work, insulin has to produce an immediate reduction in glucose availability and an increase in food intake, but the evidence reviewed so far indicates that it doesn't. Infusions of glucose normally only produce increased food intake after a delay of 20 to 40 minutes. Insulin may be effective when glucose levels are beginning to fall anyway but, as LeMagnen has shown, it is only just before the start of normally timed meals that it is possible to get any evidence for systematic changes in blood glucose levels. However, highly palatable foods will be eaten at any time. Therefore, while palatability affects digestion and absorption it is not clear how these effects feed back to influence appetite in the short term.

Another way that palatability can influence eating is through augmenting the amount eaten once intake has begun. Recent work by Geiselman (1987) has shown that foods rich in sugars like sucrose reliably produce over-consumption, relative to the animal's caloric needs, and usually lead to obesity. In this instance, when the initiation of intake is probably controlled by systemic factors, cephalic phase reflexes are believed to be responsible for the long-term increase in intake. This is due to the fact that sucrose leads to over-production of insulin, relative to the amount needed to absorb the glucose produced by its breakdown, so that blood glucose levels may be compromised.

Although it has yet to be worked out completely how palatability modifies systemic hunger signals it is clear that these systemic signals modify palatability. Grill and Berridge (1985) have devised an ingenious procedure for measuring the palatability of food to rats, based on their reflex reactions to food being placed directly into the mouth via a cannula inserted through the roof of the mouth. Substances that the rats consume promptly usually produce the 'ingestive' pattern of reactions including paw licking, lateral tongue protrusions, and mouth movements. Substances that they ultimately reject produce the 'aversive' pattern including gaping, chin rubs, paw wipes, forelimb flailing, head shakes, and locomotion. Food-deprived rats exposed to glucose injected directly into the mouth initially exhibit a pronounced ingestive pattern of reactions but as they continue to consume the glucose the pattern shifts to the aversive one and they start to reject the glucose. This indicates that food deprivation and satiation modify the palatability of foods.

Satiety

Peripheral factors

Although Stellar's two-centre model included peripheral as well as central influences on the hunger and satiety centres the peripheral influences were largely neglected for many years as being trivial. In the middle of the 1970s it began to occur to a number of researchers that peripheral factors must have an important part to play, at least in satiation, because the ingestion of food and water is often too fast for blood-borne signals, often referred to as post-ingestive signals, to have any impact before too much had been consumed. This is a serious problem because the dangers of over-consumption are physical as well as dietary. An over-filled stomach may rupture, with fatal consequences. This insight was confirmed in a number of studies and is especially clear in work on drinking. Rolls and Rolls (1982) describe studies on drinking in dogs in which water intake after a period of water deprivation is largely completed some 2 to 3 minutes after the start of drinking, yet changes in the blood plasma do not start until 10 to 12 minutes later and are not complete until 40 to 45 minutes after the start. Moreover, although drinking is terminated before the water has any impact on the internal environment the amount consumed is directly related to the amount required to restore homeostasis. The peripheral regulation of intake is, therefore, exquisitely tuned to the organism's needs. Similar results are obtained with feeding (LeMagnen 1985).

It may seem surprising that it has taken so long to demonstrate the peripheral control of intake but there are two good reasons why this is so. One of them is the preoccupation with studying intake in the laboratory rat, the other the difficulty of identifying the peripheral control signals actually involved. Rats are very convenient laboratory animals. They take up very little space, they are resistant to disease, and they are usually very tame. Their main drawback for this sort of work is that they are very slow eaters and drinkers. As a consequence, when food and water intake are studied in these animals it isn't altogether clear that intake stops before the food or water could have got into circulation. It is only when animals that eat and drink rapidly, like dogs, are used that this situation becomes clear.

Studies on the peripheral control of intake did not start in the 1970s but nearly all of them carried out before then apparently showed that peripheral factors could only play a small part in regulating input. There is, for example, the now famous experiment of Bellows (1939), who prepared dogs with a tube placed in the oesophagus so that when they drank the water passed through the mouth and out of the body. These dogs 'drank' copiously when given access to water, although they stopped eventually. Other studies showed that substances placed directly into the stomach had little effect on intake. The breakthrough that came in the 1970s was the demonstration that input is regulated by multiple controls. Although passing food or water through the mouth or into the stomach alone had little impact on intake, combining the two signals was found to have a profound effect on both eating and drinking (Smith and Gibbs 1979; Rolls and Rolls 1982).

Although allowing food or water to pass through the mouth into the stomach has a large effect on intake, this does not completely mimic normal satiety. The food or water has to enter the intestine for this to occur. In recent years there has been some debate about how intestinal feedback affects intake. Some authors maintain that activation of receptors in the intestine produces feedback to the central nervous system while others stress the role of feedback to the stomach, feedback which regulates the rate of stomach emptying.

It used to be believed that the rate of stomach emptying was constant, irrespective of the quality of the food or fluid placed there. The studies concerned invariably used physiological saline as the stomach load and did not vary the state of the intestine independently of the state of the stomach. In more recent studies on water intake it has been shown that placing water in the small intestine slows the rate at which ingested water leaves the stomach (Rolls and Rolls 1982). In studies on food intake the results are even more interesting. According to McHugh and Moran (1985), the rate at which food clears from the stomach is a function of the caloric density of the food concerned. High calorie foods clear much more slowly than low calorie foods. In fact, although the rate at which food leaves the stomach varies with the caloric load, the rate at which calories leave the stomach is constant across a wide range of caloric densities. By independently varying the caloric density of food entering the stomach and food entering the intestine McHugh and Moran have shown that the rate of stomach emptying is controlled by feedback from the intestine. More importantly, they have shown that stomach distension is a much more potent predictor of satiety than the nutritional value of the food in it. There are two sugars, glucose and D-xylose, that empty from the stomach at the same rate as each other but only glucose acts as an effective metabolic fuel. Nevertheless, equivalent stomach loads of the two sugars produce exactly the same effects on food intake on the day of testing.

When food enters the intestine cholecystokinin (CCK), one of the gut hormones, is released. Its name comes from the fact that it was originally believed just to control the gall-bladder but, as McHugh and Moran have shown, it also acts on the stomach. The pyloric sphincter, the valve at the base of the stomach that controls the rate of emptying into the small intestine, contains a large number of receptors for CCK and injections of CCK have the same effect on stomach emptying as loading the intestine with food.

The fact that intestinal feedback can affect hunger through its impact on stomach emptying doesn't mean that there are no other routes whereby it can have an effect. Studies on both eating and drinking show that infusions of food or water directly into the small intestine terminate intake, irrespective of the load in the stomach, indicating a separate role for intestinal feedback. McHugh and Moran have found that animals given stomach preloads of the sugar fructose ate no more than those given the same caloric preload of glucose, despite the fact that fructose empties from the stomach faster than glucose. In the case of water intake the feedback signal is uncertain but in the case of food intake evidence suggests that CCK released from the intestine feeds back directly to the CNS. This conclusion is, however, controversial.

The issue hinges on whether CCK alone will act as a satiating agent. Most of the early studies on its effects involved short-term measurements of total food intake in animals being fed *ad libitum*, thus confounding feedback to the CNS with feedback to the stomach affecting gastric emptying. When efforts have been made to separate these two factors the results have been mixed. According to Smith and Gibbs (1979), CCK injections will produce satiety in animals undergoing sham feeding, in which food never enters the stomach. On the other hand, McHugh and Moran report that the satiating effect of CCK only occurs when the stomach is filled, even if it is filled with saline. Inspection of their data indicates that the situation is more complex. CCK injections alone did produce a small reduction in food intake shortly after administration but the effects were considerably smaller than when there was a stomach load as well. More worrying for the people who claim that CCK has a direct satiating effect are the studies on long-term administration of the hormone. After an initial phase during which food intake is inhibited there is a return to normal levels. Furthermore, as Moore and Deutsch (1985) have shown, the effects of CCK in long-term use can be blocked by treating the animals with an anti-emetic drug. It may be that some of the effects of CCK are due to animals feeling sick after injection of the hormone.

Probably the safest conclusion to draw from all this work is that there are a number of levels of control over satiety, ranging from oral metering to feedback from the absorption of water or calories. In the case of drinking, the post-absorptive signals are probably linked to extracellular and intracellular fluid volumes but the identity of the post-absorptive signals for hunger is less clear. This is because the most likely cues are glucose level or glucose availability but, as we have already seen, the relationship between these and eating is problematic.

Systemic factors

One of the most remarkable features of drinking in rapid drinkers like dogs and humans is that although drinking stops before significant post-absorptive events can have taken place, the amount consumed is usually directly proportional to the systemic deficit. Animals do not simply continue to drink until a particular satiety signal is produced. Instead they monitor the movement of fluid through the mouth and into the gut, a process described as oral metering, and cut off intake when the amount that has been taken in matches the deficit. Clearly the reaction to peripheral satiety signals is being modified by the state of the internal environment.

It is not clear that a similar process occurs in eating. According to LeMagnen (1985), meal size is independent of the interval since the preceding meal. Instead it is correlated with the interval before the next meal. In other words, laboratory rats on an *ad libitum* schedule regulate their caloric intake by adjusting the intervals between meals rather than the size of the meals themselves. Nevertheless, there are conditions under which meal size does change.

First, after a period of food deprivation the first meal is significantly larger than normal meals in the *ad libitum* condition. It is not clear whether the amount consumed is sufficient to offset any systemic deficit completely but what these data do show is that under *ad libitum* conditions meals are terminated before the digestive system has reached the limits of its capacity to accommodate food. The problem is that rats eat so slowly the termination of eating under *ad libitum* conditions may reflect post-absorptive effects rather than oral metering. Second, alterations in the caloric density of food produce compensatory changes in the amount consumed. The compensations involve both decreases in the intermeal interval and increases in meal size. These take a day or so to come into effect, which suggests that meal termination is not simply a consequence of the post-absorptive changes in glucose or energy availability produced by eating.

Thus, satiety is influenced by the state of the internal environment. In the case of drinking there is good evidence for accurate oral metering to ensure that intake matches demand. In the case of eating, intake varies with systemic needs but it is less clear whether oral metering is equally accurate. This isn't entirely surprising given the difficulty of specifying the signal that controls food intake in the first place.

Eating in the real world

Most laboratory studies of appetitive behaviour are extremely artificial. They have to be, in order to isolate variables controlling the appetitive behaviour. Nevertheless, this does create problems for extrapolating from these studies to the conditions that occur in the normal environment. The artificiality takes three forms. The first is that experiments isolate variables from each other in ways that would never occur naturally except in pathological states. For example, blood glucose levels do not normally plummet shortly after meals, nor do they miraculously rise after periods of fasting. Consequently, studies that appear to be concentrating on a single controlling factor are, in reality, studying the conflict between that factor and other controlling variables. The second is that studies are usually conducted using monotonous and familiar sources of food and water. Rats are fed on standard rat chow and provided with water from the same drinking tube that they have been using for many weeks or even months. In the natural habitat, changes in food or water availability are usually associated with changes in their sources. Animals often only become hungry or thirsty to any degree because established food and water sources are no longer available. This is especially true of omnivorous foragers like rats, whose food sources change significantly from day to day. The third is that motivational states do not usually change independently of one another. Animals that are hungry are frequently thirsty and vice versa.

It is clear that any complete theory of appetitive behaviour has to include not only a description of the controlling variables but also how they interact with each other. In recent years there have been a number of attempts to build such models, using the control systems approach. As is the case with recent work on vision the emphasis has shifted away from experimentation to modelling, the workers concerned building computer simulations of the interactions between controlling variables and matching their results to observations of the patterns of eating and drinking observed in the normal environment (Toates 1986).

One of the aims of studying appetitive behaviours in rats and other animals is to understand our own appetites more completely. If the extrapolations are to be convincing it would help if we used realistic analogues of our own circumstances in animals studies. It is true that in many parts of the world the daily diets of people are monotonous in the extreme but in the richer countries this is clearly not the case. One of the ways in which people use their wealth is to increase the variety in their diets and, in Western Europe and North America, the variety of one's diet is often taken as a sign of socioeconomic status. Dietary variety also spills over into drinking. Laboratory rats are given water, or possibly dilute saline, to drink whereas most of us eschew plain water in favour of flavoured, sweetened, and often drugged beverages. There are few parts of the world in which it is impossible to obtain Coca or Pepsi Cola, sweetened tea is now consumed in many countries and most people in Western Europe and North America take in considerable amounts of fluid in the form of coffee or alcoholic beverages, both of which contain quite powerful drugs.

Dietary variety has been the subject of a number of studies over the past decade or so and most of them find that giving animals access to a variety of foods, cafeteria feeding, increases the size of meals relative to the amount consumed on a monotonous diet (LeMagnen 1985; Rothwell and Stock 1979). Rats also alter the type of diet they consume given a completely free choice, going for a very high fat intake compared with what is normally on offer in the laboratory. The consequences of this increased consumption within a meal depend upon whether there is a compensatory change in the intermeal interval, as the arguments of LeMagnen (1985) would demand. In fact, total daily caloric intake also increases and many animals become obese relative to controls. As I have already mentioned, high sucrose diets are also favoured by laboratory animals. Anecdotal evidence suggests that humans behave similarly and the consumption of sugars is usually associated with obesity.

The individual differences in obesity observed in studies of cafeteria-fed rats may provide insights into why some of us are more likely to get fat than others.

Motivation

Figure 5.1 Time-sharing behaviour

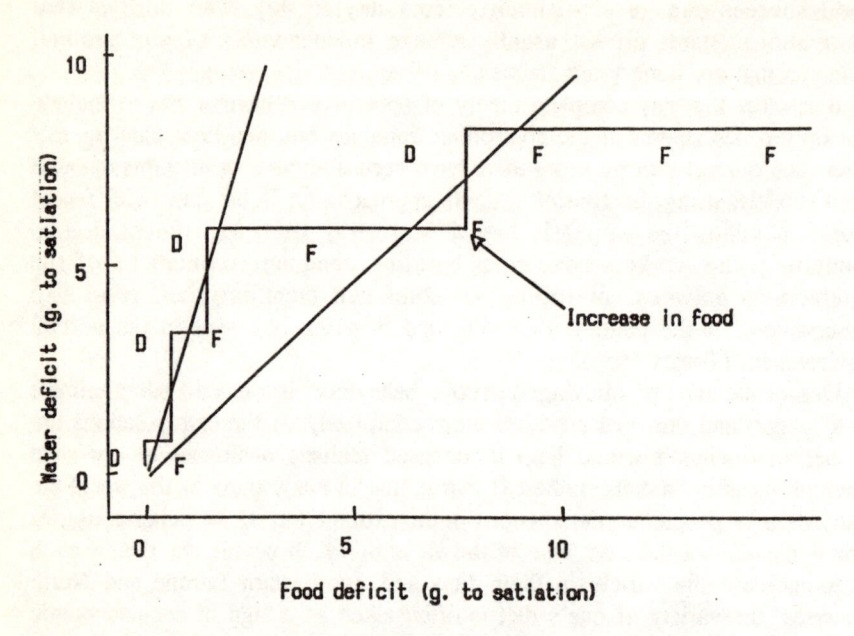

Results of a 'time-sharing' experiment, showing the way in which the transition from eating to drinking, and back again, is influenced by both the balance between the two needs and the ease of satisfying one of them. Note the increased preference for feeding when the availability of food is increased (F – feeding; D – drinking).

Rothwell and Stock (1979) suggested that the difference between fat and lean rats on a cafeteria-type diet could be attributed largely to the lean ones 'burning-off' the excess calories as heat, in a process known as 'dietary induced thermogenesis', which is believed to take place in a particular type of fat tissue, known as brown adipose tissue (BAT). There is no doubt that BAT is present in most rats and humans and that it can convert calories to heat, but there has been much debate about whether it can account for the differences between fat and lean individuals. In many instances the difference between the number of excess calories taken in by an animal and the amount of calories deposited in fat stores can be accounted for by the amount of energy required by the body to convert glucose into fat. In studies of heat output after eating in humans the correlation between normal body weight and heat generation is not significant, even when the subjects include both lean and obese individuals (Blaza 1983). The implication is that the amount of weight gained when the diet is very varied will depend simply on the amount consumed.

The consequences of conflict between motivational states have been studied for many years by McFarland and his group (McFarland and Houston 1981). Animals turn out to have a variety of interesting strategies for dealing with this problem. One is to 'time-share', which is to allocate successive blocks of time to satisfying each of the motivational demands. When thirst and hunger are placed in conflict animals tend to alternate between eating and drinking but not in a random way. The rule they operate is to start attending to the most urgent need and to continue to do so until it becomes the less urgent one, whereupon they swap over to satisfying the other need. Thus their need states keep criss-crossing the boundary between a need being dominant and being subordinate. The preference for one activity over the other can be shifted by altering the ease with which a need can be satisfied but the overall strategy remains the same (Figure 5.1). It is interesting that in all of these studies McFarland and his colleagues have used a behavioural rather than a physiological definition of need. Instead of measuring blood glucose levels, or blood osmolarity they construct their curves by measuring the amount of food or water consumed during the total test session and expressing 'need' at any point as the proportion of the total consumed that has yet to be taken in. It would be very interesting to see whether 'need', expressed in this way, correlated with any of the systemic variables discussed in the preceding sections.

Central mechanisms of motivation

Ask most psychologists what they know about motivation and they will probably tell you something about the hypothalamus, showing how far Stellar's 'two-centre' theory of motivation has become part of their mental furniture. This is unfortunate since the theory has undergone considerable revision in recent years and, while most physiologists still accept that manipulation of the hypothalamus has a profound and reliable effect on ingestive behaviours, they are far from happy with the idea that it contains controlling centres that operate in the way that Stellar originally outlined.

According to the original theory, appetitive behaviours are controlled by two antagonistic centres in the hypothalamus, one facilitating appetitive behaviour and the other inhibiting it. Moment-to-moment behaviour is then a product of the balance between the two centres. In the case of feeding, the two centres are identified with the ventromedial nucleus of the hypothalamus, the inhibitory centre, and the lateral hypothalamus, the excitatory centre. The arguments against this interpretation are well rehearsed elsewhere so I will only review them briefly. What concerns me more is to discuss how physiological psychologists are coping with the demise of the two-centre theory. This is really two issues. First, what really are the neural mechanisms underlying appetitive behaviour? Second, why do hypothalamic lesions and stimulation produce the effects that they do?

Arguments against the two-centre theory: The VMH and satiety

According to Stellar's original model appetite is the product of the continuous, dynamic tension between the VMH and LH. Eating will occur if either the VMH becomes less active or the LH more so. This leads to the simple prediction that animals with VMH lesions will be permanently hungry since the balance will be shifted permanently in favour of the LH, a prediction apparently refuted by series of studies by Miller and his colleagues (Miller, Bailey, and Stevenson 1950), which showed that rats with VMH lesions do not behave like hungry animals. For example, they are reluctant to work for food and are intolerant of unpalatable tastes. The original theory was, therefore, modified to make the VMH a satiety centre that only comes into play once eating is initiated.

There are two major problems with this hypothesis. The first is that the increase in food intake following VMH lesions isn't simply due to the animals taking larger meals. The number of meals taken increases as well as meal size and the animals tend to increase food intake during the normal sleep part of the circadian cycle. In other words, one of the main effects of VMH lesions is an increase in the number of meals. The second is that there are major changes in metabolic function that are probably the cause of both the obesity and the over-eating that is observed. Rats with VMH lesions produce more fat than controls, even when fed on exactly the same diet (LeMagnen 1985; Mogenson and Phillips 1976; Powley 1977). Thus, the idea that the function of the VMH is to terminate food intake is untenable.

Arguments against the two-centre theory: the lateral hypothalamus

Lateral hypothalamic lesions undoubtedly depress food intake, unless the subjects have previously been seriously deprived of food. The primary objection to the LH acting as a hunger centre is that the effects of lesions are so unspecific. Not only is hunger affected, but so are thirst and general activity. Indeed, food intake generally recovers quite well, if the animals are nursed properly, and the long-term residual deficits tend to be in thirst and activity levels (Epstein 1971; Stricker and Zigmond 1976). A further objection to the hypothesis is that the role of the hypothalamus itself is unclear, many studies having obtained deficits similar to the LH syndrome with lesions that completely spare the hypothalamus (Grossman 1975). The most vivid example of this sort of work are the experiments of Zeigler *et al.*(1985) which show similar effects of cutting peripheral nerves serving the mouth.

Explanations of motivational deficits after hypothalamic lesions: the ventromedial hypothalamus

The VMH presents a chicken-and-egg problem: does the increased food intake create the obesity or does the obesity create the increased intake? The arguments have now shifted in favour of the latter. Perhaps the most convincing evidence for obesity being the primary problem is the fact, mentioned above, that rats with VMH lesions get fat even when fed on the same diet as control rats. Why do VMH lesions make rats obese? Why does obesity lead to the other symptoms associated with VMH lesions?

The best explanation for VMH lesion-induced obesity is that there is over-production of the hormone insulin, which promotes the uptake of glucose from the blood and, in the absence of any metabolic work to do, its conversion into fat. Both basal and food-induced insulin release are increased by VMH lesions while stimulation has the reverse effect, lowering insulin release. The importance of the insulin release for obesity can be gauged by the fact that VMH lesions do not produce significant obesity in rats that have been made diabetic by treatment with the drug streptozotocin which destroys the cells in the pancreas that produce insulin. It might be argued that diabetic rats feel too ill to be hyperphagic but this is ruled out by the finding that transplants of islets of Langerhans, the pancreatic cells that produce insulin, eliminate the diabetes but the rats with VMH lesions still don't become obese, presumably because the transplanted islets do not have any innervation from the VMH. Further evidence that the VMH is involved in the regulation of insulin secretion is that radioactively labelled insulin is found to bind selectively to the VMH, making it plausible that the VMH monitors blood insulin levels. However, insulin receptors are also found in other areas of the brain so this sort of finding should be interpreted with caution (LeMagnen 1985).

Rats with VMH lesions don't simply over-eat, they also show changes in meal patterning and in their response to variations in palatability. Furthermore, the reduction in blood glucose availability associated with over-production of insulin might be expected to promote increased hunger, yet the evidence from Miller and his colleagues in the 1950s suggested that rats with VMH lesions were not hungrier than controls. How can these all be explained in terms of increased insulin production? Empirically, it is found that chronic insulin infusions produce the same effects on meal patterning as do VMH lesions, namely an increase in both meal size and frequency associated with an abnormal level of food intake during the sleep phase of the cycle. The increased intake during the waking phase can probably be explained in terms of reduced glucose availability or some other systemic signal related to glucose availability, but the sleep phase increase requires some other explanation because even normal rats become hypoglycaemic at this point. The best explanation is that not only does insulin promote the synthesis of fats, it also inhibits their breakdown for use as a metabolic fuel so that the lipolysis that normally forms the main source of energy during the sleep period no longer occurs.

One of the recurring problems with the VMH literature is that of comparing like with like. Rats with VMH lesions are clearly more finicky about their food than control rats fed *ad libitum*, but is this a suitable control for the effects of VMH lesions? If rats with VMH lesions are, in fact, hungrier than normal it is clearly inappropriate to compare them with free-feeding controls. They must be compared with controls that are as hungry as they are. Ascertaining how hungry a rat is is a difficult business and matching animals for degree of hungriness even more so. Rather than doing this most experiments have looked at the effects of varying food deprivation levels on response to palatability and what is typically found is that rats made very hungry by the simple expedient of depriving them of food show the same degree of finickiness as those with VMH lesions. The increased finickiness of VMH-lesioned rats is, therefore, compatible with their being very hungry (LeMagnen 1985).

Why, then, did Miller and his colleagues find that rats with VMH lesions did not appear more hungry than controls? The answer is that hunger doesn't always work according to our commonsense expectations because the relationship between hunger and performance is not linear. At low levels of food deprivation animals become increasingly prepared to work for food and increasingly prepared to tolerate adulterated food as the deprivation level increases, but there comes a point at which this relationship no longer holds. Instead, further increases in deprivation lead to finickiness and reluctance to work. This isn't totally surprising. An animal that is severely food-deprived has an emergency on its hands and has to conserve energy. It can only eat if the caloric intake associated with the food greatly exceeds the energy expended in consuming it. This will only be true with highly palatable foods for which small amounts of work are required.

The story of the VMH is an interesting interlude in scientific history, especially because the wheel has now come full circle. When Hetherington and Ranson (1940) first started studying the effects of hypothalamic lesions they expected to find endocrine disturbances and were puzzled to find increases in food intake. We now know that, as initially predicted, endocrine disturbances are what VMH lesions produce.

Explanations of motivational deficits after hypothalamic lesions: the lateral hypothalamus

In contrast to the unanimity about the effects of VMH lesions, work on the LH syndrome has produced less consistency. Some authors, like LeMagnen, continue to argue that the LH has a central role in ingestive behaviours while others, like Zeigler *et al.* (1985), maintain that the deficits are due to a sensori-motor impairment. LeMagnen (1985) acknowledges that LH lesions produce a sensori-motor deficit but argues that this is not the basis of the feeding deficit. The deficit, he argues, is due to loss of a system, located in the antero-ventral hypothalamus, that monitors blood glucose availability and regulates feeding accordingly. The most convincing evidence for this hypothesis is the decline in glucose level in the jugular vein just prior to feeding, coupled with the fact that cells in the antero-ventral LH are responsive to glucose. If this hypothesis were correct we would also expect that LH lesions would make animals selectively insensitive to the systemic signals that control hunger. Such findings have been reported a number of times (e.g. Epstein 1971), but their significance is disputed for two reasons. The first is that not all of the manipulations used to generate hunger in these experiments act like normal hunger signals. For example, the metabolic poison 2DG stimulates feeding in normal rats but not in rats with LH lesions. However, intraventricular injection of alloxan blocks the effects of 2DG in normal rats but doesn't affect normal feeding. If the LH is the centre for monitoring systemic hunger signals it is strange that it can respond to both natural and unnatural signals. The second is that, according to Friedman and Stricker (1976), rats with LH lesions are only unresponsive to hunger signals when the latter are large and are introduced suddenly. For example, while large doses of rapidly absorbed insulin fail to induce feeding in rats with LH lesions, low doses of the slowly absorbed version, protamine zinc insulin, do so.

Some of the most striking observations relevant to the LH syndrome in recent years have been coming from Zeigler's laboratory. For many years Zeigler (e.g. 1983) drew our attention to the remarkable overlap between the brain sites in which lesions would produce the LH syndrome, including the LH, and the distribution of the ascending projections of the sensory trigeminal pathways. The trigeminal, the fifth cranial nerve, carries sensory information from the face and mouth, although it doesn't carry taste information. Afferent neurons terminate in the medulla, in the principal and spinal trigeminal nuclei. Relay neurons from these nuclei ascend through the brainstem and run through the lateral hypothalamic region before terminating in a number of sites in the thalamus. More recently Zeigler and his colleagues (1985) have gone on to show that cutting the trigeminal nerve at the peripheral level has similar effects on behaviour to making lesions in the central trigeminal pathways, or LH lesions. Food intake declines and there is a change in responsiveness to the stimuli that normally promote food intake. However, there are differences between the effects of peripheral trigeminal deafferentation. The most obvious one is in meal patterning. After LH lesions rats become 'nibblers', taking small amounts of food very frequently. After trigeminal deafferentation the frequency of eating bouts diminishes while their duration may approximate to the normal. Thus although changes in sensitivity to peripheral stimuli may contribute to the LH deficit, impairments in trigeminal function cannot be the whole story.

Of course, there is no reason why the LH impairment should simply involve oro-facial insensitivity. Other modalities, especially taste and smell, may be involved as well. The attraction of Zeigler's original formulation is that it provided a neat explanation for the LH syndrome without invoking specialized circuits in the hypothalamus itself. If we wish to argue that taste and smell are also involved, this reopens the possibility of direct hypthalamic involvement since afferent connections of both the gustatory and olfactory systems reach the lateral hypothalamus itself.

Neural mechanisms of motivated behaviour – future trends

The preoccupation with centres and single controlling signals that characterized accounts of ingestive behaviour for over twenty years has now given way to a more complex, but probably more realistic picture in which multiple control signals are integrated by a number of neural control centres spread out throughout the nervous system and integrated into a hierarchical system. Some of the best evidence for this approach comes from the work of Grill and Berridge (1985) who, having established a viable technique for studying reactions to changes in palatability in rats, have investigated the role of different levels in the nervous system in controlling reactions to palatability.

One of their most surprising findings, given previous emphasis on the hypothalamus, is that rats in which the brainstem has been transected just in front of the superior colliculus and in which, therefore, the hypothalamus is disconnected from descending motor pathways, still react to variations in palatability. Moreover, their reactions are a function of both food quality and their need state, which means that information about the internal environment must be being processed outside the hypothalamus. Nevertheless, food intake in these animals is not entirely normal. Their body weights are lower than controls and they do not learn taste aversions. It is significant that these animals do not show the strongly aversive reactions to food typical of animals with lesions restricted to the LH. The fact that ablation of the LH produces symptoms not seen after the complete disconnection of the hypothalamus suggests that the LH symptoms are positive symptoms. That is to say, they are due to over-activity in a system released from inhibitory control rather than loss of a centre for integrating behaviour.

Removing the cerebral cortex and the basal ganglia, but leaving the hypothalamus intact, has the unexpected effect of producing reactions to taste that are indistinguishable from the effects of lateral hypothalamus lesions. The rats show strongly aversive reactions to food under conditions in which normal rats show a strong ingestive pattern. Needless to say, the control of food intake in these animals is grossly abnormal. These results suggest that aversive reactions are integrated at the level of the hypothalamus. LH lesions may well have their effects due to releasing these hypothalamic mechanisms for aversive reactions due to disconnecting the forebrain from the hypothalamus.

The advantage of thinking about ingestive behaviours in terms of controlling centres and single controlling variables is that it makes problems theoretically tractable and makes it possible to produce testable predictions. Once we move on to multiple centres and multiple controlling factors all things become possible, in principle. Experimental developments in our approach to ingestive behaviours must be matched by appropriate developments in theory. As with perceptual systems the best theories are those which give rise to simulations on which it is possible to test out the likely properties of motivational systems. This approach is currently being pursued by workers like Toates (1986). Simulations give us two advantages. The first is that they tell us what motivational systems are likely to look like. For example, they can tell us whether eating is likely to be initiated by a single controlling factor or a number of them. The second is that they can be used to explore anomalous findings like the effects on palatability of disconnecting the telencephalon.

Ingestive behaviours as a model for other motivational systems

There was a time when it was very difficult to identify common principles underlying 'homeostatic' motives like hunger and 'non-homeostatic' motives like sex. Indeed, some authors like Hebb (1955) went to ingenious lengths to reconcile these diverse types of motivation, although with limited success. The recent changes in our approach to motivation, with its emphasis on multiple controlling signals and multiple neural control mechanisms, largely dispose of this sort of problem and it is now possible, in principle, to discuss sexual behaviour within the same sort of conceptual framework we use to discuss eating. The multiple control system approach has proved useful even with deceptively simple motivational processes like temperature regulation, which was once thought to consist of a single control mechanism associated with a single thermostat in the hypothalamus. As Satinoff (1983) has shown, this is an over-simplification. There are, in fact, multiple neural systems involved in controlling temperature, some involving behaviour and the others involving activity in the autonomic nervous system. Some are extremely sensitive, while others only come into effect when large changes in body temperature occur.

It would, however, be unfair to imply that these changes in our attitudes to motivation have come about because of developments in the study of eating and drinking. Much of the work on other motivational systems has proceeded independently of work on food and water intake and it has only been in recent years that theorists have begun to see the common ground (Toates 1986). Far from commending the use of eating or drinking as model systems for motivation the history of work on motivation since the early 1950s illustrates the pitfalls of too narrow a preoccupation with a single system.

For many psychologists the only interest in studying eating and drinking is that they might act as model systems for 'non-biological' motives. Few of us have ever experienced severe hunger or thirst yet we continue to play out our lives by setting up goals and pursuing them with varying degrees of dedication and success. It is reasonable to ask how these other motives come about and how they affect behaviour.

One of the favourite explanations of behaviourists was that they constituted secondary drives which arose because previously neutral stimuli, like coins and banknotes, had acquired incentive properties due to being regularly associated with the satisfaction of primary drives like hunger and thirst. Those of the psychoanalytic persuasion, on the other hand, maintain that these motives arise because of conflicts between the primary drives. The intellectual contortions required to make theories like these work in every conceivable instance are only really necessary so long as we ignore the social context of our behaviour, or deny that our social behaviour has the same biological foundations as solitary actions like eating or drinking.

Our social motives, which are probably the ones that we normally experience most strongly, create numerous problems for the psychobiologist because we don't understand the conditions under which they arise and we cannot, therefore, control them successfully. Nevertheless, they can, in principle, be accommodated within the sorts of cognitive motivational models that are now being developed to accommodate more obviously physiologically based motives like the need for food or the avoidance of cold.

Overview

Motivation has been one of the success stories of psychobiology. In the space of less than fifty years we have acquired a detailed understanding of the bodily systems that control eating and drinking and have begun to map out the neural systems involved in the control of these and other behaviours. Inevitably there remain a number of questions to answer. One concerns the role of blood glucose level in the initiation of feeding. Another, more general one concerns the organization of the neural systems responsible for motivation. Finally, the resurgence of interest in the role of cognitive factors in motivation, while welcome, raises a number of serious issues about how mental representations of goal objects like food, water, warmth, or sex partners, interact with physiological variables like blood glucose levels, cellular dehydration, temperature, and sex hormone levels.

6
Emotion

The hardest part of writing about emotion is explaining to other people what it is you are writing about. Emotion is a regular part of our daily lives and, consequently, something we very much take for granted. When pressed to explain what we mean when we say we are undergoing an emotion we are likely to refer to a number of apparently disconnected things. For a start, emotions are something that happen to us rather than something we bring about. They are usually strongly linked to circumstances in that particular emotions are generally believed to be appropriate to particular situations. Emotions exist in the plural, in that we are aware of a number of possible types of emotion, such as fear, joy, or anger. They usually involve some sort of bodily reaction, be it a churning in the abdominal region or involuntary tears in the eyes. Finally, there is usually a behavioural component: a strong urge to flee the situation, a refusal to enter another situation, or an overwhelming urge to approach somebody or something.

A considerable amount of ink has been spilt in an effort to tell us what emotions 'really' are. These efforts, well summarized by Strongman (1978), can be divided into three categories. The first approach holds that the emotional properties of a situation are a qualitative dimension of the experience that is little different, in principle, from the colour of an object or its taste. According to this view, which is very much the commonsense one, our emotional reactions to a situation then cause us to behave in a particular way. This position was developed in the 1920s and 1930s by Cannon and Bard (in Grossman 1967) and by Papez (1939). The second approach, which stands commonsense on its head, holds that emotion is our perception of our bodily reactions to a situation. According to James (1884; James and Lange 1922) we are afraid because we run away, not the other way round. Finally, the last twenty years have seen the emergence of cognitive approaches which stress an interaction between our bodily reactions and our appraisal of the situation in which we find ourselves. As developed by authors like Schacter (Schacter and Singer 1962) and Mandler (1975), this approach holds that we experience emotions when we undergo bodily reactions for which there are no other explanations. In other words, our emotions are our attempts to make sense of what is happening in our bodies.

These different viewpoints have profound implications for the sorts of brain mechanisms likely to be involved in emotional states. The commonsense view suggests that there will be specific brain circuits involved in elaborating emotional experience, just as there turn out to be circuits elaborating our experience of colour (see chapter 4). Emotion as perception of our bodily reactions argues that there will be neural circuits dedicated to the control of patterns of bodily reactions and that different circuits will be activated in different reactions, but that there will be no special mechanisms underlying emotional experience. Finally, the cognitive view suggests that there will be a neural system for generating the bodily reaction associated with emotion, but only a single mechanism will be required. Moreover, it implies that emotional experience will be heavily dependent on the integrity of general purpose cognitive, as opposed to perceptual, mechanisms.

The cognitive approach will not concern us much here because it is based on the assumption that physiological mechanisms have only a minor role to play in the genesis of emotional states. Indeed, authors like Valins (in Strongman 1978) have gone as far as to suggest that emotions can be generated without any change in bodily state, providing the subject believes a change has occurred. It is difficult to interpret many of the studies supporting the cognitive approach, however, because they are usually set up to minimize the role of physiological variables while maximizing the likely impact of cognitive factors. Consequently, my strategy in this chapter is to focus on the first two possibilities and review the evidence for whether specific neural systems are involved in emotion and whether the type of emotion experienced is a function of which circuit is activated. I shall then move on to the much more problematic issue of whether these systems are involved in elaborating emotional behaviour, emotional experience, or both.

Before we can study the neural bases of emotion we have to have effective means of studying it. Our three concepts of emotion, as a subjective state, as a bodily reaction and as behavioural predisposition, suggest different methodologies. We can only really study it as a subjective state by using humans as subjects and giving them questionnaires and rating scales to find out what they are feeling and how strongly they are feeling it. This approach isn't possible with animal subjects, so we have to resort to inferential methods to determine what they are likely to be feeling from what they are doing in a particular situation, either by observing their behaviour or from measurements of autonomic responses. The main consequence of this is that people have had to use emotional states that are likely to have clear-cut interactions with ongoing behaviour and, for most researchers, that has meant studying fear. As we shall see, this may have biased considerably the way we have come to think about emotion. One of the issues to be kept in mind throughout this chapter is, therefore, the adequacy of the behavioural models used to investigate emotion.

Even if we know which systems in the brain are involved in emotion we still lack an answer to an even more basic question: why emotions exist in the first place. What exactly is the relationship between emotion and behaviour? Many psychological theories have attributed a motivational role to emotional states. If this is the case we might expect some functional and anatomical overlap between the systems responsible for motivation and those responsible for emotion. This issue is also addressed in this chapter.

Neural mechanisms of emotion: early work

Experimental studies carried out between the 1920s and the late 1940s by Cannon and Bard and later by Hess demonstrated the importance of the brainstem for the elaboration of emotional reactions in animals. Cannon and Bard (in Grossman 1967) demonstrated that removing the forebrain but leaving intact the thalamus, hypothalamus, and the rest of the brainstem produced cats that were emotionally over-reactive, flying into a rage at the slightest provocation. Later, Hess (1957) showed that low-level electrical stimulation of the hypothalamus could elicit integrated patterns of emotional behaviour in cats with intact brains. Although this work focused attention on the brainstem, a more sensitive reading of Cannon and Bard's findings indicated that the forebrain also had an important part to play in emotion since the reactions of their decorticate cats were distinctly abnormal. For one thing, the main reaction these animals exhibited was rage. None of the positive reactions cats typically show was present. In this respect the reactions are similar to the effects of forebrain removal on responses to taste described by Grill and Berridge (1985; see chapter 5). For another, the reactions were highly stimulus-dependent. They only occurred in response to physical provocation, such as touching, and rarely outlasted the stimulus.

Although he did not rely particularly on experimental findings it was Papez (1939) who provided the most comprehensive model of the neural bases of emotion for his day, and this model incorporated both brainstem and forebrain components. According to Papez, the centre for integrating emotional experience is the cingulate cortex, that part of the medial surface of the cerebral cortex that lies immediately dorsal to the corpus callosum. It is activated by input from the mammillary bodies, part of the hypothalamus, relayed via the anterior nucleus of the thalamus. According to Papez, input to the mammillary bodies comes from two sources. There is direct, sensory input via relays like the ventral lateral geniculate nucleus in the ventral thalamus, and cognitive input from the cerebral cortex via the hippocampus.

The details of Papez's model have not been substantiated by subsequent experimental research but his approach, emphasizing the role of a set of structures known as the limbic system in emotion, along with the need for integrating the activity of structures at different levels in the nervous system, set the agenda for much of the subsequent work on the neural bases of emotion. This general position was adopted enthusiastically by subsequent workers but with different emphases. For example, MacLean (1954) argued that the cingulate cortex had only a minor role in emotional behaviour and that it was the hippocampus, together with the amygdala, that were the main centres for emotional events.

About the same time that Papez was producing his limbic system theory of emotion, neurosurgeons were creating considerable excitement with their claim that they could control pathological emotional states by surgery that disconnected the frontal lobes from the rest of the brain. This technique, developed by Moniz and subsequently popularized by Freeman and Watts (see Valenstein 1980), drew people's attention to the frontal association cortex and suggested that this region too was involved in emotion.

Another significant development that set the agenda for subsequent work was the discovery of 'arousal'. Moruzzi and Magoun (1949) demonstrated that electrical stimulation of the midbrain reticular formation (MBRF) produced a consistent state of undifferentiated excitation in the cerebral cortex of cats. Subsequent work in unrestrained animals showed that stimulation also produced undifferentiated behavioural arousal, while ablation of the MBRF could produce a nearly permanent comatose state. This suggested that behaviour varied along a unitary dimension of excitation rather than falling into distinct states. It was this discovery that set the scene for many of the cognitive theories of emotion, the argument being that since physiological reactions only vary along the single dimension of arousal, the qualitative differences between emotions that we all experience must be due to cognitive elaboration rather than reflecting our perception of our physiological reactions. It should be borne in mind that psychophysiological studies carried out around the same time indicated a much more complicated picture. According to a number of researchers autonomic reactions to a situation are a function of the situation, the individual, and the measure being taken (Edwards and Hill 1967; Strongman 1978). Some consistencies were observed, such as the difference between situations in which subjects process the emotion-provoking stimuli and those in which they seek to block them out, described by Lacey (1968) but, in general, it is difficult to predict a person's autonomic reaction from knowledge of the situation alone. Nevertheless, the fact remains that more than one pattern of emotional reaction can be recorded.

Between about 1920 and 1955 a number of structures were implicated in emotion. The next section looks at the evidence for these claims before moving on to alternative interpretations of the findings.

Neural mechanisms of emotion

The hypothalamus

While the effects of hypothalamic lesions are most simply described in motivational terms, many of the effects of hypothalamic stimulation are much more readily understood in emotional terms. Since the work of Karplus and Kreidl (1969) it has been established that hypothalamic stimulation activates the autonomic nervous system, which could provide the substrate for the bodily reactions implicated in emotion by James (1884) and Lange (James and Lange 1922) in their theories on emotion. When it became technically possible to stimulate the brains of freely moving animals it soon became apparent that the autonomic reactions observed by earlier workers were part of a much richer, more complex pattern of events involving both the skeletal musculature and the autonomic nervous system. In simple terms, the animals behaved exactly like they would when exposed to emotionally provocative external stimuli (Hess 1957; Panksepp 1971). Not only does hypothalamic stimulation evoke behaviour, it also acts as either a reward or a punishment, depending on the site of the stimulation (Olds and Milner 1954), which is at least compatible with our commonsense idea that some emotional states are pleasant and likely to be sought out while others are unpleasant and likely to be shunned.

Nobody disputes the effects of hypothalamic stimulation but they do dispute its interpretation. As with the putative role of the hypothalamus in motivation there is the recurring problem of knowing whether any of the effects are really due to action on the hypothalamus itself, rather than on fibres of passage. Another problem is that it is unclear how one moves from the relatively simple events elicited by hypothalamic stimulation to the complexities and subtleties of human emotion. Is there really one neural system for joy, one for sorrow, one for fear, one for stark terror, one for grief, another for ecstasy, and so on?

As with motivated behaviour, emotional reactions can be produced by stimulation outside the hypothalamus. Furthermore, these effects persist after lesions in the hypothalamus. For example, electrical stimulation of the ventromedial hypothalamus produces 'affective attack' reactions in cats. The animal looks distinctly angry, with the typical 'Halloween-cat' posture of arched back, erect hair on back and neck, dilated pupils, and bared teeth. Cats in this state will readily attack and injure other animals that they come across but seem to find the state aversive since they will work to turn off the electrical stimulation that produces it. Similar effects can be obtained by stimulating the periaqueductal grey (PAG) in the midbrain. PAG ablation blocks the effects of VMH stimulation but the effects of PAG stimulation persist after VMH ablation (Berntson and Micco, in Carlson 1986).

For reasons which we don't yet fully understand nearly all of the ascending pathways running through the hypothalamus use neurotransmitters belonging to the class known as monoamines. There are three principle examples in the brain: serotonin (an indoleamine), and dopamine and noradrenaline (catecholamines). The neurons that contain these transmitters can be readily identified using special staining procedures, so that it is possible to determine the location of their cell bodies, the course of their axons, and the locations of their terminals. All three systems have fibres running through the lateral hypothalamus, either in the medial forebrain bundle (MFB) or adjacent tracts like the nigrostriatal bundle. All three originate in clusters of cells located in discrete nuclei in the mid- and hindbrain.

Many of the effects obtained with hypothalamic stimulation can be obtained with stimulation in parts of these monoaminergic pathways. Here are just two examples. Lateral hypothalamic stimulation produces predatory attack in rats. So does stimulation of the ventral tegmental area, which is the source of dopaminergic fibres projecting to the nucleus accumbens septi in the forebrain. Lateral hypothalamic stimulation also acts as a reinforcement, a phenomenon known as intracranial self-stimulation (ICSS). Stimulation sites in the ventral tegmental area and in the locus coeruleus, the main source of noradgrenergic fibres in the brain, also support ICSS (Panksepp 1982).

These ascending monoaminergic systems can also be manipulated pharmacologically. Drugs that block dopamine reliably suppress intracranial self-stimulation at doses that have no other detectable effects (Rolls 1975). Significantly for the discussion of emotion, antidepressants are believed to work through their effects on these pathways (Lickey and Gordon 1983; Stein 1968), although the exact mechanisms of action have yet to be worked out (Lickey and Gordon 1983). One of the oldest and crudest anti-depressants, amphetamine, simply promotes the release of monoamines from the neurons that contain them. Other antidepressants have more subtle effects. Monoamine oxidase inhibitors work by blocking the enzymes, monoamine oxidases, that promote the breakdown of monoamines in the brain so that the amount of monoamine increases. These have the disadvantage that they also lead to the accumulation of monoamines elsewhere, which, on the wrong diet, can prove fatal. Tricyclics, now the largest class of antidepressants in use, also increase the availability of monoamines in the brain, this time by blocking the mechanisms that control the re-uptake of monoamines into axon terminals in the brain.

It looks as if depression might be the result of lowered monoamine levels in the brain but there are complications to this simple story. The first is that not all cases of depression respond to treatment with these drugs. The second is that we would expect that drugs that reduced the effects of monoamines in the brain would simulate depression, and they don't. Major tranquillizers like chlorpromazine that block dopamine receptors produce motor disorders. Minor tranquillizers, like the benzodiazepines, that block noradrenergic and serotonergic function, produce a state of calm wellbeing. Finally, there are new antidepressants that have no effect on the catecholaminergic cells believed to be involved in reward and emotion. Instead, the latest evidence suggests that they work by modifying the function of a subclass of receptors for the indoleamine, serotonin, the role of which in emotion is very uncertain (Goodwin 1984).

We might get more clues about the emotional functions of monoaminergic pathways by studying the correlations between activity in monoaminergic neurons and behaviour. According to Jacobs (1987) the main correlate of serotonergic neuronal activity is level of behavioural activity. These neurons, the cells bodies of which cluster in the raphe nuclei in the pontine tegmentum and medulla, fire most strongly when the animal is active, less strongly when awake and resting, and least when the animal is asleep. One of the best correlates of noradrenergic activity is cardiac function, the activity of units in the locus coeruleus, which contains most of the noradrenergic neurons in the brain, correlating closely with the phase of the cardiac cycle. Since general activity correlates with cardiac activity there is also a correlation between noradrenergic activity and behaviour. The activity of dopaminergic neurons bears absolutely no relationship to activity level. Indeed, there is little sign that the units concerned are related to movement at all. The only exception is that cells in the substantia nigra, the source of dopaminergic input to the caudate-putamen system, are inhibited when animals make rapid movements involving most of their body, such as orienting towards a novel stimulus. Single unit recording studies therefore suggest that the monaminergic pathways are involved in motor function, rather than in emotion itself.

Of course, the distinction between hypothalamic and extrahypothalamic mechanisms isn't altogether real. Most of the areas outside the hypothalamus from which emotional effects can be elicited (see below) have extensive connections with it, either directly or indirectly. However, these observations act as a useful reminder to us to think of the brain as a set of interconnected, interacting subsystems rather than a series of isolated control centres.

The more serious issue is whether there is sufficient diversity among the reactions mediated by the hypothalamus and its allied circuitry to account for the variety and complexity of our emotional experience. Panksepp (1982) argues that there isn't and there is! What he, in fact, says is that hypothalamic stimulation in non-human animals only ever generates one of four reactions: fear, rage, panic and approach. Clearly there are too few reactions to account directly for the diversity and complexity of our emotional lives. He gets round this problem by suggesting that the complexity comes from the fact that these systems are often activated simultaneously, to give rise to secondary emotions. For example, the state we call 'anxiety', he maintains, is a product of the simultaneous activation of the fear and panic systems.

Whatever the final evaluation of Panksepp's approach, we are left with the fact that hypothalamic stimulation in animals elicits more than one type of emotional reaction. Observations like these are difficult to reconcile with theories that stress a unitary dimension of 'arousal' underlying our emotions. They also cast doubt on the value of attempts to manipulate 'emotional' states with drugs that largely affect our autonomic nervous systems alone (e.g. Schacter and Singer 1962), since these treatments can never generate the integrated packages of skeletal and autonomic reactions produced by central stimulation. They don't, however, let us know whether the experience of emotion is due to the activation of specialized centres in the brain or to feedback from bodily reactions.

The cingulate cortex

Papez's theory gave pride of place to the cingulate cortex as the centre of emotional experience. Cingulate cortex lesions certainly alter spontaneous emotional behaviour in animals, although the direction of the effects is often unpredictable (see Grossman 1967 for descriptions of early studies). When formal behavioural test procedures are used the results are similarly variable. McCleary (1966) has shown that the effects of cingulate cortex lesions on 'emotional' reactions depend critically on the way those reactions are measured. At the time it was widely held that avoidance learning was based on an intervening state of fear: animals avoided noxious stimuli like electric shock by fleeing from the environmental stimuli that were associated with and predicted the shocks because the stimuli generated a fear state from which the animals were trying to escape. Two avoidance learning paradigms were used: active and passive. In active avoidance learning the noxious stimulus was presented unless the animal did something, usually jumping between one part of a shuttle box and the other. In passive avoidance learning the noxious stimulus is avoided by refraining from an action, usually putting the head into a food-well recessed into the side of the test chamber. Since both behaviours are supposed to be based on fear, both should be similarly impaired by lesions that disrupt emotions like fear. Unfortunately they are not. Cingulate cortex lesions impair active avoidance learning but facilitate passive. Combined with the results of stimulation studies showing that cingulate cortex activation enhances ongoing behaviour (Kaada 1951, in Grossman 1967), these studies were interpreted in terms of changes in 'response modulation', a motor phenomenon, rather than in emotion.

If the cingulate cortex does have a motor function it is not directly related to single unit activity in the region. Gabriel and his colleagues (Gabriel, Foster, Orona, Saltwick, and Stanton 1980) have studied single cell activity in the cingulate cortex in rabbits undergoing discriminative avoidance learning, in which one stimulus signals the impending delivery of electric shock, which can be avoided by running, and a second stimulus signals the absence of shock. Cells in the cingulate cortex fire differentially to the two stimuli as learning progresses but when the animals are presented with a reversal of the original discrimination, the behaviour to the two stimuli changes before the response of the cingulate cells. This suggests that the cingulate cortex processes information about the emotional significance of stimuli, rather than directly controlling movement. Thus the cingulate cortex is still seen as part of the circuitry for emotional reactions, but there is uncertainty about its exact role. One possibility is that it controls autonomic mechanisms involved in preparation for movement, rather than movement itself (see Mogenson 1987 for evidence).

The hippocampus

When the entire temporal lobe, including hippocampus, amygdala, and overlying neocortex, is removed from monkeys they undergo profound changes in their emotional reactions (Kluver and Bucy 1939). Typically the animals fail to show fear and anger to events that normally provoke them. Removal of the hippocampus alone produces less reliable effects (see Grossman 1967), some authors finding an increase in emotional behaviour, others a decrease. Studies using formal avoidance learning procedures also produced apparently inconsistent results. In some studies avoidance learning is impaired, in others it is facilitated (McCleary 1966). To confuse the picture further, hippocampal damage in humans is associated with memory defects, not emotional changes (Parkin 1987).

The picture of hippocampal function that has emerged over the fifty years since Papez published his theory has been an extremely confusing one, and only a few brave authors, such as Gray (1982), and O'Keefe and Nadel (1978) have dared to try to pull together all of the strands of the literature. Few of these attempts are entirely convincing: they all leave some disturbing loose ends for which there are no satisfactory explanations.

The apparent inconsistencies in the effects of hippocampal lesions on avoidance learning can be tidied up quite considerably by attending to the distinction between active and passive avoidance, as described in the previous section. In contrast to cingulate lesions, hippocampal lesions impair passive avoidance learning and facilitate some forms of active avoidance learning. Gray (1982) offers an ingenious explanation for this, which involves abandoning conventional versions of two-factor learning theory. According to Gray, only passive avoidance learning actually involves fear. Active avoidance learning, in contrast, involves the hopeful anticipation of shock avoidance, which he views as equivalent to the anticipation of reward in conventional, appetitive learning. Thus the effects of hippocampal lesions are quite compatible with its being involved in fear, but not more positive emotional reactions. The problem is that hippocampal lesions don't facilitate performance on all active avoidance tasks or impair performance on all passive avoidance measures. O'Keefe and Nadel (1978) have put forward an alternative interpretation of these findings, which is that the effect of hippocampal lesions depends on whether the animal has to remember where something happened. In a typical passive avoidance task, on which the animals are impaired, the animal has to remember where it received an electric shock, whereas in active avoidance tasks it has to remember which stimuli were associated with the shock. They argue that animals with hippocampal lesions are impaired on active avoidance tasks in which the animals have to remember where something happened but unimpaired on passive avoidance tasks in which the noxious stimulus is predicted by another environmental stimulus.

In any event, Gray's argument appears to be undermined by the fact that hippocampal lesions also impair extinction when appetitive motivation is used. There are a number of other lines of evidence to show that the hippocampus is particularly important for mediating responses to the withdrawal of reinforcement. Rats with hippocampal lesions show abnormally prolonged extinction in a range of instrumental learning tasks (Gray 1982). Furthermore, activation of the hippocampus by electrical stimulation of the septum, using regularly spaced pulses that induce a characteristic 7.7 Hz theta wave in the hippocampus, simulates the effects of non-reward in rats. Stimulation like this during continuously reinforced acquisition produces resistance to subsequent extinction normally characteristic of partial reinforcement during learning, a phenomenon known as the partial reinforcement extinction effect. Conversely, blocking the theta rhythm, by using randomly spaced pulses of current in the septum, has the converse effect. Animals that have experienced non-reward during acquisition behave as if continuously reinforced if the stimulation is given on the trials in which the reinforcement has been omitted. Again, Gray has an ingenious response to these findings: he argues that the processes occurring during non-reward are the same as those occurring during aversive stimulation.

It seems counterintuitive to believe that the same processes occur in non-reward as in punishment, but Gray's position is not based on intuition. It is based on a number of sources of converging evidence that show that manipulations that affect an animal's response to non-reward also affect its response to punishment. One of the most telling of these is that minor tranquillizers like Valium have effects on both and the effects are in the same direction as those of ablation of the hippocampus. Valium given to rats abolishes the partial reinforcement extinction effect, facilitates some forms of active avoidance learning, and impairs passive avoidance learning.

The real issue is not whether the hippocampus is necessary for normal emotional reactions in animals but what part it plays in them. Is it, as Gray argues, part of a larger circuit devoted to mediating anxiety responses or is it a more general-purpose cognitive mechanism that happens to be important for anxiety reactions under some conditions because they activate the cognitive processes mediated by the hippocampus? The biggest challenges to Gray's type of position come from work on the spatial functions of the hippocampus and on memory failures in humans with hippocampal damage.

Figure 6.1 A radial arm maze

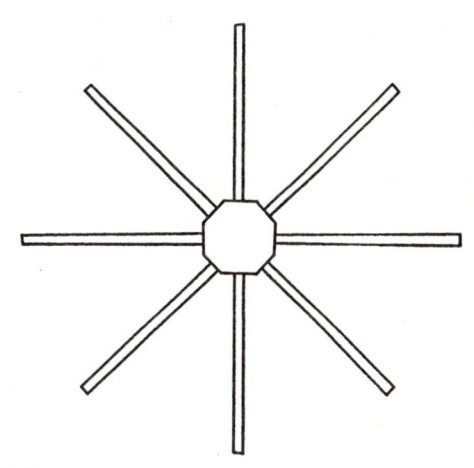

The rat is placed on the central platform
and allowed to explore the arms.

In a series of electrophysiological studies in the 1970s Nadel and O'Keefe demonstrated that many hippocampal cells in rats would only fire when the animals were in a particular part of the test apparatus. These cells were very sensitive to changes in the layout of the room in which the apparatus was placed, or the orientation of the apparatus relative to the room, but peculiarly insensitive to changes within the apparatus, such as the elimination of possible odour cues by cleaning, or rotation of a symmetrical apparatus such as an elevated radial arm maze (Figure 6.1). Following these studies, it was shown that hippocampal lesions produce deficits in spatial ability and spatial memory. One of the most convincing demonstrations involved a 'milk-maze' (Morris, Garrud, Rawlins, and O'Keefe 1982). Rats were placed in a large container of milky water which contained a platform hidden just under the surface at a consistent location in the tank. The rats swim around until they find the platform and then climb on to it to escape from the water. Providing the position of the platform, relative to the layout of the test room and the container, was kept constant from trial to trial normal rats learned rapidly to swim to the platform, no matter where they were placed in the water at the start of the trial. Rats with hippocampal lesions were unable to learn this task. They were, however, able to swim rapidly to the platform when they were placed in clear water so that the platform was visible.

The spatial mapping hypothesis is attractive but still doesn't fit all of the data without the liberal application of a shoe-horn. At the single unit recording level, for example, there are many other studies showing that hippocampal cells respond to events other than places. In one series of studies Vinogradova (1975) has shown that hippocampal units will respond to almost any event providing it is novel. In other studies Thompson and his colleagues (Thompson 1983) have shown that the activity of many hippocampal units correlates with the emergence of the conditioned response during classical conditioning of the nictitating membrane (the second eye-lid) response (NMR) in rabbits.

Lesion studies also present difficulties. For one thing, there are tasks on which animals with hippocampal lesions are impaired that do not embody any discernible spatial element, such as responding on a differential reinforcement of low rate (DRL) schedule on which the animals are only reinforced if they have refrained from making any response for a fixed period. For another, they are not always impaired when there is a spatial element present. Olton (1983) has used a version of the multiple arm radial maze to demonstrate this. In the normal version of the test all of the arms are baited and the rats allowed to enter the arms in any order they like to retrieve food. After a number of trials the animals never re-enter an arm once they have removed the food from it, indicating that they can remember the location of the arms they have just visited. Rats with hippocampal lesions make large numbers of errors on this task, regularly re-entering arms from which they have removed the food. In Olton's variation half of the arms were never baited, so that, after a number of trials, the rats never entered them to look for food. With the remaining arms they carried out an efficient search, entering each only once. After hippocampal lesions the rats made re-entry errors with arms in which they had previously encountered food on that trial but there was no increase in errors involving entering the arms that were never baited. According to Olton, then, the hippocampus is not important for all forms of spatial ability.

The picture we are left with is that the hippocampus is essential for some form of cognitive activity that is involved in some emotional reactions, rather than being directly tied to a particular type of reaction, as argued by Gray. What is that cognitive activity? Many of the recent accounts of hippocampal function stress its role in memory. Since the mid 1950s it has been recognized that temporal lobe damage in humans that includes the hippocampus produces severe impairments in some forms of memory (Scoville and Milner 1957) but this has been argued away as a peculiar feature of human memory rather than reflecting a direct memory function for the hippocampus. For example, Weiskrantz and Warrington (in Parkin 1987) argued that the memory deficit in humans was due to the same underlying impairment that produced the response perseveration observed after hippocampal lesions in non-human animals. According to these authors, response perseveration in humans reduces the efficiency of memory through proactive interference. They have since modified their position, however (Warrington and Weiskrantz 1982).

The main reason for explaining away the human memory deficit was that hippocampal lesions didn't seem to produce memory impairments in non-human animals. For example, visual discrimination learning proceeds at the normal pace and, although single unit activity in the hippocampus correlates strongly with the classically conditioned nictitating membrane response, the response is not affected by hippocampal ablation. Recently we have seen two ways of resolving this difficulty. The first, favoured by Mishkin (1982), is the observation that the memory deficits in humans are associated with combined ablation of the hippocampus and amygdala (see below), rather than destruction of the hippocampus alone. Mishkin and his colleagues have carried out a number of studies showing that combined destruction of the hippocampus and amygdala in monkeys results in severe impairments in many forms of learning that are not seen after either lesion in isolation.

Meanwhile Gaffan (1977) and Olton (1983) have been arguing that the learning studies typically used with animals are not proper analogues of the memory tests used with humans. They point out that, in studies of human memory, it has been necessary to draw a distinction between two types of memory. These two types go by different names according to which author you read but the gist of what they are saying is that your memory for what happened, termed variously, 'working' or 'episodic' memory involves different systems from your memory for facts and skills, termed variously 'procedural', 'reference', or 'semantic' memory. Most studies of learning in animals involve procedural memory, while the tasks on which patients with hippocampal damage are impaired involve 'working' or 'episodic' memory. On the human side this is demonstrated by the remarkable ease with which patients with amnesia after hippocampal damage can acquire new skills and reactions yet remain unable to recall the conditions under which those skills and reactions have been acquired (Weiskrantz and Warrington 1979; and see chapter 7). On the animal side, Gaffan and Olton have developed tests of reference or working memory. For example, Gaffan (1977) has developed a recognition memory paradigm for use with monkeys. They are presented with a series of stimuli, one after the other, and have to respond differently to them according to whether or not they have appeared previously in the sequence. Normal monkeys can master this quite well. After section of the fornix, the main output pathway of the hippocampus, an operation that simulates many of the other effects of hippocampal damage, their performance is appalling. Olton's argument is based on the performance of rats with hippocampal lesions on variants of the radial arm maze (see above).

No doubt the debate about the functions of the hippocampus will run and run. Not everybody accepts the memory hypothesis (e.g. Gray 1982) and, to be fair, the hypothesis does leave some unanswered questions, especially about the fact that hippocampal lesions don't affect the classically conditioned nictitating membrane response, while the activity of single units in the hippocampus correlated strongly with the conditioned response. One of the best answers to this sort of problem comes from Kesner and DiMattia (1987). They point out that memory involves learning about a number of different aspects or attributes of the learning situation, not all of which are relevant to performing the task. For example, even tests that are heavily dependent on procedural memory will activate the working memory system in intact animals.

We would not, therefore, expect a strong relationship between the neural systems that are activated during a particular task and those that are essential for its performance. However, were the performance requirements changed, perhaps the importance of these other systems would emerge. For example, rabbits with hippocampal lesions may, like amnesic humans (Weiskrantz and Warrington 1979), continue to display the classically conditioned response but fail to remember anything about the apparatus in which they have been tested.

Amygdala

The hippocampus, hypothalamus, and cingulate cortex were the main components of the Papez circuit but since that theory was first put forward a number of other structures have been implicated in emotion. One of the most important of these has been the amygdala. Our attention was first drawn to the amygdala by Kluver and Bucy (1939), who reported dramatic changes in emotional behaviour in monkeys after temporal lobe ablations that included the amygdala (see above). The changes included a remarkable tameness coupled with a tendency to try and eat or mate with anything that came to hand. They also seemed unable to learn from experience in that they would pick up the same inedible object again and again and try to eat it.

It soon emerged that, while amygdala lesions alone would also produce changes in emotional behaviour, the effects were far from predictable. In some studies amygdala ablation resulted in increased emotional activity, while in others it resulted in a reduction. Why? There are three possibilities. The first is that the lesions created scar tissue that irritated surrounding tissue, in effect acting as a stimulation site rather than a lesion. The second is that the effects depend on which part of the amygdala is destroyed. The third is that it depends on the prior experience of the animals and the immediate circumstances in which the behaviour is being observed.

The possibility that a lesion in one region might create scarring or other neurological abnormalities that activate adjacent areas is a recognized hazard of neurosurgery, and one that experimental neurosurgeons are at pains to avoid whenever possible. That it is more than a hypothetical possibility when it comes to the amygdala is demonstrated by the study of Grossman (1963), who disrupted the amygdalae of cats by a single injection of a cholinergic drug. For months afterwards the cats suffered epileptiform activity in the amygdala and, behaviourally, were vicious, responding to any form of stimulation with attack. They would even attack without provocation.

Ursin (1965) demonstrated that the amygdala is not functionally homogeneous. In electrical stimulation studies he showed that activation of the rostral part of the amygdala produced fear or flight reactions while activation of the caudal amygdala produced anger and defensive reactions. In a subsequent lesion study he showed that ablation of the rostral amygdala reduced fear and flight reactions. The correlation between defensive reactions and caudal amygdala destruction was less clear-cut, however. Reductions in anger and defensive reactions were seen after lesions that spared this zone. The functional subdivision of the amygdala is supported on anatomical grounds (Mogenson 1987). The basolateral nucleus of the amygdala projects to the ventral striatum, via which it can exert an influence over the skeletal motor system. The medial and basomedial nuclei project to the ventromedial hypothalamus and median eminence (part of the base of the hypothalamus), via which they can exert control over the endocrine system. Finally, the central nucleus projects to parts of the hypothalamus and brainstem which give it access to the autonomic nervous system.

Finally, the importance of context and experience has been demonstrated a number of times. Rosvold *et al.* (1954) studied the effects of amygdala lesions on group-living monkeys which had established a dominance hierarchy. Removing the monkey at the top of the hierarchy, subjecting it to amygdala ablation, and returning it to the social group usually resulted in it losing its place in the hierarchy, the animal going from the top to the bottom. This didn't occur with one monkey. Instead it became more dominant after the operation. When they looked at the group in more detail they found that the next animal in the hierarchy was peculiarly unaggressive and didn't bother to challenge the lesioned animal, while this animal continued to be as aggressive as ever. Bolhuis *et al.* (1984) found something similar in a study on rats. Rats, being sensible animals, rapidly learn who not to fight with. If a male rat has a fight with another male and loses, it refrains from fighting with it the next time they encounter each other. Indeed, it displays distinctly submissive behaviour. Rats with lesions in the corticomedial division of the amygdala are not as wise. They continue to pick fights with other rats that have previously beaten them and fail to exhibit appropriately submissive behaviour.

Analogous effects have been obtained with feeding. Rats are notoriously suspicious of strange foods. When given a choice between novel and familiar foods they are as faddy as an average five-year-old human and stick resolutely to what they know. This avoidance of the unfamiliar is known as neophobia. Gradually, repeated exposure to the novel foods breaks down the neophobia and the normal rat starts to eat it in increasing quantities, unless something untoward happens, like becoming ill after eating the food. After lesions in the basolateral amygdala rats do not display neophobia, boldly going where no rat has gone before as far as food is concerned. They also fail to learn to avoid foods that have previously made them ill (Ashe and Nachman 1980).

One way of characterizing the effects of amygdala lesions is that they affect the appropriateness of an animal's behaviour, rather than the amount of it. Consequently, if an animal with amygdala lesions is placed in a situation in which it is appropriate to behave emotionally it is likely to appear under-emotional. If it is put in a situation where it is appropriate to behave unemotionally, it will look over-emotional. Kesner and DiMattia (1987) suggest that these effects arise because amygdala lesions prevent animals from learning about the emotional consequences of their own actions. As with the hippocampus, the amygdala is increasingly being seen as part of a cognitive system that is important for mediating emotional behaviour, rather than as a centre for the elaboration of emotional behaviour or experience.

The prefrontal cortex

At about the time Papez was promulgating his theory of emotional experience, Moniz was proposing the disconnection of the prefrontal cortex from the rest of the brain as a means of controlling abnormal emotional behaviour in humans. Legend has it that he was stimulated by some remarks made by Jacobsen, at a conference in 1935, about the calming effect of prefrontal cortex lesions in monkeys. Jacobsen's primary interest was in the cognitive effects of the ablations and he was reporting a severe impairment in delayed response performance. He noted that normal monkeys performed very well on his task but often displayed severe temper tantrums when they made mistakes. After frontal ablations the error rate shot up but the animals no longer seemed to mind. At the conference Moniz remarked that the emotional changes were exactly those that would be needed to alleviate many of the emotional symptoms associated with psychological disorders in humans. Shortly afterwards he started carrying out prefrontal leucotomies as a means of treating psychological problems, although to his dying day he denied that he got the idea from Jacobsen.

Prefrontal leucotomy is surgically less invasive than the ablations being done by Jacobsen. In a leucotomy a knife is inserted into the brain and waggled around to cut the fibre tracts that connect the frontal cortex to the rest of the brain, but no brain tissue is removed. Although originally developed by Moniz it was eagerly taken up by Freeman and Watts, in the USA, who developed 'improvements' in the surgical procedures designed to speed up the rate at which the operations could be carried out. Within two decades of Moniz having first suggested the idea, the number of patients that had been subjected to prefrontal leucotomies ran into tens of thousands. Until the 1970s, however, few systematic follow-up studies were conducted. When they were done there were two remarkable findings. One was that most patients enjoyed little relief from their psychiatric symptoms. The other was that they suffered relatively little psychological impairment (see Valenstein 1980). The only group of patients to enjoy a reliable relief of symptoms after prefrontal leucotomy were those suffering from chronic pain.

If Moniz's suggestion was not based on Jacobsen's remarks then it is unclear what he did base his proposals on, since most other studies on the prefrontal cortex would have argued strongly against the procedure. One of the earliest reported cases of prefrontal cortex damage in humans, that of Phineas Gage (in Kolb and Whishaw 1985), was associated with serious deterioration in the victim's personality, so serious that a responsible and likeable person had to be fired from his job because of a combination of carelessness and an inability to get along with his colleagues, and ended his days pathetically displaying himself and the object that had caused his injury in fairgrounds to earn a living.

Since then experimental studies on animals and systematic analyses of brain-damaged humans have confirmed the deleterious effects of prefrontal damage on psychological function. Jacobsen's delayed response impairment has been repeatedly confirmed (Gross and Weiskrantz 1964). In the simple version of this task the monkey is shown two food-wells and is allowed to see food being placed in one of them. At this stage a glass screen separates the monkey from the food so that it cannot reach out and touch it. Both food-wells are then covered, so that the monkey cannot see which one contains the food. An opaque screen is lowered between the monkey and the wells so that not only can it not touch them, it cannot see them either. The screen is left in place for a number of seconds and then it and the glass screen are removed together so that the monkey can both see and reach out to the food-wells. It is then allowed to displace one of the covers of the food-wells. If it goes for the previously baited one it is allowed to retrieve the food. If it goes for the unbaited well it gets no food and an error is recorded. Normal monkeys perform very well on this task. After prefrontal cortex ablation they do not, even with very short delays. The simplest interpretation of this deficit is that there is an impairment in short-term memory. Not all of the prefrontal cortex is important for this sort of ability. Small ablations that include the sulcus principalis produce the deficit readily. Large ablations that spare the sulcus principalis have little effect (Gross and Weiskrantz 1964). In contrast, lesions of the orbitofrontal part of the prefrontal cortex produce severe impairments on things like discrimination reversal learning (Mishkin 1964). In these tasks the animal is trained to choose one stimulus consistently in order to obtain reward. When it has reached a performance criterion of about 90 per cent correct, the reinforcement contingency is altered so that the animal now gets rewarded for selecting the previously unrewarded stimulus. Normal animals usually take a few more trials to learn the reversal of a task than they took to learn the original version. In monkeys with orbitofrontal lesions this tendency is exaggerated. These behavioural studies therefore suggest that the prefrontal cortex in primates has a number of functions that depend on the sub-area involved.

One might expect that prefrontal lesions in humans that include the sulcus principalis would produce a short-term memory deficit. This happens when the patients have to remember the order of presentation of stimuli (Milner 1964; Petrides and Milner 1982) but they rarely display the sort of severe memory impairment one might expect. Instead, the most reliably reported effects of prefrontal damage are response perseveration and impairments in spatial ability. For example, Milner (1964) reported that patients with prefrontal damage had difficulty with a card-sorting test (the Wisconsin Card-Sorting Test). In this task the patients are presented with a pack of cards which are marked with symbols that vary along a number of dimensions, such as shape, colour, and number. The subject's task is to guess which dimension the experimenter wants them to sort along and sort the cards accordingly. The experimenter then tells the subjects whether they have sorted each card according to the concept they have in mind and the subjects have to modify their sorting categories according to the feedback they get. Once the subject is sorting reliably according to one rule the experimenter then changes the dimension to sort along and the subjects have to alter their sorting behaviour accordingly. Non-brain-damaged humans rapidly learn how to do this task. Patients with prefrontal damage acquire the first rule fairly promptly but, from then on, fail to change rules as quickly as controls, sticking to dimensions that are clearly inappropriate.

Teuber (1964) demonstrated impairments in spatial ability. The task involved setting a luminous rod to the vertical in an otherwise darkened room. Frontally damaged patients have no problem when they too are sitting vertically, but when the chair in which they are sitting is tilted they make much bigger errors than controls. Teuber argued that this spatial deficit is the real consequence of prefrontal damage and that the perseveration deficit is due to incidental damage to adjacent structures after the brain damage studied by the other workers. The reader is directed to the original papers for details of this debate.

Given the fundamental role of emotion in the behaviour of mammals we would expect the brain systems involved in it to be present in all species. All of the structures discussed so far, the hypothalamus, hippocampus, cingulate cortex, and amygdala, all have homologues in every known mammal. In contrast, it is possible that prefrontal cortex appears only in primates. Another name for prefrontal cortex is frontal granular cortex, because of the distinctive appearance of the fourth layer of the cortex which contains a large number of granule cells. Adjacent parts of the frontal lobe, the frontal agranular cortex, lack this distinctive fourth layer. In rodents, like rats, there is no sign of a region of granular cortex anywhere in the frontal region. All of the cortex in the frontal region is resolutely agranular. Furthermore, all of the anterior cortex in rodents projects to the cerebellum, via the pons, giving it access to the motor system (Legg and Glickstein 1984). The frontal granular cortex in monkeys, in contrast, has no significant projections towards the cerebellum (Glickstein *et al.* 1985).

Summary

The balance of evidence suggests that the prefrontal cortex is involved in cognitive processes essential for normal emotional behaviour, rather than being a centre for emotional experience or expression. Similar conclusions apply to many of the other parts of the limbic system implicated in emotion. Those regions that do not have a cognitive function appear to be involved in the autonomic and motor expression of emotional behaviour. Thus, at present there are no good candidates for a centre for emotional experience.

Emotion and motivation

Common sense tells us that some emotions are pleasurable, and we pursue them, and that others are unpleasant, and we avoid them. We therefore expect emotional states to have motivational properties. For many years psychologists were happy with the idea that we, and other animals, would work to escape from aversive emotional states like fear, but were less happy about our ability to work in order to produce pleasant ones like happiness. Willingness to work to escape unpleasant states is enshrined in two-factor avoidance learning theory (see above). Willingness to work for pleasant states has now also been accepted, although initially begrudgingly.

From the commonsense point of view it is not surprising that brain stimulation often produces motivational and emotional effects through the same stimulation site. What is more remarkable is that animals will work to produce electrical stimulation through sites through which it also elicits increases in motivation, since motivational states are often considered to be aversive. Typically, stimulation sites associated with signs of pleasure are those from which appetitive behaviour can also be generated and the stimulation of which acts as a reward. The finding that stimulation which produces signs of displeasure usually also generates escape or avoidance behaviour and acts as a punishment seems more reasonable. To give concrete examples, rats will work to turn on stimulation of the lateral hypothalamus that has, independently, been shown to produce predatory attack behaviour but will work to turn off stimulation of the ventromedial hypothalamus that has been shown to produce affective attack (Panksepp 1971).

Deutsch argued that the paradoxical effect of animals seeking out apparently increased motivation was an artefact of the type of stimulation used. He suggested that intracranial self-stimulation comes about because there are certain sites in the brain where the mechanisms for arousing motivational states and the systems that signal their satisfaction are overlapped, so that electrical stimulation will activate both. The effect of stimulation is to create the motivational state and then to signal its satisfaction, thus creating a vicious circle of drive and its reduction that acts as a powerful reinforcement. The idea that ICSS involves both drive induction and reduction was taken up by both Gallistel (Gallistel, Shizgal, and Yeomans 1981) and Rolls (1975). Gallistel separated drive induction from reinforcement by using a discrete trial procedure in which the drive-inducing stimulation was presented in one end of a runway at the beginning of a trial and the reinforcing stimulation at the other end at the end of the trial. Running speed, the target behaviour, varied independently with changes in both the motivating stimulation and the reinforcement, thus indicating that stimulation through the sites used has an independently motivating effect. Rolls explored the system electrophysiologically. He placed electrodes in a variety of sites known to be effective for ICSS and then tested the animals behaviourally to ensure that

ICSS was obtained. In animals in which ICSS was obtained he studied the effects of stimulation through that site on single unit activity in other parts of the brain. Hypothalamic stimulation sites activated units in both the mesencephalic reticular formation and the limbic system, which is compatible with the idea that two separate systems are being activated in ICSS. However, stimulation through effective sites in the limbic system only normally activated other sites in the limbic system itself. This work suggested that a pure intracranial reward effect could be obtained.

This observation is supported by a number of differences between the ICSS produced by hypothalamic stimulation and ICSS produced by limbic system stimulation. For example, hypothalamic ICSS shows little sign of satiation. The animals will work for hours on end, only stopping to sleep. In contrast, limbic system ICSS shows a progressive decline in response rate. Hypothalamic ICSS is affected by the motivational state of the animal, increasing with food deprivation and decreasing with satiation. Limbic system ICSS is independent of motivational state (Rolls 1975).

The overlap between the systems involved in motivation and those involved in emotion is probably not accidental. The work on ICSS tells us that one of the functions of emotions is probably to give us feedback about the consequences of our actions that modifies our behaviour and makes it more adaptive.

Overview

We started out with three models for emotional experience and emotional behaviour. The first, espoused by people like Cannon and Bard, and by Papez, holds that emotional experience is a direct consequence of activating central mechanisms, rather in the same way that the experience of colour is due to activating specific mechanisms in the CNS. The second, developed over a century ago by James, is that emotional experience depends on our emotional behaviour. The third, developed recently by people like Schacter and Mandler, holds that our varied experiences of emotional states are due to cognitive mechanisms trying to make sense of variations in arousal level.

Despite the large body of psychophysiological evidence in its favour the third hypothesis can be ruled out immediately. The fact of the matter is that this sort of attributional model was put forward to explain the absence of qualitative differences between emotional states at the physiological level. This is true so long as the analysis is restricted to activity in the autonomic nervous system. It stops being true as soon as it is extended to the skeletal motor system, since distinctive patterns of emotional behaviour can be generated in animals by appropriately sited electrical stimulation of the brain. Certainly, there aren't enough patterns of emotional behaviour to account for all of the subtleties of human emotional life but Panksepp's (1982) ingenious suggestion, that many of our emotions are composites of 'pure' emotional states, takes care of this problem.

The psychophysiological literature is important for one thing, which is showing that manipulations of the motor system alone are capable of producing emotional experience in humans. In most of the relevant studies a state of autonomic activation is combined with a psychological manipulation designed to produce some form of overt emotional behaviour (e.g. Schacter and Singer 1962). This appears to be sufficient to induce a genuine emotional state. These findings, therefore, suggest that there is no need to postulate central mechanisms for the direct appreciation of the emotional significance of stimuli. This is just as well since we have yet to identify the central substrate of emotional experience.

What we have, in fact, found are central mechanisms for the generation of emotional behaviour coupled with cognitive mechanisms necessary for the elicitation, and possibly the appraisal, of those emotional behaviours. It does begin to look as if James's (1884) insight was correct.

7
Memory

Memory is a bit like the computer I am using to write this book: something one only thinks about when it goes wrong but so sophisticated in its workings the marvel is that it ever works at all. When we think of memory we think of a store into which we dump ideas and information for retrieval at a later date. We notice memory when we can no longer locate the things we know we have put into the store. A little thought tells us that memory is more complicated than that. For a start, consciousness and memory are inextricably interlinked. At any time we are conscious not only of what is happening immediately around us but also what has happened in the recent past. Activities like listening, speaking, writing and reading would be impossible without this type of memory. Furthermore, memory isn't just the retrieval of information from a store, it is an experience associated with that retrieval, or its failure. We often have the experience of *déjà vu*, the sense of remembering something as having happened before when it is, in reality, happening for the first time. Most of us are also afflicted with tip-of-the-tongue experiences, in which we know something is in our memory store but we are unable to get at it. According to Warrington and Weiskrantz (1982), patients suffering from memory failures due to brain damage, known as the amnesic syndrome, often have the reverse experience: they can remember things but have no experience of retrieving that information from their memory stores. Memory is clearly more than a large filing cabinet.

It is important to recognize the complexity of memory because most work on its neural mechanisms has been carried out in an unreservedly behaviourist framework in which people study the neural bases of learning phenomena like instrumental and classical conditioning. Much of it is done using simplified 'model' systems, often involving invertebrate species or subcomponents of the mammalian CNS. This is fairly inevitable, since we have to start somewhere, but it does create problems about the generality of some of the findings.

The aim of most memory research is to find out what memories are made of. This is a deceptively simple question to ask. What it comes down to is really two questions. First, what changes occur in individual brain cells when memories are laid down? Second, how do those changes encode information such as the name that goes with the face you are looking at? In other words, we want to know about the neural and the behavioural codes for memory. To study these we first have to identify locations in the brain where memory-related changes actually take place. One possibility is that they take place throughout the brain, with every cell contributing, to some small degree, to every memory. At the other extreme, memory may involve specialized memory systems which are localized in particular neural regions. Let us, therefore, start with the question of the localization of memory.

Are memory traces localized?

The filing cabinet analogy of memory leads us to the idea that the brain contains some sort of memory store, in which we collect information for future retrieval. Since so many other psychological functions seem to involve specialized areas of the brain it is reasonable to ask whether there are similarly specialized areas for memory. The obvious, but not necessarily the best, way of testing this is to remove parts of the brain and find out which are essential for memory. The study being obvious, it has been done many hundreds of times but without a clear consensus emerging. There are three sorts of outcome reported in these studies. Most of them, starting with Lashley (1963), have found that vast areas of the brain could be removed with little impact on memory and that what effect there is was very much more a function of the amount of brain damage than its location. Some studies have found quite severe impairments in memory function, but other evidence indicates that it isn't the memory store that has been lost. Finally, very recently there have been a small number of studies that indicate loss of memory function itself after localized brain damage. Let us look at these in turn.

Negative findings

The most widely used behavioural paradigms in memory studies are instrumental learning and classical conditioning tasks. Memory for performance on these tasks is remarkably resistant to damage to the cerebral cortex, and the effects that are obtained are very much more a function of the amount of cortex that is removed than the location of the damage. Moreover, when effects are obtained it is not altogether clear that they are due to loss of memory as such.

Lashley (1963) set the scene for this type of work by showing that the retention of maze habits in rats was not significantly affected by small cortical lesions. Larger lesions produced effects that were proportional to their size, but were in no way related to their locus. This gave rise to the laws of mass action and equipotentiality, respectively. By the end of his career Lashley (1950) had despaired of ever finding the location of memory traces for things like maze habits. With tasks that depended on a single sensory modality, such as visual discrimination learning, the situation was slightly different. In this case, removal of a single cortical area, the primary visual cortex, was apparently sufficient to abolish memory for the task in rats. It is important to note that the ability to perform the discrimination task used in these studies was not affected by the ablations. Experimentally naïve animals would learn these discriminations as fast as, or even faster, than controls and animals trained preoperatively would relearn them in as many test trials as they took to learn the task in the first place.

Needless to say there are complications. First of all, both mass action and equipotentiality appear to operate within the visual cortex, in that the lesions have to be above a critical minimum size but that their location within the area doesn't matter. This isn't particularly surprising. The tasks concerned are fairly simple brightness discrimination tasks, with stimuli extending across most of the visual field, that normal rats learn very quickly. Since the visual cortex always contains an orderly map of the visual field, and cortical lesions tend only to affect detection of stimuli falling within that part of the visual field represented by the damaged region (Kolb and Whishaw 1985; Weiskrantz and Cowey 1970), only very large visual cortex ablations would remove sufficient of the visual field representation to compromise detection of these large stimuli. Two more recent observations are much more worrying for the memory hypothesis. The first is that it is possible to protect rats against the effects of removing the visual cortex by training them with light-diffusing hoods over their eyes, so that they have no pattern vision prior to the operation (Bauer and Cooper 1964). This suggests that the primary effect of removing the visual cortex is to alter the cues that the animals are using to access the memory trace, rather than removing the trace itself. This is supported by the second observation, stemming from an ingenious study by LeVere (1980; LeVere and LeVere 1982). If the actual memory trace is destroyed by removing the visual cortex then rats that have been trained preoperatively should be indistinguishable post-operatively from naïve animals with the same ablations. If an animal had, for example, been trained preoperatively to approach a dark stimulus and avoid a light one and was then required, post-operatively, to avoid the dark and approach the light, a procedure known as reversal learning, we would expect it to be indistinguishable from a naïve animal meeting the requirement to approach the light and avoid the dark for the first time. If, on the other hand, a memory trace for the preoperatively learned task remained we would expect this to interfere with learning the reversal. LeVere used this reversal learning approach to test for residual memory after visual cortex ablation in rats and found that learning a brightness discrimination task preoperatively significantly interfered with ability to learn the reversed version post-operatively. This suggests that some form of memory trace survives destruction of the visual cortex and that the lesions interfere with access to it. The reader should note that LeVere's findings do not completely rule out the possibility that the visual cortex contains a memory trace. One possibility is that visual discrimination learning sets up multiple memory traces, some of which are lost after visual cortex ablation, giving rise to the memory losses observed by Lashley and others, and some of which are retained, giving rise to the interference with reversal learning observed by LeVere.

Studies on the role of the cortex in classical conditioning have produced similarly negative results. Indeed, most forms of classical conditioning proceed quite happily without any neocortex at all and, with only one or two exceptions, removal of cortex does not produce a post-operative retention loss. As Lashley pointed out many years ago, these findings contradict Pavlov's conclusion that classical conditioning involved the formation of links between the different areas of the neocortex activated during the conditioning procedures. If one accepts the original sort of associationist model put forward by Pavlov it isn't entirely surprising that classical conditioning survives ablation of the neocortex. After all, most of the sensory and motor mechanisms involved in these simple behavioural tasks also survive cortical ablation and probably involve subcortical systems even in intact animals. These findings are, however, very surprising in the light of more recent accounts of classical conditioning that place so much emphasis on cognitive processes in this form of learning (Rescorla 1975). While subcortical areas like the reticular formation may be capable of mediating stimulus-response associations there is little evidence that they contain sophisticated cognitive mechanisms capable of forming 'representations' of conditioned and unconditioned stimuli, or determining the degree to which the conditioned stimulus is correlated with the unconditioned stimulus.

This raises the disturbing possibility that, although classical conditioning forms a single behavioural paradigm, it, in fact, taps into a range of neural mechanisms of varying cognitive sophistication. There is also the possibility that different embodiments of the paradigm, such as heart-rate conditioning in humans and eye-blink conditioning in cats, are dependent on entirely separate neural mechanisms, so that it is wholly inappropriate to talk about 'classical conditioning' as a single process, as Pavlov originally thought.

Memory loss with an intact store

In 1957 Scoville and Milner reported on a patient, HM, who had undergone bilateral removal of the medial parts of his temporal lobes in order to control his temporal lobe epilepsy. Judged in terms of his epilepsy the surgery appears to have been a success but the relief of his symptoms was overshadowed by a profound impairment in HM's memory. Things he had learned about before his surgery were still there but he was unable to form any new long-term memories. The effects on HM were devastating. He lives in a constant present, having no recollection of what he was doing a day ago, a week ago, or even five minutes ago. HM's case is dramatic but the only unique feature of his case is the irony that the memory impairment was induced by surgery designed to cure another neurological disorder.

In fact, it has been known for about a century that people can suffer from profound memory impairments as a result of brain damage or brain disease. Korsakoff (see Victor, Adams, and Collins 1971) described a syndrome, usually associated with chronic alcoholism, that included a dense memory impairment. This has become known as the Korsakoff syndrome. Subsequently, Alzheimer reported another memory disturbance in older people, usually associated with abnormal structures, known as plaques and neurofibrillary tangles, in the cerebral cortex. The disorder, known as Alzheimer's disease, isn't restricted to a memory disturbance as there are also changes in personality, but the memory loss has attracted considerable attention. Memory loss is also found in some infectious diseases of the brain, most notably viral encephalitis. Thus a number of insults to the central nervous system, ranging from the effects of chronic alcoholism to neurosurgery, can produce severe impairments in memory. These impairments are known as the amnesic syndrome.

The amnesic syndrome has been investigated extensively in recent years. For more details on these investigations the reader is referred to Parkin (1987) and Mayes (1988). A number of important points emerge from these studies. The first is that short-term storage of information is rarely affected. The patients score as well as matched controls on standard tests of short-term storage, like the digit-span test. The second is that there are usually difficulties in accessing memories formed before the disease or injury (retrograde amnesia) as well as in forming new memories (anterograde amnesia). However, old memories are still available. The third is that the deficit in long-term storage is not usually total. The patients can learn new skills as rapidly as controls and other memories can be laid down, although much less efficiently. The most striking example of skill learning involves the Tower of Hanoi problem. In this task the subject is presented with a board containing three spikes. On one of the spikes there are five disks arranged in descending order of size. The subject's task is to transfer these disks to one of the other spikes so that they are in the same order. The task is complicated by the requirement that, during the transfers, it is not permitted to place a large disk on top of a smaller one at any point. If you know the solution to this problem it is quite easy and can be solved in thirty-one moves. If you don't know the solution it can take all night. Patients like HM can learn tasks like this. After a number of trials, they are capable of doing them in the minimum number of moves. Most amnesic patients are also capable of acquiring new verbal memories, although the progress is very slow and the memories not very durable.

What emerges from these studies is the sense that the site or sites of memory storage are no more compromised in these patients than in patients with other forms of brain damage, but the mechanisms for creating and accessing memories are severely deranged. Although the amnesic syndrome doesn't tell us anything about where memories are stored in the brain it does tell us about some of the processes underlying memory. These suggest that there are different forms of memory, since some aspects of memory are much more affected than others. They also emphasize the importance of 'control processes', that is, factors which determine whether information currently available to subjects will be turned into stable memories. These may include cognitive processes, like encoding information properly or attending to salient features, as well as neural events such as those believed to underlie memory consolidation. All of the recent accounts of the amnesic syndrome suggest that it is these control processes that are defective. However, a recent attempt at modelling memory processes suggests a simpler explanation for many of these findings (Meir and Domany 1987). Although we have no evidence that the model these authors have used is a realistic account of human memory, their finding that a memory network (see below for more details on networks) will break down when the ratio of memories to be stored to the number of cells in the network exceeds a certain number suggests that amnesia may simply be due to a general loss of efficiency in the nervous system reducing the number of elements available for memory formation. This would provide an adequate account of the amnesias associated with other cognitive disorders, notably the amnesias associated with Korsakoff and Alzheimer's syndromes. It is a less acceptable explanation of the much more circumscribed memory losses associated with disorders like viral encephalitis and medial temporal lobe removal. However, there is now evidence that the amnesias associated with cognitive disorders are qualitatively different from these others (Parkin 1987).

The amnesic syndrome is a phenomenon of human memory. Ever since it was highlighted by Scoville and Milner (1957) there has been debate about whether analogous memory impairments could be found in animals. The structures most severely damaged in the amnesic syndrome usually lie within the limbic system. The bilateral temporal lobe removals undergone by HM, for example, included the hippocampus and amygdala, while the Korsakoff syndrome usually involves degeneration in the mammillary bodies and/or anterior thalamus. As we saw in the previous chapter, there is some evidence that parts of the limbic system in animals are involved in memory processes but the deficits are much less convincing than the amnesic syndrome. Either they rely on complex test procedures and the animals concerned usually take many trials to master the rules involved (Gaffan 1977) or they appear to be specific to a single domain, such as spatial information (Morris *et al.* 1982).

Mishkin (1982) has argued that the deficits obtained in animal studies are much less profound than the amnesic syndrome because the latter involves simultaneous damage to two systems, the hippocampus (and its connections) and the amygdala (and its connections). He supports this by demonstrating severe impairments in visual discrimination learning and other tasks in monkeys after combined ablation of the hippocampus and amygdala, but not after ablation of either structure alone. There are two problems with Mishkin's position. The first is that it is unclear that the deficits he describes in animals are really analogous with the amnesic syndrome. There is an equally good argument to be made that the deficits are analogous with the agnosias (difficulties in object recognition) often seen in brain-damaged patients. The second is that it requires a fairly imaginative approach to the data to interpret the memory losses seen in Alzheimer's syndrome, or after damage restricted to the anterior thalamus, as resulting from effects on the hippocampus and amygdala, or their projections. Mishkin has argued that his results are consistent with what is known about the aetiology and pathology of Alzheimer's syndrome. One of the most consistent findings in the brains of patients with Alzheimer's syndrome is that it looks as if the cells in the basal nucleus of Meynert, which provides a diffuse, cholinergic innervation of most of the forebrain including, according to Mishkin, the hippocampus and amygdala, have degenerated. It is possible that Alzheimer's syndrome is due to disruption of the hippocampus and amygdala as a consequence of the loss of this cholinergic input.

Positive findings?

Thompson (1983) published a review paper intriguingly entitled 'The engram found?', in which he described studies on the neural systems involved in acquiring a classically conditioned response. Using a test procedure in which the conditioned closure of the inner eye-lid, the nictitating membrane (NMR), is produced in rabbits by pairing a noxious stimulus to the region of the eye with a light or sound stimulus, this group has studied the role of a number of neural systems in conditioning. Electrophysiological studies (see the next section) have revealed that single unit correlates of the conditioned response (CR) appear in a number of sites in the CNS, including the hippocampus and cerebellum. Ablation of the hippocampus has little effect on the acquisition or retention of this CR but extensive destruction of the cerebellum does. The impairment isn't a simple motor deficit, however, because there is no effect on the unconditioned response.

This work opens the exciting possibility that the memory traces underlying this type of conditioned response are located somewhere in the cerebellum. The problem is, where? The cerebellum is a fairly regular structure, consisting of a layered cortex, a set of subcortical nuclei, the deep cerebellar nuclei, which are the primary destination of the output of the cortex, and two main input stations, the inferior olive and the pons. The large cortical removals made by Thompson *et al.* involved both the cortex and the deep cerebellar nuclei. Subsequent work showed that the same effects could be produced by lesions restricted to the deep cerebellar nuclei. There remains a debate about whether the cortex itself is involved in forming the CR. Everything we know about the anatomy and physiology of the cerebellum tells us that it should be, but Thompson and his colleagues (1983; Woodruff-Pak, Lavond, and Thompson

1985) claim that the CR persists after ablation of the cortex, providing that the deep nuclei remain intact. Yeo *et al.* (1985), in contrast, provide convincing evidence that ablation of part of the cerebellar cortex alone can abolish the CR, while leaving the unconditioned response (UCR) intact. Recently, Thompson modified his position, claiming that appropriately sited cortical lesions do affect the CR, but that the animals can relearn, provided training is extended (Lavond, Steinmetz, Yokaitis, and Thompson 1987).

The reason why the title to this section has a question-mark in it is that, until additional single cell recording studies are done, it is premature to conclude that the cerebellum is the site of the memory trace. Given how widespread correlates of the CR are in different parts of the brain, another possible explanation of these findings is that the associations are formed diffusely throughout the CNS but their expression depends on the cerebellum because it is part of the motor system. Another reason for caution is the very fact that it is the cerebellum involved. The cerebellum is part of the extrapyramidal motor system, and these results are the first hint that it might be involved in something essentially cognitive like learning. Other studies on the cerebellum have indicated that it plays an important part in adjusting the amplitude and latency of reflexes, rather than producing reflexes to new stimuli (Gellman and Miles 1985). It is possible that the NMR, in fact, involves adjusting the size and latency of a defensive reflex, closing the nictitating membrane, that can be elicited by all novel visual or auditory stimuli rather than reflecting the formation of new associations. This is still of interest, since it involves a form of neural plasticity, but it means that the work is irrelevant to those interested in what psychologists conventionally think of as learning, which involves the formation of novel associations.

If the cerebellum is, in fact, the site of the association between the conditioned stimulus and the unconditioned stimulus then a number of interesting predictions follow, given what we know about the anatomy and physiology of the cerebellum. It is generally agreed that information about the unconditioned stimulus would have to enter the cerebellum via the 'climbing fibre' system that originates in the inferior olive while the conditioned stimulus would have to enter via the 'mossy fibres' that originate in the pons. This means that pontine damage, or cutting the mossy fibre system as it leaves the pons, should have the same effects as destruction of the cerebellar cortex or deep cerebellar nuclei. At present the findings are equivocal. In those studies that have found positive results there is the possibility that other pathways have been damaged along with the intended lesion site (Lewis, LoTurco, and Solomon 1987). In those studies in which only the mossy fibre input to the cerebellum has been cut there has been recovery of the conditioned response, but here there is always the possibility that the interruption of the mossy fibre pathway was not always complete (Yeo, Hardiman, and Glickstein 1986b). Damage to the appropriate part of the inferior olive should have a much more interesting effect. Since this is supposed to act as the input route for the unconditioned stimulus its destruction should have the same consequences as simply removing the unconditioned stimulus, namely the conditioned response should extinguish. Once again, there is a difference of opinion between Thompson and Yeo. Thompson has reported that lesions of the inferior olive produce extinction (McCormick, Steinmetz, and Thompson 1985) while Yeo finds that they produce immediate loss of the conditioned response (Yeo, Hardiman, and Glickstein 1986b). Given what is known of cerebellar physiology, Yeo's findings seem the more likely but his reasoning removes one of the most obvious and most powerful tests of the role of the cerebellum in learning. The debate between Yeo and Thompson highlights the difficulties of doing experiments that are both sensitive to the complexities of the physiology of the systems being studied and provide a critical test of a hypothesis.

Localizing the memory trace for the conditioned NMR to the cerebellar cortex would be a great achievement, but it doesn't solve all of the problems for those trying to study the cellular bases of memory. There are a number of cell types in the cerebellar cortex, with highly organized, predictable patterns of interconnections. The memory-related changes could be occurring at one or all of these stages and, in order to study the cellular bases of memory, we need to be able to localize memory-related changes to the level of individual cell types, not just to areas of the brain. Further work, using electrophysiological methods like intracellular recordings and methods for labelling the individual cells from which recording have been made, will be necessary to settle these issues.

Alternative approaches

Although the lesion method is the most obvious way of approaching the problem, it may not be the best. It all depends on the organization of the memory systems of the brain. If there is a single memory store which is necessary either for all memory, or for all the memory processes required for a particular task, then lesions will identify this store. If memory operates redundantly then the lesion method will prove unduly conservative.

At this point it is important to distinguish between task-related and brain-related redundancy. Following in the footsteps of people like Pavlov there has been a tendency to assume that there is a simple mapping between behavioural test procedures, psychological processes, and neural processes, so that it is possible to speak about the neural bases of what are essentially experimental procedures like classical conditioning. As I have already pointed out, the psychological processes operating during classical conditioning are actually extremely varied and complex. For example, in some situations organisms form associations between the conditioned stimulus (CS) and the CR, while in others the association is between the CS and the unconditioned stimulus (UCS) (Gormezano and Kehoe 1975). Furthermore, it is generally agreed that classical conditioning involves registration of the degree to which the CS predicts the UCS, rather than simply resulting from the pairing of the CS and UCS (Rescorla 1975). Thus even an apparently simple procedure like classical conditioning will call into play a number of subsystems, all of which may have a memory component. As a consequence, classical conditioning may produce memory-related changes in a number of neural centres, even though any one of them may prove irrelevant for performance of the CR once learning has taken place.

How do we get round this problem? One solution is to change methods, the other to retain the lesion method but devise psychological tests that only involve a single psychological subsystem. A number of authors have responded to the challenge by using electrophysiological test procedures, rather than lesions. Recently Kesner and DiMattia (1987) have rejuvenated the lesion method by offering a more sophisticated analysis of the psychological processes involved in learning and their possible neural substrates.

Electrophysiology

Let us start by looking at studies on classical conditioning. As mentioned above, Thompson (1983) studied the effects of cerebellar lesions on NMR conditioning because the activity of single units in the cerebellum correlated with the emergence of the conditioned response. Unit activity in a number of other sites also correlates with the emergence of the CR, including the hippocampus (as also mentioned earlier), the motor cortex, the reticular formation, and the deep layers of the superior colliculus. Not only does the response of the single units to the CS change during the course of learning, but single unit activity is also predictive of whether a CR will occur or not. To demonstrate this point, Thompson and his collaborators reduced the CS intensity to around threshold, so that a CR was produced on some trials but not on others. There was a clear difference between the response to the CS on those trials on which a CR was emitted and those on which it was absent. Unfortunately, the distinction was not perfect. There was a response to the CS on both types of trial but the unit response when the CR failed to occur was less than when a CR was emitted. Although Thompson and his collaborators have established that unit activity in the cerebellum, and elsewhere, changes in parallel with the emergence of the conditioned NMR, it is far from clear that it reflects the learning process as such. In addition to correlating with the conditioned NMR, unit activity in the cerebellum and hippocampus is also usually correlated with the unconditioned response. Therefore, a more accurate description of their results is that unit activity is usually associated with movements of the nictitating membrane, irrespective of their cause.

Thompson's work is unique for the range of recording sites studied. In most other experiments the investigators have tended to concentrate on specific areas of the brain. For example, Woody (1986) has studied the single unit correlates in the motor cortex of cats of another form of classical conditioning, the conditioned eye-blink response. Woody's work is important because it raises the very interesting question of what a single unit correlate of conditioning should look like. So far we have assumed that conditioning involves changes in excitability that can be picked up at the level of each unit. Each unit involved is expected to increase its response to the CS to above the level that can be produced by neutral stimuli. Woody finds that, in the motor cortex, the response of individual cells to the CS does not rise above their response to other stimuli but the number of cells that will fire in response to the CS increases. In other words, the learning-related changes only occur when one looks at the behaviour of a population of neurons, rather than at the individual cells.

One reason why Woody was able to sample less recording sites than Thompson was that the response used by Woody occurs at a much shorter latency than the NMR, 20 ms for the component of the blink response he studied, as compared with 80 to 300 ms for the NMR. Consequently, there is less scope for complex interactions between different parts of the CNS prior to the eye-blink. In the case of Thompson's work we have the problem of understanding the relationship between the CR-related activity in the cerebellum and the CR-related activity elsewhere in the CNS. There are three possibilities. The first is that changes elsewhere in the CNS are caused by those in the cerebellum, the second that changes in the cerebellum and those elsewhere are independent, and the third that the changes in the cerebellum are secondary to those elsewhere.

The simplest way of settling this issue is to carry out a latency analysis, comparing the response latency at different recording sites (Woody 1986). If the responses in, say, the superior colliculus occur before those in the cerebellum the former cannot be caused by the latter. Of course, this sort of analysis does not prove that it is the areas with the short latency responses that cause the responses in those with longer latencies, but it does enable us to rule out some models. The difficulties of interpreting short-latency responses are illustrated by an experiment by Olds, Disterhoft, Segal, Kornblith, and Hirsh (1972) who trained rats to approach a food hopper when a tone sounded, by pairing the tone with the presentation of food. They recorded responses to the CR in a number of sites during the learning process and found that short-latency learning related changes occurred in the posterior nucleus of the thalamus, not a structure thought of as part of the memory system of the brain.

Another approach would be to ablate one area and look for changes in single cell correlates of learning in other regions. Clark, McCormick, Lavond, and Thompson (1984) did just that. Rabbits were prepared with microelectrodes implanted in the hippocampus and trained on the NMR. After they had reached criterion, lesions were made in the cerebellum. These lesions abolished the CR, along with the hippocampal correlates of the learning, making it look as if the changes in the hippocampus were secondary to associative changes in the cerebellum. Detailed inspection of their results reveals a different, more complicated story. As mentioned above, the units whose activity correlates with the CR also respond in association with the UCR. Following cerebellar lesions that result in loss of the CR there is, in addition to loss of unit activity in the interval between the CS and UCS, a reduction of activity associated with the UCR. Nevertheless, the UCR remains constant. Another unexpected finding emerged when the UCS was shifted from the left to the right eye. Most of these studies are carried out using unconditioned stimuli applied to only one side of the head, and the effects of cerebellar damage are obtained with lesions restricted to that same side. If the UCS is shifted to the other side, and the movements of the nictitating membrane on that side recorded, the cerebellar damage on the other side has no effect on the conditioned or unconditioned response. When the UCS is returned to the side of the lesion and movements of the nictitating membrane on that side are recorded, there is still no sign of a conditioned response. However, when you record from the hippocampus you find that units on the same side as the cerebellar lesion start to respond as the CR emerges with training on the opposite eye. Moreover, when training is returned to the eye on the same side, the responses to the CS persist, even though there is no response on that side.

Taken in conjunction with the fact that unit activity in the hippocampus and cerebellum is associated with the UCR as well as the CR, these findings suggest that the picture of an association between the CS and UCR being built up in the cerebellum and distributed to other sites in the brain is too simple. On the other hand, the dissociation between movements of the nictitating membrane and hippocampal unit activity after cerebellar lesions suggests that the unit activity doesn't simply reflect movement either. Clearly, more data are required to establish that an association is being established in the cerebellum.

One of the interesting features of Thompson's electrophysiological results is that there is no hint of any response to the CS or UCS. All of the responses are tied to the movements. In a series of studies on the electrophysiological correlates of avoidance learning, in contrast, Gabriel, Foster, Orona, Sattwick, and Stanton (1980) found that learning-related changes in unit activity in the cingulate cortex were closely tied to the CS. The subjects, rabbits, were tested on a discriminative avoidance response in a running wheel. There were two stimuli, both tones. One, CS+, was followed shortly by a shock to the feet; the other, CS−, by nothing. Running in the period immediately after the CS+ avoided the shock altogether, while running when the shock had come on terminated it. Movements in response to the CS− had no effects. The rabbits learned rapidly to run in response to the CS+ and to stay still in response to the CS−. Right from the start of training, units in the cingulate cortex responded to the tones with a biphasic response pattern having two peaks of activity, one at around 50 msec and one at around 120–150 msec. As training proceeded, the responses produced by the CS+ and CS− became distinguishable. No change occurred in the short-latency component of the response but, as training proceeded, the longer latency response to the CS− diminished significantly.

Clearly these changes in unit activity reflect the development of an association between the conditioned and unconditioned stimuli but the relationship between the unit activity and behaviour was very obscure. In some units the differential response to the two conditioned stimuli emerged before the behavioural response and then faded with more prolonged training. In other units the differential response emerged after behavioural differentiation had appeared. The dissociation between the unit responses and behaviour become even more obvious when the animals were put on to reversal training, in which the previous CS+ became the CS− and vice versa. As reversal training proceeded, differences between the responses to CS+ and CS− disappeared but the response to the CS− did not drop below the response to the new CS+. These observations suggest that activity in the cingulate cortex was reflecting something that the animals had learned, but that this was not directly related to their behaviour.

Improved task analysis

Kesner and DiMattia (1987) argue forcefully that you cannot equate learning paradigms with individual psychological or neural processes. Instead, they argue, learning takes place in a context and, as animals learn, they learn about that context as well as about the contingencies set up by the experimenter. Thus all learning situations have a number of properties, or 'attributes', about which the animals will learn. These attributes include when something happened, where it happened, what the animal felt when it happened, what it did when it happened, and which objects were present when it happened. The art of designing psychological experiments is to develop tasks in which performance is almost exclusively dependent on one of these attributes.

I have already discussed the evidence that learning about the spatial context of an action depends on the hippocampus. Most of this work is based on studies of 'cognitive maps', which involve establishing durable internal representations of where things are relative to other parts of the environment. Kesner and DiMattia (1987) have gone beyond this to show that the hippocampus is also important for remembering where things are when their position changes from trial to trial. They have modified Olton's radial arm maze procedure to control the sequence in which the rats can gain access to each arm by placing doors at the start of each arm. In one experiment the rats were allowed to enter, and take a reward from, each of five of the eight arms of the maze in turn. Shortly afterwards they were presented with two open arms, one of which had been opened during the first phase and one of which had been kept closed. An additional reward was available for entering the arm that had previously been opened. Normal rats can learn to perform this task at around 90 per cent accuracy. After hippocampal lesions their performance falls to around 60 per cent. They have also shown that the hippocampus is not essential for maintaining cognitive maps, even though it may be essential for establishing them in the first place. Using the milk-maze task to measure spatial ability (Morris *et al.* 1982), they have shown that rats trained on this task prior to hippocampal ablation are not particularly impaired post-operatively relative to controls, while rats learning the task for the first time post-operatively do much worse than controls.

Memory for response appears to depend, in part, on the caudate nucleus. Rats were trained on two different tasks on a twelve-arm radial maze. One task emphasized the ability to make the response that was reinforced on the previous trial; the other emphasized the ability to go to the place that was associated with reinforcement. Caudate lesions produced a severe impairment on the first task, and the animals showed no sign of recovery. On the second task they were only slightly inferior to controls.

This work is ingenious for the way in which it applies the sorts of inferential methods currently being used in human neuropsychology to tease apart memory processes in animals. Readers should be cautious about interpreting this work, however, since there are potentially serious differences between the methods used to demonstrate the different memory systems. For example, in studies on the hippocampus the deficits only appear when the animals are learning the task post-operatively, or have to remember different items on different trials. On the other hand, in the studies on the caudate nucleus the animals had to learn a rule, such as turn left on leaving this arm or go to the arm near the desk, that remained the same throughout the experiment. In other words, one set of studies involves remembering events while the other set involves learning a rule.

Summary

The search for the engram continues. The most promising line of research is the work of Thompson and of Yeo on the role of the cerebellum in the classically conditioned NMR but, at present, there are many gaps in the data. Kesner and his collaborators have shown that many forebrain structures are essential for learning about various attributes of the environment, but it is too soon to say that the memory traces concerned are embodied in the structures he has been studying.

What are we to do in the absence of hard evidence for localizable memory traces? One thing is to use simplified systems, containing small numbers of identifiable cells, to study the cellular bases of 'memory' and leave worrying about how such components could be put together to mediate normal memory till later.

Model systems

Some invertebrate animals have such simple nervous systems it is possible to view them under the microscope and identify individual neurons. Since the layout of the nervous system varies little from animal to animal it is, in fact, possible to identify the same cell in different specimens. One such animal for which we have a fairly complete 'wiring diagram' of the nervous system is the sea hare (*Aplysia Californica*). Kandel and his colleagues, among others, have taken advantage of this to study learning-related changes in identified cells (Carew and Sahley 1986; Farley and Alkon 1985; Hawkins and Kandel 1984). This simple nervous system is capable of three forms of learning: habituation, sensitization, and 'classical conditioning'. In the habituation experiments a moderate stimulation to the siphon region produces withdrawal of the gill and siphon. With repeated stimulation, the response fades and the gill and siphon remain static. In the sensitization experiments the stimulation of the siphon is interspersed with much stronger stimuli to the tail. The net result is that the response to stimulation of the siphon is augmented rather than diminished. In the 'classical conditioning' experiments the CS is light stimulation of the siphon and the UCS is strong stimulation of the tail that evokes gill and siphon withdrawal. After a number of pairings the siphon stimulation alone is sufficient to evoke the response. I have put 'classical conditioning' in inverted commas because there is some debate about whether this corresponds to what most people think of as classical conditioning. The problem is that the CS is also capable of eliciting the UCR, providing it is sufficiently intense. Indeed, with stimuli matched for intensity, it is easier to evoke the reflex with the CS than with the UCS. Nevertheless, this procedure has some features in common with conventional classical conditioning, such as the importance of using the CS and UCS in the right sequence. If the sequence is reversed (UCS followed by CS) no behavioural change occurs.

There are two ways in which these changes could come about. The first is that there could be a change in the amount of neurotransmitter released by the sensory neurons that relay the information about the stimuli, that is, a presynaptic change. The second is that there could be a change in the response of the motor neurons to the transmitter being released by the sensory cells, that is, a post-synaptic change. Most of the evidence favours the former possibility. Habituation is associated with a reduction in the duration of the action potential in the sensory neurons, sensitization and classical conditioning with an increase in the duration of the action potential. By using more sophisticated techniques, like 'patch clamping', it has been possible to identify some of the processes going on within the cells that make these changes possible.

Habituation involves a reduction in the rate at which calcium ions move into the cell as the action potential reaches the nerve terminals. Sensitization and classical conditioning involve the reverse, an increased influx of calcium.

This is associated with a reduction in the outward movement of potassium. The significance of all of these events lies in the fact that calcium levels are known to control the rate of release of neurotransmitter substances at nerve terminals. High levels of calcium within a cell promote increased transmitter release while low levels are associated with a reduction in transmitter release. Hawkins and Kandel (1984) present models of how the changes in the movement of calcium across the cell membrane might be controlled.

There is one problem with these models. The processes they describe all involve proteins interacting with each other at the nerve terminals but proteins are quite unstable compared with the durability of memories. For these processes to form the basis of memory it is necessary to have an additional mechanism to replace the proteins, as they are broken down in the cells, in exactly the same quantities as they are lost. Goelet, Castellucci, Schacher, and Kandel (1986) offer the interesting speculation that this involves changes in the readout from the genetic code in the cells.

According to Kandel and his colleagues both sensitization and classical conditioning involve 'heterosynaptic facilitation', by which they mean that activity at one set of axon terminals augments activity at another set. For example, in classical conditioning in aplysia the activity in the tail sensory neuron terminals augments the release of neurotransmitter from the siphon sensory neuron terminals. A number of lines of evidence suggest that this facilitation is mediated by the release of the neurotransmitter serotonin from the terminals of the tail sensory neurons. Interestingly, many of the cellular effects associated with learning can be mimicked by applying serotonin to the cells concerned.

The advantage of work on aplysia, and on other invertebrate models (see Carew and Sahley 1986) is that is possible to study cellular processes in identifiable neurons during analogues of real learning procedures. The disadvantage is that the nervous systems concerned are not mammalian nervous systems, and there may be differences between them and our own. Hawkins and Kandel (1984) argue that this isn't so, and that the cellular mechanisms they have identified in aplysia are universal, but this position can only be sustained if we know about the cellular mechanisms involved in learning in mammals, which is where we came in. Faced with the problems of localizing the memory traces involved in learning in intact mammals a number of groups have taken to working on preparations of slices of mammalian nervous system. One of the most popular of these is the hippocampal slice.

As long as the input pathway known as the perforant path and the granule cells of the dentate gyrus remain intact, it is possible to demonstrate a learning-like phenomenon known as Long-Term Potentiation (LTP) in hippocampal slices (Teyler and DiScenna 1987). In LTP studies stimulation is applied to the perforant path and unit activity recorded from the granule cells. Low-frequency stimulation produces action potentials of a fixed amplitude.

Following bursts of high-frequency stimulation the amplitude of the action potentials elicited subsequently by individual stimuli is greatly augmented and remains elevated for many days after the original treatment. Although LTP was first demonstrated in the rabbit hippocampus, it has since been studied in a wide range of neural systems and species and appears to be a very robust experimental phenomenon. Whether you call it learning is a matter of personal taste.

Berger (1984) suggests that LTP may be related to learning in intact animals. He produced LTP in the hippocampi of intact rabbits by high frequency stimulation of the perforant path. A second group received the same number of stimuli to the perforant path, but at a frequency too low to produce LTP. Following this, the two groups were trained on the classically conditioned NMR, as described above. Rabbits in which LTP had been produced learned the NMR significantly faster, and produced more CRs, than the controls. This is a very surprising finding. We would expect memory to depend on the pattern of activity in a system. Either different cells should be active following discriminable events, like tones and shocks, or their patterns of firing should be different. Since the stimuli used to produce LTP involve most of the perforant path and have no obvious temporal code, it is difficult to see how they could generate a memory that encodes information. These results would also lead us to expect that hippocampal ablation would abolish the NMR which, as we have already seen, it doesn't. Berger's results look much more like what you would get if the amount of hippocampal activity were important for learning, rather than the hippocampus constituting the site of the memory trace.

What of the cellular processes underlying LTP? As with sensitization and classical conditioning in aplysia, LTP is calcium-dependent. It doesn't happen if the slices are bathed in a solution that is deficient in calcium and biochemical analyses have shown that LTP is associated with an influx of calcium into both pre- and post-synaptic elements. An important difference between LTP in hippocampal slices and learning in aplysia is that LTP seems to depend on changes in the post-synaptic membrane, rather than in presynaptic function. The post-synaptic changes involve an increase in the number of receptor sites for a class of neurotransmitters called excitatory amino acids. Initially it was thought that the transmitter involved was glutamate but it is now known that LTP depends on a related substance called N-methyl-d-aspartate which, mercifully, is abbreviated to NMDA. As a consequence of this work people are beginning to argue that the NMDA receptor is crucial to memory functions.

One of the best demonstrations of this is the recent study by Morris, Anderson, Lynch, and Baudry (1986), who selectively blocked the functions of the NMDA receptors in rat brains by chronically infusing the animals with the drug AP5 while training them on the milk-maze test of spatial learning that I described earlier. This drug, but not an inert form of the same substance, produced a statistically significant impairment on this task. Acquisition of a visual discrimination task was not affected by similar infusions in other animals. This is an attractive result but some aspects of the findings give cause for concern. The first is that the effects of the drug treatment were very small, much smaller than those obtained with hippocampal lesions as such (Morris et al. 1982). The second is that the visual discrimination task was so difficult, some of the controls failed to learn it in the time given, making it difficult for any drug effect to appear.

LTP is widely acclaimed as a model for learning but nobody is seriously suggesting that normal learning involves high-frequency, unpatterned stimulation of the perforant pathway. If we are going to consider the cellular events evoked by LTP as part of the normal memory process in the intact brain we are in urgent need of a mechanism for generating the same changes during learning in intact animals. There is now evidence that activity in the noradrenergic fibres that run from the locus coeruleus, in the hindbrain, to the hippocampus is the factor involved. Hopkins and Johnston (1984) demonstrated that the magnitude of the LTP they obtained could be modulated by the application of noradrenaline to hippocampal units. More recently Gray and Johnston (1987) have shown that noradrenaline increases the flow of calcium into hippocampal cells. Calcium influx, you will remember, is a critical part of the cellular events underlying LTP.

The idea that neurotransmitters can modulate the magnitude of memory-related changes in the CNS is potentially important for understanding some memory deficits in humans. One of the most consistent features of the brains of patients with Alzheimer's syndrome is that a small nucleus in the base of the forebrain, the nucleus basilis of Meynert, has degenerated. It is widely accepted that this is the cause of the memory loss that these patients suffer. The nucleus basilis of Meynert is a very small nucleus containing cells that project their axons to sites throughout the forebrain. All of the cells use a single neurotransmitter, acetylcholine. Since the nucleus is so small and contains so few cells, each cell must project to many others. It is hard to believe that such a small nucleus could form a memory store. Its connections with the rest of the brain make it a much better candidate for a structure that can modulate the activity of cells in the rest of the forebrain. Perhaps it modulates memory-related changes and its degeneration reduces the efficiency of memory formation. If that is the case, we still need to understand the mechanisms by which it would do this. We know that noradrenaline can modulate memory-like events in the hippocampus but we know little about the capacity of acetylcholine, the neurotransmitter used by the cells of the nucleus basilis of Meynert, to produce similar effects.

We should remember that most of the phemonena studied with these model systems are relatively short-lived compared with the normal lifetime of a human memory, which may extend into decades. As Kandel and his colleagues are only too aware, stable long-term storage must involve some sort of change in the regulation of the readout from the genetic material of the cells involved in learning. The next, but realistically realizable, goal of this sort of work is to analyse these changes.

The behavioural code: localized versus distributed memories

If we accept the behaviourist assumption that learning and memory involve nothing more than the strengthening of stimulus-response associations, then the problem of the behavioural code does not arise, since changes in synaptic 'resistance' of the sort described above are the memories. Unfortunately life isn't that simple. Memories must consist of more than S-R associations. One reason for believing this is that most of the effects of brain damage on memory are incompatible with the S-R model. Another is that most serious attempts at modelling how memory works demand that memories be distributed over networks of cells, rather than residing in single associations. Consequently, knowing about the cellular changes involved in memory formation is about as useful for understanding how memory works as understanding transistors for knowing how computers work. What really matters is knowing what happens when you put the components together into larger clusters.

Stimulus-response psychology tells us that memories are nothing more than a mass of newly formed connections between the input and output stages of the brain. Since these stages are well localized it is reasonable to assume that the mechanisms that form the connections between them will be similarly localized. In S-R terms it is certainly difficult to see why the connections between the visual and motor cortices should be so widely distributed that it is impossible to disrupt conditioned responses by removing the cortex in between. By itself, this isn't a very strong argument. Positions based on negative evidence never are. It is always possible to explain away failures to produce learning and memory deficits in terms of inappropriate selection of task, lesion site, or both. A much stronger reason for accepting that memories involve networks of neurons is that that is the only way to build working models of how our memories behave.

Approaches to memory have now changed and we now talk about 'representation' in memory (Roitblat 1982). In simple terms this means that our memories consist of a set of internal models of the outside world, rather than a set of connections between inputs and outputs. The important features of models are that they contain more information than is normally accessed on any occasion, that partial information can call up the whole model, and that we can manipulate our representations to extract information that was not explicit in the input. Take, for example, our representations of space. When I use my representation of the layout of the City University I only ever take advantage of part of it at any one time. If I am going to the library I don't normally think about how to get to the swimming pool, yet I know the way to the pool from my office and I know my way from the library to the pool.

I can also call up the whole representation on the basis of partial cues. If you were to show me a picture of the university precincts before some of the buildings had been put up, I would be able to tell you what now stands on particular sites. Finally, if I were to visit part of the university I hadn't previously visited I would be able to use my representation to get from the new part to somewhere familiar, even though I had never been formally instructed on the route nor had ever followed it before. Representations need not all be spatial. Take, for example, family relationships. We all know who our relatives are, even if we don't think about them all at the same time. If we are given a name, we can usually say what relationship that person bears to us. If we are told that somebody is our mother's sister, we can immediately say that that person must be our aunt.

Representational skills like this are so self-evident to us it is remarkable that psychologists spent so many years denying their existence. They may have been wrong, but they weren't perverse in their error. To them, representation was a mental concept and they could neither explain how mental events could influence behaviour nor imagine how such mental events could be implemented in the brain. We now know that it is possible to build machines that represent 'knowledge', and even acquire new knowledge. While the brain may not work exactly like the machines we are making today, the fact that such machines exist gives us the confidence to believe that mental processes can be implemented in the brain and gives us some ideas about how the brain might do it.

Efficient representation of knowledge can be most effectively achieved in computers that operate according to the principles of Parallel Distributed Processing (PDP, see Johnson-Laird 1987). The theory of PDP systems is extremely complex, and beyond the scope of this book. Nevertheless, they have some general features that are relevant to our present discussions. The most important feature is that any piece of information is represented by a large number of elements in the system. The second is that, by allowing for feedback between parts of the system to modify the strength of the connections between the elements it is possible to get such systems to learn new concepts. For example, Rumelhart, Hinton, and Williams (1986) have developed a programme that simulates a multilayered network system which can 'learn' about family relationships. What this means is that memory systems in the brain are also likely to use large numbers of elements to represent information, with the representation distributed across the elements of the network so that no single element embodies the representation. As was pointed out in chapter 3, such a system would be highly resistant to damage and, when damaged, would respond according to the laws of equipotentiality and mass action.

At the present time, network theory is very much in its infancy. Nobody has yet constructed a system that can simulate all of the properties of human memory and there are those who argue that they never will. Nevertheless, the approach shows great promise because it can simulate one of the most significant features of our memory, what is known as 'content addressability'. Up to now one of the main differences between our memories and those of computers is that we can access information very rapidly on the basis of what we are trying to recall, whereas computers have had to work on the basis of where in the system a particular item of information is stored. For example, most of us can say very quickly who is the prime minister of the United Kingdom and, equally rapidly, give the capital city of France. Computers normally find this sort of thing very difficult. When asked a question they have to search their data-banks serially, giving rise to extensive delays in retrieving information that increase with the size of the information base.

From the point of view of the psychobiologist the real challenge is relating the abstract algorithms of the computer scientists to the 'wetware' of the brain. We need to know which cells are likely to be involved in a particular network and how they connect up (McNaughton and Morris 1987; Rolls 1987). Since it is now widely accepted that the brain has a modular structure, with different forms of information being processed in different zones, we also need to know how these systems are integrated to form higher-order networks.

Overview

Despite many decades of research, little progress has been made on localizing engrams in the central nervous system. There is one possible exception, which is the recent demonstration that some forms of motor learning depend on the cerebellar cortex (Yeo *et al.* 1985) but it is unclear how far the learning tasks used in these studies are representative of general learning mechanisms. The failure to localize the memory store has had two effects. At the theoretical level we have started to conceptualize memory as a distributed process involving neurons spread over a wide area of the CNS. Such networks have a number of desirable features, such as resistance to degradation following damage and content addressability. At the practical level, memory researchers have turned to model systems that involve demonstrable neuronal plasticity in response to experience and have made great strides in untangling the cellular mechanisms involved in this plasticity. The hope is that these mechanisms are identical with those that operate during normal memory formation.

The recent theoretical approaches to memory require considerable development before they achieve widespread acceptance. At present the gulf between the computer algorithms and the 'wetware' of the brain is enormous. We now know a considerable amount about the cellular events underlying many forms of neuronal plasticity but there is still some way to go. For example, we don't know whether these processes are universal or specific to the model systems that have been studied, although what we do know encourages us in the belief that the processes are universal. The big task facing researchers in this field is to explain how cellular processes occurring in or near the cell membrane get translated into the permanent changes in the expression of the genetic code believed to be necessary for long-term memory storage.

8
Plasticity

Our ability to think, act, and feel depends on our brains being wired up in the right way at the right time. Wiring up a brain is likely to be a fairly tricky business. There are millions of cells involved, with the capacity to make billions of synaptic connections. Imagine the problems of getting the right cells into the right place and ensuring that they then make the right connections. Anyone who has owned a complex electronic device like a computer will also be aware that, in addition to being complicated to put together in the first place, it is also likely to go wrong, especially if maltreated. On the other hand, our brains go on working well for decades without appreciable deterioration of function, and will often work remarkably well even when damaged. How do our brains get wired up properly in the first place and how do they stay that way? Many people now believe that the answer lies in the inherent plasticity, or modifiability, of the brain. During development the brain adjusts its connections in the light of the environment in which it is operating. Throughout life cells seem to be able to modify themselves to compensate for losses of inputs or outputs. This chapter is about this remarkable flexibility in the organization of the brain that underpins all of our other behavioural capacities.

The development of the brain

It has often been argued that explaining behaviour in terms of what happens in the brain is a hopeless task because the brain is such a complicated device; it would be impossible to describe all of the connections in the brain and record all of the patterns of activity in the cells. If the brain is so complicated that we, with all of the resources at our disposal, cannot describe all of the connections in it, how does the genetic code inside the sex cells that fuse to form the human embryo specify all of the connections that will be present in the adult brain? The answer is that it cannot. The genetic information that we receive from our parents at the moment of conception is simply too limited ever to specify something as complex as the brain. Given what we know about the physical basis of the genetic code, the DNA (deoxyribonucleic acid) molecules that inhabit the nuclei of all of the cells of our bodies, it is possible

Plasticity

to calculate how much DNA would be required to code the production of a human brain. The depressing conclusion of such calculations is that each spermatozoa would have to be the size of a golf-ball (Changeaux 1985). If the genetic code cannot specify how they get wired up, how is it possible for our brains to be wired together in such a predictable and reliable way?

Clearly the genetic code cannot work this way. Instead of specifying all the connections, what it specifies is a set of rules for wiring the brain up. Modern work on the development of the brain has shown that two rules are specified genetically: the time at which different cell groups, such as those destined to form the cortex or the hypothalamus, emerge and the relative positions taken up by cells and their terminals at the end of the process. Elegant studies using radioactive tracers to identify the cells born on a particular day have shown that the brain develops in an orderly sequence, with the cells in some areas appearing and making their connections before the cells in other areas (Changeaux 1985; Jacobson 1978). Inevitably, the distribution and pattern of connections of the earlier cells limit the distribution and connections of cells born later. Other work has shown that, in most systems, the fibres growing into a region distribute their terminals so that they are in the same relative positions as their cell bodies (Changeaux 1985; Jacobsen 1978).

This sort of developmental mechanism is remarkably economical, but it is scarcely likely to be very accurate. It will give a broadly similar overall pattern to all brains in the same species but it will not lead to a properly formed mature nervous system because there will be all sorts of errors incorporated along the way. For example, there may be a mismatch between the number of cells formed in an afferent pathway, such as the optic tract, and in the number in the relay nucleus, such as the lateral geniculate nucleus, to which it projects. As a consequence there will either be optic tract fibres unable to make contact with relay cells or relay cells without optic tract contacts. Some mechanism is required to eliminate this imbalance. The evidence we have strongly suggests that this 'fine tuning' of the connections of the nervous system depends on experience during the post-natal period.

There is another limit on the genetic programming of the nervous system, which is that there appear to be developmental events that depend on social experiences rather than the physical environment. The most obvious example here is language learning, which appears to be an irreversible process that occurs early in human life and which depends on an interaction between the linguistic environment of the child and an innate mechanism for acquiring language. Analogous processes occur in other species. These include imprinting in precocial birds and song-learning in some song-bird species.

The fine-tuning of the brain

If we want to describe what happens during neural development we have to study a system that is well described and understood in the adult. The visual pathways are such a system. Their anatomy is known in great detail and many thousands of publications have been devoted to describing the physiological properties of cells at different levels of the visual system, running from the retina to visual association cortex (see chapter 4).

In animals like monkeys and cats the cells of the mature primary visual cortex (V1) have a number of clearly identifiable properties, not present at earlier stages in the system, which can be used as markers in developmental studies. The most useful of these are binocularity and orientation selectivity. In the adult, most cells of the visual cortex respond to input from both eyes (binocularity), even though the information is clearly segregated at lower levels in the visual pathways. A number of authors have studied the factors that affect the emergence of binocularity (e.g. Sherman and Spear 1982; Wiesel 1982). The cells are also very fussy about the orientation of the stimuli with which they are presented and, unlike cells at earlier stages, will only readily respond to bars and edges within a limited range of orientations (orientation selectivity). The factors affecting the emergence of orientation selectivity have also been the subject of a number of studies (Hirsch and Leventhal 1978).

Binocularity

One of the reasons why the developing CNS needs fine-tuning is that there are initially too many connections between cells. This exuberance of growth is likely to be translated into cells responding to too many inputs early on in life and then gradually losing their responsiveness according to the pattern of inputs they experience. We would, therefore, expect that most cells in the visual cortex of newborn animals would be binocularly responsive and that some of this responsiveness would be lost as the animal matures. This is, broadly speaking, what happens. In newborn animals, or those that have had no visual experience, most of the visually responsive cells in the visual cortex are binocular. Subsequent visual experience determines what happens to this initial binocularity (Wiesel 1982).

In the adult brain the degree of binocularity can vary quite widely. Some cells will only respond to the ipsilateral eye and some only to the contralateral, but most respond to both eyes to some degree. Hubel and Wiesel (1977) devised a system of ocular dominance ratings for evaluating the degree of binocularity of cells in the cortex. This scale runs from 1, completely dominated by the contralateral eye, through 4, equally activated by both eyes, to 7, completely dominated by the ipsilateral eye. Figure 8.1 illustrates the distribution of ocular dominance normally encountered in cats.

This pattern is remarkably easily disrupted by depriving animals of input through one eye early in life. This was first systematically studied by Hubel and Wiesel (1970), who sutured closed one eye in kittens and then determined the ocular dominance rankings of cortical cells when these kittens had grown into adulthood. Following monocular deprivation nearly all of the cells in the

Figure 8.1 Distribution of ocular dominance in the normal cat

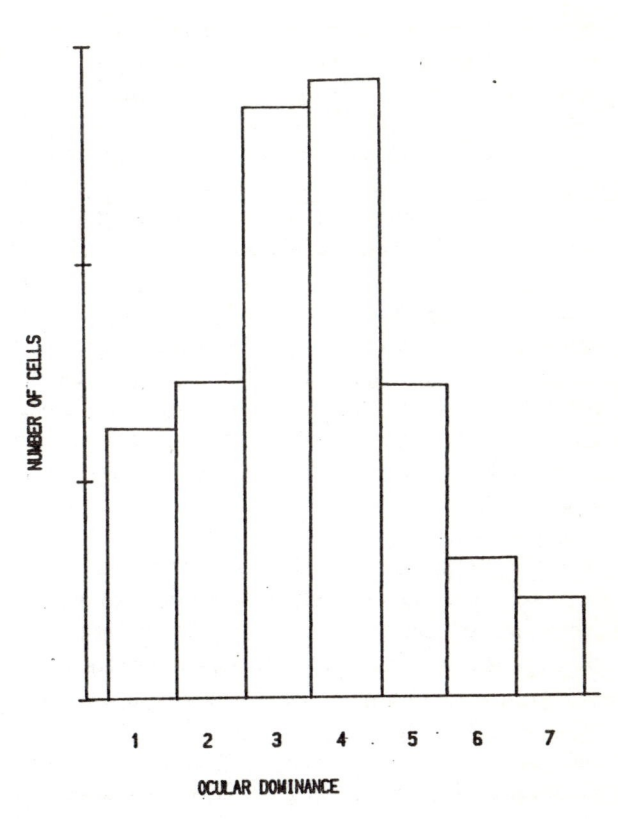

visual cortex were responsive to the non-deprived eye and unresponsive to the deprived eye. They found that even very brief periods of monocular deprivation very early in life had long-term effects on ocular dominance. Similar results were obtained when comparable experiments were carried out on monkeys (LeVay, Wiesel, and Hubel 1980).

In parallel with these physiological effects monocular deprivation also alters the anatomical organization of the visual pathways. Some of these effects are visible below the level of the visual cortex. For example, in cats the cells of the layers of the lateral geniculate nucleus (LGN) that receive input from the deprived eye are shrunken, when compared with the layers that receive input from the non-deprived eye. At the level of the cortex, the terminal fields of the input fibres that relay input from the deprived eye are much smaller than those that relay information from the non-deprived eye (Hubel and Wiesel 1977; Wiesel 1982).

This is most clearly demonstrated in monkeys. If a radioactively labelled amino acid is placed in one eye it is carried along the optic nerve to the LGN. At the LGN the amino acid moves across the synapses and is carried, in the geniculocortical fibres, to the visual cortex. It is, therefore, possible to ascertain which parts of the cortex receive input from a single eye, by determining the location of the radioactive label. In normal monkeys this procedure gives rise to strips of labelled cortex, representing the injected eye, separated by unlabelled strips of the same width, representing the uninjected eye. These strips are called ocular dominance columns. After monocular deprivation early in life the strips representing the deprived eye become narrower and those representing the non-deprived eye become broader. This suggests that inputs from the non-deprived eye take over cortical territory normally associated with the deprived eye.

Corresponding effects are seen at the level of the terminations of individual geniculocortical cells. In newly born kittens each cell has a diffusely organized set of terminations spread over a wide area of the cortex. As the cat matures these terminals cluster into patches with blank areas in between. Monocular deprivation prevents the emergence of patches and the terminals of LGN cells associated with the non-deprived eye are as widespread as in the neonate, although there appears to be less of them (Wiesel 1982).

Monocular deprivation studies are interesting not only because they tell us that early experience is important for visual system development but also because they let us explore the mechanisms by way of which early experience works. Indeed, one of the advantages of studying binocularity is that the effects of manipulations like monocular deprivation are so clear-cut that it is possible to carry out quite elegant studies on the variables that affect its development and still get interpretable results. Why does monocular deprivation produce such severe effects? There are two possibilities, each of which has different implications for the normal process of development. The simplest explanation is disuse: synaptic connections that are not confirmed by experience are lost. The second is competition: the inputs from the non-deprived eye displace those from the deprived eye.

Disuse can be ruled out quite quickly by the fact that binocular deprivation has far less severe effects than monocular deprivation. This suggests that it is the imbalance between the inputs from the two eyes in the monocular deprivation case that is critical, rather than the lack of input from the closed eye alone. Guillery (1973) has carried out some elegant studies on the cat that confirm this. These studies rely on the fact that the LGN in this species is divided into layers that receive input from the contralateral and ipsilateral eyes alternately (Figure 8.2). The contralateral eye goes to layer A, the ipsilateral eye to layer A1. The LGN is wired up so that the visual field maps in the two layers are in register, which is to say that when the cat is looking at a point, the part of the A layer that is stimulated by that point via the contralateral eye is immediately above the part that is stimulated by it through the ipsilateral eye. However, the visual fields of the two eyes are not completely identical. For example, the contralateral eye sees further into the peripheral visual field than the ipsilateral eye. As a consequence, there is part of the A layer of the LGN, representing the far periphery of the visual field,

Plasticity

Figure 8.2 The relationship between the visual field of the two eyes and the lateral geniculate body

The right visual field of the left eye (dashed line), projects on to lamina A1 of the LGN. The right visual field of the right eye (continuous line) projects on to lamina A of the LGN. Since the right visual field of the right eye extends further into the periphery than that of the left eye there is a region in lamina A of the left LGN that represents on the right eye. This is the monocular segment (MS).

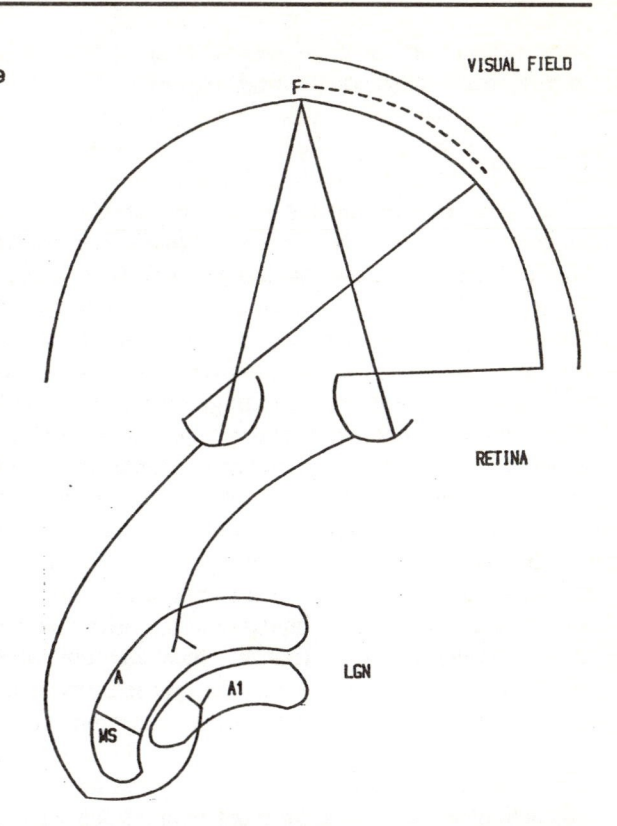

for which there is no associated part of the A1 layer. There can therefore be no competition between the cells in the A layer and the A1 layer for cortical targets, so we would expect monocular deprivation to have less severe effects on this monocular part of the A layer than on the rest of the LGN. This is what Guillery found. Whereas the cells in the rest of the A layer shrink when the contralateral eye is closed, the cells in the monocular segment do not.

Other experiments indicate that normal binocular development requires more than both eyes being active at some time: they have to be active at the same time. This can be shown in two ways. First, Wiesel (1982) and others have studied the effects of surgically inducing squint by cutting one of the eye-muscles in newly born animals. The consequence of inducing a squint is that stimuli no longer act on corresponding points on the two retinae so that, when the inputs from one eye to a cortical cell are active, those from the other eye won't be. As a consequence, the inputs from both eyes will be active at some time but rarely simultaneously. The physiological consequence of squint is that cortical cells respond exclusively to either one eye or the other. Binocularity is absent. A similar effect can be achieved by using alternating deprivation, in which both eyes are opened but never simultaneously. We can therefore conclude that the maintenance of the binocular connections we are born with in our visual systems depends on simultaneous activation of inputs from corresponding points in our two eyes.

Orientation selectivity

Given that one of the main errors that normally occur in the prenatal development of the CNS is an over-production of synaptic connections it is not altogether surprising that the majority of the cells in the visual cortex are binocular. By the same token we wouldn't expect many of them to be orientation selective, since this requires a degree of selectivity in the inputs to the cortical cells that might be beyond the scope of genetic preprogramming. Reflecting this line of reasoning, much of the debate about orientation selectivity has concerned whether experience creates this property, as opposed to simply modifying a predetermined pattern. One thing on which most observers agree is that the orientation selectivity seen in adults depends on being exposed to bars and edges of all conceivable orientation early in life.

Early studies by Hirsch and Spinelli (1970) and Blakemore and Cooper (1970) suggested that the visual cortex was readily modifiable by experience. After being exposed to a limited range of orientations while they were kittens, adult cats had visual cortices in which the cells would only respond to the orientations to which they had been exposed early on. There are two possible explanations for this. The first is that orientation tuning is completely plastic so that the visual cortex models itself on the environment present post-natally (the plasticity hypothesis). The other is that orientation tuning is, in the first instance, determined prenatally but requires subsequent experience to confirm the connections (the confirmation hypothesis). These explanations make different predictions. For one thing, the plasticity hypothesis suggests that the visual cortex of the newborn kitten will be completely devoid of orientation selective cells. For another, the plasticity hypothesis suggests that, with novel early environments, it will be possible to create novel receptive field characteristics in developing animals. Finally, the plasticity hypothesis implies that all the cortex will be committed to the orientations that have been experienced early in life.

Most of the evidence now favours the confirmation hypothesis, although there is some dissent. As early as 1963 Hubel and Wiesel had reported that the visual cortices of kittens raised from birth without visual experience until their eyes had opened had orientation tuning characteristics similar to those observed in adult cats. The main differences between kittens and adults were that the cells were much more sluggish in the kittens and some cells failed to respond to visual stimuli altogether. Pettigrew (1974) disputed this conclusion. Using Hubel and Wiesel's methods he was able to confirm their data but argued that they hadn't measured orientation selectivity properly. Although we talk about orientation selectivity as if it is a completely independent property of receptive fields, it is often measured using moving stimuli, bars or edges, with the stimuli being moved at right angles to their long axes. A vertically oriented bar would be moved from right to left or left to right, a horizontally moving bar would be moved up or down. As a consequence, orientation is usually confounded with direction. Pettigrew's point was that Hubel and Wiesel were measuring direction selectivity when they claimed they were measuring orientation selectivity. When he tested for orientation selectivity using bars and edges moved other than at right angles to their long axes Pettigrew found that it was the direction of movement rather than the orientation of the stimuli that determined responses. Subsequent work (Sherk and Stryker 1976; Wiesel 1982) indicated that, while there are differences between the visual cortex in kittens and in adult cats, orientation selectivity could be demonstrated even when defined by more stringent criteria. In monkeys the situation is clearer. The visual system is behaviourally functional at birth and the cells of the visual cortex show distinct orientation selectivity in newly born animals. On balance, work on orientation selectivity favours the confirmation hypothesis, suggesting that it is a genetically determined property of the visual cortex.

How far can the properties of the visual cortex be modified by experience? According to the plasticity hypothesis it should be possible to create completely new receptive field properties. We know that this isn't completely true without ever having to study the developing visual system because cells in the visual cortices of normal adults don't respond to all possible features of the environment. For example, cells in V1 don't selectively respond to corners or stars, and those with non-oriented binocular receptive fields in monkeys are restricted to the cytochrome oxidase blobs of the upper layers (see chapter 4). A limited version of the hypothesis might still be true. Blakemore and VanSluyters (1973) claimed that it was possible to create a new class of receptive field properties in cats by raising kittens in an environment in which the only features were blobs of varying sizes. As adults the animals had visual cortices that would only respond to blobs. This is a very dramatic demonstration of the power of the environment to modify the properties of the visual cortex but it is not altogether clear that blob detection represents a new property or a distortion of what is normally present. The other side of this coin is that we would not expect cortical cells to be tuned to stimuli that were not experienced in infancy. In a study in which kittens were exposed only to moving stimuli of a fixed orientation, direction, and velocity Tretter, Cynader, and Singer (1975) found that the orientation and direction of movement determined the subsequent tuning of cortical cells but the preferred velocity bore little relationship to the velocity used during the initial exposure phase. The degree of modifiability of the visual cortex isn't as great as the plasticity hypothesis demands.

Finally, do all cells become committed to the stimuli that have been experienced during early development? According to Blakemore, all of the cells one records from in the visual cortices of animals raised in restricted visual environments respond to the stimuli used. There appears to be no unresponsive cells. The problem here is making sure that any unresponsive cells have been given a fair chance of appearing in the group studied by the experimenters. To do this you have to be very circumspect about proper sampling procedures and it is in the nature of electrophysiology to discourage proper sampling. It is extremely difficult to isolate individual cells from their backgrounds and it takes a considerable amount of effort to characterize the receptive field properties of the cells that have been isolated. This does tend to bias electrophysiologists towards the cells from which they can record most easily. As a consequence most electrophysiological studies report on cells scattered throughout the cortex, often with large gaps between cells along the same electrode penetration. These gaps can be quite variable in size. Under these conditions it is hard to swear that there are no unresponsive cells or silent areas. Stryker and Sherk (1975) attempted to get round this by moving their recording electrode a fixed distance and then characterizing the response properties of the cells they found, no matter how difficult it was to do so. According to these authors, when you do this in cats that have been raised in restricted visual environments there is no bias towards cells that respond to the experienced orientation. This suggests that rearing in a restricted environment may depress the responsiveness of cells that would otherwise have been visually responsive, rather than shifting their receptive field characteristics to those experienced early in life.

This leads us to another methodological problem, which is the possibility of experimenter bias. It is the exception, rather than the rule, for experiments like these to be carried out using the sorts of double-blind control procedures that are commonplace in psychology. Usually the person doing the electrophysiology is fully aware of the rearing conditions. Blasdel, Mitchell, Muir, and Pettigrew (1977) are an exception. They used a double-blind procedure in which the animals were reared in one laboratory and shipped to another for the electrophysiology. Their results fell half way between Blakemore's and Stryker and Sherk's. Cells responding to all orientations were found in the visual cortex but there was a clear bias towards the one experienced. Again, these results favour the idea that early experience confirms genetically predetermined response properties.

There is a considerable amount of plasticity in the developing visual cortex, but that plasticity is limited. Leventhal and Hirsch have argued that this is because the properties of cells that respond to horizontal and vertical edges are largely innately determined while responsiveness to oblique orientations is determined by experience. In support of this they report that kittens exposed to vertically oriented bars and edges develop cells that respond to horizontal and vertical but not oblique orientations. If they are raised with oblique stimuli then they have cells that respond to horizontal or vertical as well as to this orientation.

Mechanisms of plasticity

The conditions under which developmental plasticity in the visual system takes place had been largely established by about 1980. Since then effort has been directed to unravelling the cellular mechanisms involved. There are two important features of developmental plasticity that deserve comment because they constrain the sorts of cellular process likely to be involved. The first is that even short periods of restricted experience can have very severe effects if they occur at the right time. The second is that these effects are largely irreversible by subsequent normal experience. Both point to cells in the visual cortex passing through a state that renders them particularly susceptible to the effects of restricted input. This state probably lasts a matter of weeks in kittens and never recurs in the animal's life.

Pharmacological studies by Kasamatsu (1983) have shown that this plasticity depends on the level of the neurotransmitter noradrenaline (NA) in the visual cortex. Depleting noradrenaline, by infusing the neurotoxin 6-OHDA into the visual cortices of kittens during the sensitive period, blocks the ocular dominance shift that normally accompanies monocular deprivation at that time. Moreover, infusing the cortices of these animals with NA restores the plasticity. One of the most exciting features of this work is that noradrenaline infusions into the visual cortices of adult cats have been found to induce plasticity. These adults show small, but measurable, ocular dominance shifts in response to monocular closure. This work suggests that cortical levels of noradrenaline are important for developmental plasticity.

Noradrenaline may not be the whole story. Recent work by Tsumoto, Hagihara, Sato, and Hata (1987) has shown that NMDA receptors, a cellular subsystem believed to be important in adult memory formation (see chapter 7), are more effective in influencing visual responses in the cortices of kittens during their sensitive periods for plasticity than in adult cats. Although the effect was small it does raise the interesting possibility that, at the level of the single brain cell, the mechanisms involved in developmental plasticity and adult learning are the same. However, it remains to be seen whether manipulations of the NMDA receptor system affect plasticity and, if they do, whether they are independent of the noradrenaline inputs to the cortex implicated in the control of plasticity by Kasamatsu and Pettigrew.

The idea of being able to manipulate cortical plasticity pharmacologically is exciting because it opens the way to dealing with some of the problems that arise from abnormal early experience. For example, congenital squint usually results in long lasting visual difficulties even though the squint has been corrected surgically. These difficulties are probably due to abnormal development of the visual system during the time of the squint. Combining corrective surgery with pharmacological treatment to re-instate plasticity temporarily in the visual cortex might overcome these difficulties.

The social environment and the brain

One of the lasting contributions of the behaviourists working in the 1940s and 1950s has been to demonstrate the implausibility of behaviourist explanations of some of the more important facets of human behaviour. This is especially true of Skinner's (1957) book, *Verbal Behaviour*, which attempted to demonstrate how the various properties of human language could come about as the result of reinforcement contingencies in the social environment but ended up convincing people of the opposite. As Chomsky (1959) pointed out in his review of Skinner's book, reinforcement contingencies cannot explain the extraordinary speed with which we acquire language when we are very young. As Lennenberg (1967) subsequently pointed out, it is difficult to see why we are the only species with symbolic communication if the trick lies in reinforcement contingencies alone. The alternative is that we come pre-equipped with the ability to learn a language, a Language Acquisition Device (LAD) as Chomsky termed it. The challenge for psychobiology is to explain how the brain can come pre-equipped to learn something as culturally dependent as language.

Of course, there have been some attempts to repudiate this position, by showing that non-human species can acquire symbolic communication when their behaviour is shaped by the appropriate reinforcement contingencies. However, in many ways these studies simply serve to re-emphasize the difference between humans and other animals when it comes to language. For one thing, the level achieved by their subjects, which are usually great apes like chimpanzees or gorillas, probably just about matches that of a mentally deficient 3-year-old human. Furthermore, the amount of effort and training required to instil this level of skill is far in excess of the amount received by the average child. Finally, these animals learn their skills progressively. There is no sign of the sudden spurts of ability we see with human children (Patterson 1978).

The problem with arguing that language is unique to humans is that we cannot study it as easily as we can study other psychological processes. Not surprisingly, we don't know enough about the neural bases of language even to begin to understand how the neural mechanisms change as a result of exposure to the linguistic environment. If we want to study culturally dependent early learning we are forced to turn to animal models in the hope that they will shed some light on the matter. Even if these models don't tell us anything directly about human language they can at least tell us whether age-related learning mechanisms like the LAD are possible and, if so, whether they have any common features that might extend to human language learning. Two widely studied model systems are imprinting and song-learning, both of which occur in birds.

Imprinting

Imprinting is a form of attachment learning that occurs in the recently hatched chicks of precocial birds like geese, ducks, and domestic chickens. Following relatively brief periods of exposure to distinctive objects the chicks start to follow them around, show signs of distress at their absence, and are calmed by their presence. Usually the imprinting object has to be another animal, preferably a member of the same species, but the range of possible imprinting objects is quite large. For example, most people have seen pictures of the ethologist, Lorenz, being followed by goslings that had imprinted on him. Domestic chickens are even less fussy than geese in that they will imprint on inanimate objects like flashing lights. Imprinting is biologically important for two reasons. In the early stages of life it keeps the chick in contact with its mother, thus bringing it to food and keeping it out of danger. Later in life it provides the bird with a sexual identity, telling it what sort of creature it should look for to mate with. We know a lot about imprinting as a behavioural phenomenon but it is only relatively recently that people have turned to studying its neural bases.

Horn (1985) argues that imprinting forms an ideal model system for studying the neural bases of learning in general. One of the reasons for this is that the neural systems involved in imprinting seem to be highly localizable. Horn's group's approach to localizing the systems involved in imprinting has been quite original. They argue, justifiably, that learning and memory must involve the synthesis of proteins in the brain and that you can, therefore, localize the sites at which memory formation is taking place by looking for the regions in which protein formation is at its highest. Protein synthesis relies on the production of messenger molecules in cells called ribonucleic acid (RNA). Horn's group monitors protein synthesis by measuring the production of RNA in different regions of the brains of domestic chicks that have been exposed to imprinting stimuli. Following imprinting, but not after exposure to a wide range of other conditions that are often confounded with imprinting, protein synthesis in a small part of the forebrain, the intermedial and medial part of the hyperstriatum ventrale (IMHV), is reliably enhanced. Ablation of the IMHV prevents imprinting and spontaneous single unit activity in IMHV is correlated with the strength of imprinting. More recent work from this group has looked at the cellular changes in this region during learning.

What we don't yet know is why changes in activity in the IMHV are associated with imprinting. Imprinting is very stimulus-specific. An animal that has imprinted on one stimulus will not respond to other stimuli. We would therefore expect the neural mechanisms involved in imprinting to distinguish between effective and ineffective stimuli. Since most studies of imprinting have employed predominantly visual stimuli we would expect the critical neural structures to have visual response properties that distinguish between stimuli. In fact the IMHV doesn't seem to contain visually responsive cells at all. It isn't that the cells are not selective for visual stimuli, but that visual stimuli fail to activate them altogether. It is possible that these results are an artefact of the methods used, for example the anaesthetics used in the experiments, but it is puzzling how a system that is so reluctant to respond to visual stimuli could encode information about the appearance of objects.

Little has been said about the sensitive period. Under normal conditions imprinting only occurs if the exposure takes place when the bird is at the right age. Exposure earlier or later than this time is relatively ineffective. It is tempting to argue that the sensitive period in imprinting occurs for the same reasons as the sensitive period in other forms of developmental plasticity, namely neurochemical modulation. At the moment the evidence points to modulation by noradrenaline (Horn 1985) but it isn't clear that noradrenaline levels in the IMHV change with the sort of inverted-U-shaped function that would be necessary for the control of a critical period.

Song-learning

Nottebohm (1980) has been responsible for much of the work on the neural mechanisms of song-learning in recent years. One of his earliest, and most interesting, findings was that song control in canaries depends on a single motor nerve, the hypoglossal or twelfth cranial nerve. Moreover, it is much more dependent on the left hypoglossal nerve than on the right, suggesting that there is hemispheric asymmetry of function in birds as well as humans. Quite a lot of detective work was required to identify the central mechanisms involved in the control of singing. One clue was that song control depends on the birds being able to hear other birds singing, so some connections from the auditory system seemed to be necessary in the circuit. Another constraint was that the system had to project to the motor neurons in the hypoglossal nucleus for the singing to take place. Guided by these insights, Nottebohm and his colleagues have traced a circuit for the control of singing. At the centre is a forebrain region called the hyperstriatum ventrale, pars caudale which projects to the robust nucleus of the archistriatum which, in turn, projects to the hypoglossal nucleus. Lesions at any point along this pathway abolish normal singing in canaries. Auditory input depends on projections from field L of the forebrain, which is the auditory receiving area, to HVc and the robust nucleus.

The importance of these areas for song was confirmed by a number of other observations. It is only male canaries that develop song, the females singing little or not at all. If these areas are important for singing we might expect differences between them in males and females. This is exactly what they found. In males the HVc is about three times larger than in the female, while the robust nucleus is about two-and-a-half times as large. As mentioned above, the left hypoglossal nerve is more important than the right. This asymmetry also extends into the nervous system in that damage to the HVc or robust nucleus on the left has far more severe effects on song than damage to the corresponding areas on the right.

Song develops fairly slowly in canaries, acquisition of song starting about forty days after hatching and continuing for about nine months. Initially the birds produce a fairly simple 'subsong' which involves a low amplitude sound in which the frequency is shifted up and down. Some two to three weeks later the bird produces its 'plastic' song in which simple song elements are linked into syllables and phrases which are fairly variable in their structure. It is only by the end of eight or nine months that the adult song, consisting of about twenty-five syllables, appears. This gradual evolution of the song is paralleled by the anatomical differentiation of the HVc and the robust nucleus. In very young birds these regions simply cannot be differentiated from surrounding brain tissue but are completely identifiable and of normal adult size by the time that song development is complete. This degree of differentiation only takes place in male birds, the nuclei concerned remaining small in the female. This sex difference depends on the male sex hormone, testosterone. Males that have been castrated do not develop song and the relevant nuclei remain small, while females treated with testosterone do develop song and the relevant nuclei become enlarged.

This work therefore indicates that song-learning depends on an identifiable set of neural mechanisms in the canary. Subsequent work will undoubtedly elucidate the cellular mechanisms involved in song-learning and tell us something about the way that the motor programmes involved in song generation are represented neurally. Of course, it is a long way from either imprinting or song-learning in birds to language acquisition in humans, but this work should re-assure us that neural mechanisms capable of acquiring culturally determined information like the identity of one's family or the song of one's social group are actually possible. This should encourage us to search for neural mechanisms specific to language-learning in our own species rather than trying to account for it in terms of general learning mechanisms.

Recovery from brain damage

Throughout our lives we are losing cells from our brains. Usually this takes the form of a steady loss from all areas but occasionally there are traumas that lead to the sudden loss of a large group of cells. The steady loss usually goes unremarked. As we get older most of us become aware of some deterioration of mental function, but it is rarely so great as to cause alarm. Trauma to the CNS is a different story. Usually the initial effects are very obvious and distressing but it is remarkable how often the long-term effects are relatively minor. Why are psychological functions so resistant to the effects of losing brain cells? How do psychological functions survive the steady loss associated with ageing and why do functions that are initially lost after trauma re-appear with the passage of time or with training?

If we accept the arguments now being put forward that perception and memory are the result of activity in networks of cells, then the problem of the progressive loss of neurons disappears. It is in the nature of networks that their functions are highly resistant to the loss of individual elements. When damaged they undergo graceful degradation of function, in proportion to the number of elements lost (see chapter 3). The relationship between function and the number of elements lost is not linear. That is to say, a large number of elements have to be lost before there is any appreciable deterioration in function and then the system suddenly becomes very unreliable. It has been suggested that this is precisely what happens in dementias like Alzheimer's syndrome, where there is widespread disruption of cellular function in the cerebral cortex (see chapter 7).

The really challenging issues stem from the recovery of function that occurs after trauma to the CNS. Why are there often only minor long-term effects from brain damage that wipes out a large mass of brain tissue? The rub here lies in the word 'often'. The amount of recovery one observes is quite variable. Some patients have little residual impairment while the others have a lot. Our first task is to identify the variables that affect the amount of recovery that occurs.

Variables affecting recovery from brain damage

Age

It is intuitively obvious that brain injuries sustained early in life, before the adult patterns of connections have been formed completely, will have qualitatively or quantitatively different effects from those sustained in adulthood. The difference could go either way, however. On the one hand, a developing brain has more scope for correcting faults induced by localized damage but, on the other, the fact that connections are still to be formed means that there is more scope for additional errors to be built into the system. It is widely held that brain damage in infancy is followed by less severe effects than comparable damage in adults, but this conclusion has been challenged in recent years.

A lot of the clinical literature favours the idea that recovery from early damage is more complete than recovery from later damage. For example, there are numerous reports showing that individuals who sustained damage to the left hemisphere before the age of 2 are more likely to recover the capacity for language than those who sustain left hemisphere damage after the age of 2. This still happens when the damage involves removal of an entire hemisphere. St James-Roberts (1979) argues forcibly that these conclusions are based on inadequate data and that when proper controls are included in the studies the differences between early and late left hemisphere damage or removal are much less clear-cut. He points out a number of problems with the literature. They include the fact that we use different techniques to measure language function in children and adults, that children and adults develop brain damage for different reasons, and that the surgical complications are often greater in adults than in children.

Clearly, we need experimental evidence from studies in which the age of brain damage is dissociated from these other confounding variables to address this problem properly. This means studies on animals. Advocates of superior recovery from early injuries gained a lot of support from the studies reported by Kennard in the late 1930s and early 1940s. Kennard ablated the precentral gyrus, which comprises the electrically excitable motor cortex, in infant and adult monkeys. Not surprisingly, given that this region of cortex is the origin of the main descending motor pathways from the neocortex, such lesions produce severe motor impairments in adults, notably spasticity and an absence of movement of the distal (hand and arm) muscles contralateral to the damaged side. In individuals operated on as infants these effects were either greatly attenuated or absent altogether. However, a more detailed examination of Kennard's reports shows that while there were residual differences between infant and adult operates, the difference between the two decreased as the infants aged. Spasticity increased with age and although the animals were capable of making forced grasping movements when objects were placed in their hands, they did not develop the tendency to make voluntary grasping actions.

Goldman (1974) has argued that Kennard's findings were due to confounding the age at which the lesions were made with the age at which the animals were tested. Since different brain systems mature at different rates lesions in infants may produce relatively small effects simply because the system involved does not make a particularly great contribution to the target behaviour in normal animals at the age at which they are being tested. To explore this she studied the effects of ablating the dorsolateral prefrontal cortex in monkeys on delayed response performance, a task usually sensitive to these lesions in adults. As we would expect from Kennard's findings, animals operated on as infants and tested shortly after were not particularly impaired on this task, in stark contrast with animals operated on and tested as adults. However, when animals that had been operated on as infants were allowed to grow into adulthood before being tested, very severe impairments were remarked on the same task. Given that the animals operated on as infants had had more time to recover from their injuries than animals operated on as adults, this finding is very impressive.

A further complication to Kennard's position is evidence that, in some instances, brain damage in infancy may produce severe impairments not seen in animals operated on as adults. Schneider (1979) has shown that lesions in infants can lead to abnormal patterns of neuronal growth in pathways that normally innervate the damaged area and this can lead to behavioural abnormalities. For example, after destruction of one superior colliculus in infant hamsters, the optic tract fibres from the contralateral eye that normally innervate that colliculus recross the midline of the brain to make synaptic contacts with the medial aspect of the surviving colliculus. These contacts are functional in that synaptic transmission occurs but they lead to maladaptive behaviour. When food is introduced into the affected visual field the animal turns away from it, rather than towards it as normally happens.

There may also be enhanced innervation of areas that do not normally receive a large input from the affected area. For example, the optic tract supplies only a small number of terminals to the lateral posterior nucleus of the thalamus in normal rats. Cowey, Henken, and Perry (1982) have shown that ablation of the superior colliculus in young rats leads to a considerable increase in this innervation and there is some evidence that this is correlated with an impairment of visual function. Thus brain damage in young animals can produce abnormal development in the nervous system associated with deficits in performance not seen after comparable lesions in adults.

Lesion variables

Lesion site is likely to be one determinant of the degree of recovery of function. According to Finger (1978) another major factor is the 'momentum' of the lesion. This concept can be traced back to Hughlings Jackson who, a century or so ago, observed that the severity of the symptoms resulting from brain injury in humans was a function of both the size of the lesion and the rate at which it had developed. For example, a slowly developing tumour in Broca's area was considered less likely to disrupt speech than sudden loss of that area due to a stroke or focal injury. This is an attractive notion, if only because it provides a means of explaining away exceptions to the conventional findings on localization of function, but clinical studies alone cannot demonstrate that lesion momentum is the sole critical factor.

The problem is that the rate of development of a lesion is normally confounded with (a) the source of the lesion (tumour versus stroke, for example), and (b) the side-effects of whatever caused the focal injury. An example of a side-effect would be the rapid build-up of intracranial pressure that follows a cerebral haemorrhage. Once again, experimental results are needed. Finger uses the serial lesion technique in which the effects of ablating a structure in one go are compared with those of producing a similar quantity of damage spread over a number of stages. Frequently this involves removing all of a cortical area, such as the primary visual cortex, on one side of the brain, leaving the animal to recover and then removing the comparable area from the other side. There is a subtle version in which one removes a small part of the same area on both sides and then removes the rest in a subsequent operation. The use of this paradigm has revealed extensive transoperative sparing of skills and habits following two-stage lesions. For example, retention of an avoidance response signalled by light is poor if the visual cortex is ablated in one go, but performance is within the normal range if the lesions are made in two stages. The list of experiments finding a serial lesion effect is impressive but there are some anomalies. For example, while serial lesions of the visual cortex spare a light intensity discrimination task when the light is a cue in a go/no-go avoidance task, there is no sparing when a two-choice simultaneous brightness discrimination task is used. Similarly, Schultze and Stein (1975) found that two-stage lesions of the caudate nucleus facilitated performance on a passive avoidance task relative to both one-stage lesions animals and sham-operated controls. The one-stage group was not impaired relative to the controls.

Post-operative experience

One thing on which most authorities agree is that if adult operates are given adequate care and attention in the immediate post-operative phase, then many of the immediate post-operative symptoms decline or disappear, suggesting that the passage of time is important for recovery. However, passage of time is confounded with the passage of events, so it is possible that recovery is related to post-operative experience. The evidence indicates that the quality of post-operative experience is important in determining the amount of recovery. For example, a number of studies have shown that the loss of a simultaneous brightness discrimination habit following serial ablation of the visual cortex can be prevented if the animals are given additional training between the two operations.

Specific post-operative training may also lead to the re-emergence of a skill after one-stage lesions. For example, Spear and his colleagues (Spear 1979) have shown that the loss of pattern discrimination performance produced in cats by total ablation of areas 17, 18 and 19 of the visual cortex can be partially reversed by seventy-five days of training on the task. Just allowing seventy-five days to pass was not sufficient. Zihl and VonCramon (1985) have reported an analogous phenomenon in humans with visual cortex damage. Practice in detecting light flashes presented in the scotomata of patients with V1 damage led to shrinkage of the scotomata, but only during those periods when the patients were practising on the task.

Mechanisms of recovery

Having looked at the variables that affect the amount of recovery we now have to consider why recovery should take place at all. Over the years neurologists have thought up a number of possible explanations for recovery of function. Before we look at these we have first to consider the possibility that recovery is in some sense illusory because the initial effects of brain damage exceed what we would expect from a sober appreciation of the likely functions of the area that has been damaged.

As early as 1917 VonMonakow (1969) was proposing the existence of 'diaschisis', a reduction in reactivity in nerve cells due to loss of input from a damaged region. According to VonMonakow the affected cells eventually adapt to the loss of those inputs so that the partially denervated regions recover their functions. Recovery is then due to surviving systems returning to normal levels of operation rather than any replacement of the system that has been lost. Diaschisis would account for the findings on lesion momentum, since it would be less when lesions developed slowly. The main drawback to the hypothesis is that there is no evidence for it. There is no widespread loss of responsiveness in the CNS after localized brain damage (Marshall 1985).

LeVere (1980) has put forward a behavioural explanation for the initial over-estimation of the effects of localized damage. He makes the very sound point that even partial damage to a system may alter its function to such an extent that it becomes untrustworthy to the animal or patient concerned. As a consequence the individual ceases to use the system altogether, even though it is capable of some function, leading us to over-estimate the initial effects of the damage. For example, patients with damage to the brain regions involved in speech may find speaking difficult but retain comprehension. Nevertheless the patients' difficulties may lead them to avoid conversation altogether, thus making their impairment seem more severe than it actually is. LeVere's evidence comes from the effects of visual cortex damage on 'memory' for simple visual discrimination tasks in rats that I have described already in chapter 7.

Bearing in mind that there may be less to explain than we think, let us look at the other explanations for recovery of function that have been put forward. These include: vicariation, system substitution, regeneration, collateral sprouting, and denervation supersensitivity.

Vicariation

Vicariation is the yardstick against which all other theories of recovery of function are measured. It is also the one for which there is no evidence. According to this hypothesis, recovery takes place because other brain regions alter their functions to take over the role of the system that has been lost. It predicts that, following recovery, brain areas not previously found to be important for a task become important and that recovery is associated with these areas changing their functions in some way. There is some evidence for the first prediction. For example, Spear (1979) has shown that the recovery of pattern discrimination performance after ablation of areas 17, 18, and 19 in the cat, depends on visual cortex in the suprasylvian sulcus. This area is not important for pattern vision in otherwise intact cats. However, the second prediction is not supported. Although the receptive field properties of this area are changed by the first lesion, recovery is not associated with any further changes in this area. There are certainly no signs of receptive field properties similar to those seen in areas 17, 18, or 19 emerging.

System substitution

In reality it is unlikely that areas of the brain would acquire new functions. The amount of rewiring of the brain it would require would be prohibitive and those areas would lose their normal functions as a result of the change, thus inducing other deficits. A more likely explanation is that the animals adopt different stra- tegies for solving the same tasks, thus bringing different brain systems to bear on them. This would account for Spear's findings without having to postulate any change in the function of the suprasylvian visual area. It is supported by the fact that recovery or preservation of function after brain damage is regularly associated with changes in the effects of lesions elsewhere in the nervous system, even though those other areas have not changed their functions.

Regeneration

Although new nerve cells are not formed after the development of the nervous system is complete, it is possible for cells to produce new axons if the old ones have been damaged. This is known to occur reliably in the peripheral nervous system. There is now evidence that it can also occur in the central nervous system but only under limited conditions (Marshall 1985). What is the difference between the central and peripheral nervous systems? Is it that genetic preprogramming forbids regeneration in the CNS or is there something about the physical environment of cells in the CNS that interferes with the regenerative process?

One of the obstacles to regrowth in the CNS is that the axons have to grow through other brain tissue to make their connections and this other tissue seems to inhibit regrowth. Regrowth can be facilitated by placing the right sort of tissue adjacent to the damaged parts. For example, cut central noradrenergic fibres will grow into pieces of smooth muscle that normally receive a noradrenergic input. Central transplants of embryonic brain can also induce regrowth. If the fimbria of the hippocampus is cut in a rat the fibres do not normally regenerate. However, if transplants of embryonic hippocampus are placed by the cut fibres, cholinergic fibres from the host will grow into the embryonic tissue and, if given enough time, will grow through it and back into the host hippocampus.

When we injure our skin through cuts and abrasions the surface is often marked by a thickening we call a scar. Scarring also occurs in the CNS after localized injury. It normally takes the form of proliferating glia cells, and these glia may inhibit the regrowth of axons in their vicinity. The evidence for this is that lesions made using neurotoxins like 6-OHDA, that do not cause scars, are often associated with regeneration. However, because most of this work has been done on monoamine pathways we don't know how general this finding is. We don't, for example, know whether the pathway from the

Plasticity

thalamus to the cerebral cortex would regenerate if severed using a non-scarring method.

Regeneration is only possible if the cell bodies survive the injury. In most instances they don't. Under these conditions there is little scope for adjustment to brain damage unless some other adaptation occurs. One possibility is to replace the lost cells with transplants of tissue from other animals. Until recently this was considered a bit of a fantasy, something to be written about in science fiction novels rather than by practising scientists. In less than a decade the whole scene has changed and we are now taking the issue of transplants seriously, so seriously that people are beginning to get worried about the possible sources of transplant material.

Transplantation of tissue from other adult animals doesn't work, partly because of the activation of the host's immune system and consequent rejection of the grafted tissue. Transplantation of foetal tissue, on the other hand, can work. It is a relatively straightforward bit of neurosurgery to get a bit of fetal brain tissue into the host's brain and get it to survive. The problem is to get it to make functional contacts with the host brain tissue. However, this has now been done with systems as diverse as the hippocampus, basal ganglia, and the cerebellum (Marshall 1985; Sotelo and Alvarado-Mallart 1987). Mostly, when people talk of functional connections they mean anatomical and physiological evidence of contact between the graft and the host. The degree of behavioural recovery following transplants is less clear. Low, Lewis, Bunch, Dunnett, Thomas, Iversen, Bjorklund, and Stenevi (1982) carried out septal transplants into rats that had previously undergone suction lesions of the fimbria and fornix. The animals were subsequently tested on an eight-arm radial arm maze of the sort described previously in chapters 6 and 7. Normal rats rapidly learn not to visit arms from which they have already taken food during a trial. Rats with transection of the fimbria and fornix do not. Nor do rats that have been given septal transplants, unless they are also given injections of a drug like physostigmine that increases the availability of acetylcholine at the synapses. Even then the transplant recipients did not do as well as intact controls given physostigmine. Thus transplants may provide for some recovery of function but the benefits observed so far are limited.

At the moment transplantation of neural tissue is most likely to be effective when dealing with systems that exert a tonic influence over others, like the projection from the substantia nigra to the basal ganglia. The day when functioning chunks of neocortex can be transplanted is still a long way off.

Collateral sprouting

Although damaged axons have relatively little chance of regrowing, undamaged axons can grow new axon terminals to replace those that have been lost. This growth, which is known as collateral sprouting, has been demonstrated at a number of sites in the CNS. Whether sprouting will be converted into recovery of function depends on the system involved. If a completely different set of axons are sprouting, such as the sprouting of optic tract axons seen after removal of the visual cortex in rats, the sprouting may well interfere with recovery, although there is no hard evidence for this. If the sprouting involves spared axons of the same type as those damaged by the lesion it may compensate for the lost axons. This is especially likely to be true of the widely distributed ascending monoaminergic pathways, in which the number of active terminals is more important than the identity of the neurons involved (Marshall 1985; Stricker and Zigmond 1976).

Denervation supersensitivity

It is now well established that cells deprived of some of their inputs will increase their sensitivity to the transmitters released by their surviving inputs. In fact, the changes that occur at the synaptic level are complex and may involve both an increase in sensitivity and an increase in the release of transmitters by the surviving terminals. Again there is evidence that these mechanisms are involved in the recovery that takes place following damage to the ascending monoaminergic pathways in the brain (Marshall 1985).

Conclusions

True recovery of function is probably less common than we would like to think. It is most likely to occur in diffusely organized systems like the ascending monoaminergic pathways in which the amount of activity is more important than the identity of the cells that are active. Otherwise 'recovery' is probably due to a combination of initial over-estimation of the effects of the damage and changes in behavioural strategy leading to dependence on different neural mechanisms.

Overview

The brain is a remarkably adaptable structure, both in infancy and during adulthood. Development cannot take place without the regulating hand of the environment playing its role and, in adulthood, plasticity is required to compensate for losses of brain cells due to ageing and trauma. Nevertheless, plasticity is limited. It takes place within the boundaries set down by our genetic inheritance. No amount of environmental enrichment will make a chimpanzee function like a human and no amount of deprivation will make a human function exactly like a chimpanzee.

9
Consciousness

One of the major requirements of a good scientific theory is that it is capable of explaining our day-to-day experiences of what happens in the world. The explanations may not always be intuitively obvious but they have to work. For example, physical theories tell us that objects that appear to us to be solid are, in fact, composed of billions of atoms separated by relatively large interatomic spaces so that solidity is, in some sense 'illusory'. The reason why we accept these theories is that they include descriptions of forces that operate between the atoms so that they lock together into rigid structures that interact with other objects to give the property that we call solidity. Theories in psychobiology must also explain what happens in the real world, rather than just accounting for laboratory-based phenomena. The one thing that unites human beings is our experience of being conscious. Psychobiology must be capable of explaining that experience.

When talking about consciousness it is hard not to get lost in a fog of philosophical obscurity as people attempt to explain what consciousness 'really' is. Fortunately, while it is unrealistic to expect everyone to agree about everything on this topic, there are a few points on which most of us can agree. Most people will accept that the main obstacle to neurobiological explanations of consciousness is the fact that consciousness is, by definition, unitary while the brain consists of billions of individual cells organized into functional modules that can operate with a considerable degree of independence. Another point of agreement is that we use the term 'consciousness' to refer to two different things. One way we use it is to describe variations in our awareness of the outside world. We distinguish between states in which we are conscious and those in which we are unconscious. We also distinguish between events of which we are or are not conscious. Another way in which we use it is as an explanation of our behaviour, distinguishing between consciously mediated voluntary actions and unconsciously mediated involuntary reactions. Although we may not agree on what consciousness actually is, we may be able to get a handle on why it is by studying these two problems, the control of awareness and the control of action.

One of the main stumbling blocks in understanding the neural bases of consciousness is that it is something quite different from the stuff of nerve cells. The brain consists of millions of nerve cells, each one a separate living entity working in concert with its neighbours. Where is 'consciousness' in all this? Some solve the problem by saying, simply, that it isn't and that mind and brain are distinctive entities, capable of interacting in some unspecified way (Eccles 1973). Dualism, the idea that mind and body are separate entities, has a very respectable intellectual history and, not surprisingly, is remarkably difficult to refute in a convincing manner. Why is that? It is difficult to refute because all of the evidence for it comes from our failure to come up with convincing alternative explanations. So long as we lack a convincing materialist explanation for consciousness we are obliged to accept the possibility of dualism. Be that as it may, we are certainly not obliged to accept its reality. From the point of view of the scientist, dualism is an admission of defeat. In that spirit I intend to assume that a materialist explanation for consciousness is possible and will not deal with the dualist position any further. The alternative is that consciousness must be something that comes out of the concerted action of nerve cells as a group. This is what people like Sperry (1979) mean by consciousness being an 'emergent property' of the brain. An emergent property is something that arises because of the way elements are combined together in a system, rather than being a property of the individual elements themselves.

Whether or not consciousness is an emergent property of the brain is a philosophical issue. Fortunately it is a fairly straightforward one since, once we accept that individual nerve cells are not conscious, consciousness has to be an emergent property of their activity. There is nothing magical about emergent properties. Indeed, the whole purpose of modern science is to explain the properties of the objects we find around us in terms of the emergent properties of simpler, more fundamental components of the universe. Take, for example, the radio I am listening to while writing this. It, being a fairly old machine, consists of a cluster of transistors, resistors, diodes, capacitors, and inductances, connected to a length of wire called an aerial and to a magnet attached to a cone of paper that together form a loudspeaker. None of these components has the ability to translate the electromagnetic signals emanating from the radio station into music. Only by combining them in the right way do these components acquire that property. It is, therefore, an emergent property. We could go further. Each transistor consists of a material like gallium arsenide. Organized in the transistor in the right way, the gallium arsenide functions to amplify electrical signals, but amplication is a property of the gallium arsenide and the way it is organized rather than of the gallium arsenide alone. At this level we again have an emergent property. Since emergent properties are the stuff of science, to describe something as an emergent property is not to explain it but simply to say that it needs an explanation. In the context of consciousness, that means that we need to know why and how the organization of the human brain gives rise to consciousness.

Consciousness also raises a number of methodological issues that link into the philosophical ones. For present purposes one of the most contentious is the possibility, or otherwise, of using non-human animals in its study. Psychologists have now just about reconciled themselves to the fact that consciousness cannot be disposed of as a problem in humans but many are reluctant to accept that it is also possessed by animals. Indeed, some authors have argued that it is a relatively recent acquisition in our own species (Jaynes 1982). Each of us knows that humans are conscious because we are conscious and we are humans but, since we are not cats, dogs, rats, or budgerigars, we don't have any direct knowledge of them. From a scientific point of view this anthropocentrism is misplaced. The fact of the matter is that the only creature of whose consciousness I can be assured is my own. Describing other people as conscious is not a statement of fact but an attribution I make, using behavioural signs to make inferences about their inner states. This means that, logically, I am entitled to use the same signs to attribute consciousness to a laboratory rat as I am to attribute it to the person sharing the office next to mine.

The reason why people object to attributing consciousness to other species is because they perceive a relationship between consciousness and language. One of the things that we do that other animals don't is to use symbolic communication to indicate to each other our conscious states. As a consequence it is hard to deny the consciousness of our fellow human beings. Nevertheless it is counterproductive, at this stage in the development of our knowledge, to move to the argument that consciousness is only possible with language. Apart from pushing adherents of this view into the nonsense that people who lack language must also lack consciousness it also smacks of scientific nihilism because it denies the possibility of being able to collect the data that could shed light upon the issue. Until we have the data to show either that consciousness is not a product of the brain at all, or that there is something special about the functional organization of the human brain that means that only that particular organ is capable of sustaining it, it makes much more sense to make the assumption that enables us to do research, which is that animals other than us are conscious. Nevertheless, there may be qualitative differences between us and other species that reflect differences in our cognitive abilities.

The unity of consciousness

In psychobiology we now take it for granted that the brain is the seat of the mind and of consciousness but the idea is of relatively recent origin (Blakemore 1977). One reason for this is that the brain is not as essential for consciousness as other organs. Injury to the heart produces a rapid and reliable loss of consciousness, whereas damage to the brain may impair mental function without loss of consciousness, unless the damage is severe and involves the brainstem. We now know that damage to the heart leads to loss of consciousness because the brain is deprived of oxygen, but that is a fairly recent discovery. Another reason why people were reluctant to consider the brain to be the seat of the mind is that consciousness is unitary while even cursory examination shows that the brain is not, the bulk of the human brain consisting of the two cerebral hemispheres. It is not really surprising that people looking for the seat of consciousness were more inclined to link it to unified systems like the heart or, when they attended to the brain, to unified components like the ventricular system or the pineal gland. The evidence that mental processes depend on the brain is now overwhelming, but this does create the problem of accounting for how such a fragmented system can be the basis of a unified consciousness. In recent years we have seen two serious, scientific approaches to this problem. The first approach holds that the unity of consciousness occurs because it depends on activity in a single, unified subsystem in the brain. The second holds that the unity of consciousness is, in some sense, illusory and that the phenomenon we call consciousness consists of a number of mental, and hence neural, events occurring in parallel.

Since most of the brain is bilaterally organized, there are few structures capable of linking the functions of the two cerebral hemispheres. A notable exception is the reticular formation of the brainstem, which occupies the central core of the brain from the medulla to the midbrain. Not surprisingly it has been suggested that this system is responsible for consciousness (Thompson 1965 ; Kilmer, McCulloch, and Blum 1969). I shall review later the evidence that the reticular core controls the level of consciousness. What concerns us here is the separate possibility that it is activity in the reticular core of the brain that represents consciousness. Two lines of evidence support the argument. The first concerns the anatomical organization of the reticular system and its connections, the second the effects of brain damage on consciousness.

The reticular formation (RF) gets its name from the fact that it has a net-like appearance when appropriately stained sections are viewed under the microscope. It is difficult to discern much other structure in it, other than the fact that, in some places, there are clusters of very large cells. The net-like organization stretches the length of the RF and extends across the midline. As a consequence it looks as if input arriving at any point in the RF could be readily conveyed to all other parts of the system, allowing for the sort of level of integration of input and output that we associate with consciousness. Input comes from all over the cerebral cortex, as well as from subcortical sensory and motor pathways. Auditory and visual information could converge on the same cells, as would descending information from the motor system. Its outputs seemed to be similarly diffuse, running rostrally into the thalamus, into 'non-specific' nuclei that have widespread connections with the cerebral cortex. Anatomically, the reticular formation seemed well placed to carry out the sort of integration required of a centre of consciousness.

The neurological data also seem to fit with the story. As I have already pointed out, damage to the cerebral cortex usually leads to cognitive and motor impairments without any long-term loss of consciousness. Damage to the brainstem, in contrast, usually results in coma that is often permanent. Furthermore, it was once thought that people who had undergone disconnection of the two cerebral hemispheres following the cutting of the corpus callosum and other forebrain commissures (commissurotomy) enjoyed a degree of integration of mental function that could only be explained in terms of the activity of the two hemispheres being co-ordinated at a subcortical site such as the RF.

Our view of the reticular formation and its likely functions has shifted significantly in recent years and such a simple view is no longer tenable. At the anatomical level the reticular formation is much more organized than was once thought. Although the whole cerebral cortex projects to the reticular formation, the projections from different parts of the cortex are quite strongly segregated (Valverde 1962). Furthermore, it is now clear that much of the reticular formation forms part of the motor system controlling cranial nerve motor nuclei (Travers and Norgren 1983). As a consequence, the amount of reticular formation available to form the seat of consciousness has shrunk. For example, the control of the muscles of the face involves a projection from the cerebral cortex to cells in the medullary reticular formation which, in turn, project on to cells in the facial and trigeminal motor nuclei.

At the neurological level, more recent studies have shown that the amount of integration between the two hemispheres is much less in commissurotomy patients than was first thought. Some integration can take place at the subcortical level, although it is unclear whether it is the reticular formation itself that is involved, but the transfer of information is limited. For example, Gazzaniga (1985) describes a situation in which commissurotomy patients are presented with an array of four Xs, two in the left visual field, thus projecting to the right cerebral hemisphere, and two in the right visual field, thus projecting to the left hemisphere. When asked to give a verbal report of what they can see the patients only report the Xs in the right visual field, the ones that are received by the left hemisphere. However, when asked to move their eyes to whichever of the four stimuli was highlighted on a particular trial the patients could move their eyes to stimuli in both the left and right visual fields. Thus the patients were capable of directing accurate movements to stimuli of which they claimed to be unaware. Thus, under these conditions there is integration of motor control but not of consciousness. Even the integration of motor control is limited, however. Gazzaniga describes another patient in whom the right hand, controlled by the left hemisphere, would find itself in conflict with the left hand, controlled by the right. This patient was conscious of what her right hand was intending to do but was constantly surprised by the antics of her left hand. These observations suggest that the integration of behaviour and of consciousness takes place predominantly at the cortical level, rather than in the brainstem.

Another way of achieving integration is to allow one hemisphere to dominate the other. Over the years a number of authors have argued that the integration of consciousness depends on the left hemisphere and this, in turn, relates to its role in the control of language. Some of the best evidence for this comes from the commissurotomy patients I have already mentioned. Gazzaniga's patient with the recalcitrant left hand, for example, reported that she was conscious of what the hand associated with the left hemisphere, the right hand, was doing but knew nothing of the intentions of the hand associated with the non-linguistic right hemisphere, the left hand. The importance of language is indicated by another patient who showed signs of bilateral representation of language after his operation and who was also capable of reporting his state of consciousness from either hemisphere.

Why should language be so important for consciousness? The first point to get clear is that authors like Gazzaniga draw a sharp distinction between language and speech. What is important about human language, they argue, isn't simply the facility for communication but the capacity for formulating and representing inferences about what is happening in the world. This dissociation is illustrated by one of Gazzaniga's patients who possesses speech capacity in both hemispheres after commissurotomy. Although the right hemisphere is capable of identifying objects and naming them, it is incapable of using language to draw logical inferences. For example, when the left hemisphere is presented, via the right visual field, with the words 'pin' and 'finger' the patient is able to draw the inference that the outcome will be to bleed. The right hemisphere is incapable of producing such an inference, even though it is capable of defining 'bleed' when the word is presented to the left visual field. The reason why Gazzaniga and others give pride of place to language in consciousness is that they believe consciousness, or, to be more specific, self-consciousness, is a running commentary, represented in the medium of language, of what we and our brains are doing at any moment. This commentary is necessary because our brains really consist of a set of largely functionally autonomous modules working in parallel, the activities of which need to be integrated and co-ordinated in order for us to achieve our goals. When the corpus callosum is cut the right hemisphere can work independently of this left hemisphere monitor, with the consequence that the left hand can develop a will of its own without the patient being aware of what it is about to do. To the extent that mental events are really occurring in parallel, while our conscious experience is of a continuous stream of ideas and impressions occurring sequentially, the integrity of our conscious experience is illusory.

The idea that consciousness arises out of the need to integrate the diverse activities of parallel brain mechanisms is an attractive one. Clearly, a structure with as much parallel organization as the brain is going to need some mechanism to co-ordinate the activity of its parts, or else neural anarchy will ensue. This is especially true when the parallel activity of the brain has to be converted back into serial activity in the muscles to produce movement (Calvin 1987). Why should that process of integration have the subjective properties we call consciousness? Why should that integration depend on language? The answer to the first question is currently beyond our understanding. The answer will, no doubt, come through when we are able to produce serious models of the integration process. The relationship between consciousness and language is not much clearer, but there are some things that can usefully be said.

The first is that the use of verbally based introspective reports makes many of the studies circular. If you ask someone to give a verbal explanation for their behaviour they can scarcely be expected to report on events that have been disconnected from their verbal mechanisms by, for example, commissurotomy. Considering consciousness as something that must be verbalizable is a matter of definition, however, and not an empirical matter. The second thing is that all of the things that need to be done by the mechanisms of consciousness in humans need to be done in non-verbal animals as well. They too need to co-ordinate the activities of their 'social' brains. They too need to be able to plan actions to anticipate the future. They too need a self-concept to be able to operate effectively. In order to defend resources successfully they need to be able to distinguish between self and not-self. To be able to mate effectively they need to be able to identify animals that are like themselves. The sophisticated strategic decision-making that is now known to underlie behaviour in most non-human species means that cognitive models have had to replace the older reflex models of these activities. The range of cognitive abilities that reflect inferential processes that non-human species turn out to be capable of is impressive. The recent work on spatial ability in rats, for example, shows that this species is capable of quite sophisticated inferences provided they are restricted to the spatial domain (Kesner and DiMattia 1987; Morris *et al.* 1982). In primates the evidence is more impressive. Good evidence for self-awareness can be found in chimpanzees. If a chimpanzee is anaesthetized and has part of its fur painted while unconscious it is quite capable of using a mirror to inspect the regions that have been painted (Rowell 1972). This is only possible if the animal is capable of making the inference that what it is seeing in the mirror is itself. This impression of the cognitive abilities of primates is re-inforced by work done on chimpanzees. In addition to being able to acquire communication skills they are also capable of using sophisticated concepts like number (Matsuzawa 1985; Woodruff and Premack 1981). Of course, there may be differences between the cognitive processes in man and in other animals, but there is no compelling evidence to presuppose that one set involves consciousness and the other doesn't.

A further difficulty with accepting that language is the basis of the integration of consciousness is that there isn't a clear mechanism for explaining how the various modules of the brain connect to the language system. One possibility, discussed by Gazzaniga, is an attributional process in which we observe our own behaviour in various situations and use our language system to draw inferences about what must have been causing us to act in that way. He argues, for example, that this is how emotion works. Emotion, he argues, starts with a non-verbal mechanism responding to a situation and generating a motor reaction that involves both the autonomic and the skeletal motor system. The verbal system then 'notices' what is happening and seeks to interpret the reaction in terms of what is going on. If, for example, you feel lethargic and on the verge of tears and someone has just given you some bad news, your verbal system will interpret the bodily reaction as depression caused by the bad news. In some ways Gazzaniga's own data from split-brain patients argue against this position. When these patients find their left hands, the ones connected to their right, 'non-verbal', hemispheres, doing things, they don't spontaneously start making attributions about what that hemisphere is trying to do. Instead they find themselves in a conflict between what the two hemispheres are trying to do, and describe their left hands as being out of control.

Clearly the integration of consciousness depends on the information transmitted between the two hemispheres by the corpus callosum, rather than on an attributional process dependent on monitoring one's own behaviour, but how is this achieved? What we know about the anatomy of the corpus callosum suggests that this integration must be achieved in two stages. Since the majority of the callosal fibres run between corresponding cortical areas in the two hemispheres, the first stage must involve relaying information between the corresponding areas. In the second stage, information must be relayed across the left hemisphere to the language system. If this is true then circumscribed lesions in the left hemisphere should have a far more severe effect on cognitive function than similar lesions in the right. The reason is that a right hemisphere lesion leaves intact the corresponding region in the left hemisphere and its connections with the language mechanisms. A left hemisphere lesion, on the other hand, will both disconnect the left hemisphere from the language system and isolate the intact right hemisphere. It is significant that many language deficits can be produced by focal left hemisphere lesions but not by damage to corresponding regions in the right hemisphere, and that the most effective lesion sites are those that involve both transmission pathways across the left hemisphere and callosal terminals arriving from the opposite hemisphere (for examples see Kolb and Whishaw 1985).

One unresolved problem with this sort of model is defining the relationship between action and language. Common sense tells us that our verbally expressed thoughts are the causes of our actions. Attributional models reverse the logic and insist that actions are the causes of our thoughts but, as we have seen, this doesn't happen that much in split-brain patients, suggesting that either thought and action occur in parallel or thought causes action. If integration is occurring at the neural level directly, as the split-brain literature suggests it must be, then we are faced with the question of whether the information delivered to the language system stops there or whether the language system can, in turn, modify what these other modules are doing. Gazzaniga implies that it can, but doesn't spell out how the process occurs. The problem, in the end, is that language is a psychological concept rather than a neural one, so we come back to the problem of explaining how a psychological event can influence the modules of the brain.

What the split-brain literature does is to throw into relief the fact that we have two concepts of consciousness, one as the basis of verbally reported subjective experience and the other as the basis of purposive action. Gazzaniga's data show that these two aspects can be dissociated. Rather than arguing that consciousness 'really' is one or the other, it seems much more sensible to accept that what we call consciousness has a number of separate aspects and that these aspects do not all depend on the same neural mechanisms (Oakley and Eames 1986).

The control of awareness

Most human beings spend approximately a third of their adult lives in a state of unconsciousness known as sleep. Non-human animals enter into a comparable state, some for a much larger proportion of their time than we do (Allison and Cicchetti 1976). If we could work out what happens when people go to sleep, what distinguishes a sleeping from a waking brain, we may be able to say something about the brain mechanisms underlying our conscious experience. Since sleep is a universal phenomenon it provides a convenient model for studying variations in awareness, and I will, therefore, concentrate on it in this section.

It is intuitively reasonable to assume that a sleeping brain is less active than a waking one, but is that true? If it is true, is sleep associated with a reduction in activity throughout the brain or are some systems more affected than others? This is a very easy question to ask but, until recently, it has been a difficult one to answer owing to the technical difficulties involved.

When most of us think of brain activity we think in terms of electrical activity. The simplest form of electrical activity we can measure is the electroencephalogram (EEG), which reflects the summed activity of many millions of cells at a time. As is well known, the electroencephalogram exhibits a complex series of changes as we fall asleep (Figure 9.1) but it is difficult to say whether these changes in the amplitude and frequency of the brain waves are a sign of increased or decreased activity at the level of the individual brain cells. In fact, these changes in the EEG probably reflect variations in the degree of synchrony between groups of brain cells rather than variations in their overall activity. This is borne out by single cell recordings of spontaneous activity in the cerebral cortex of cats and monkeys. Typically the transition from waking to sleep is associated with a shift from an apparently random pattern of activity in cells to a bursting pattern with silent periods between the bursts. Although the pattern of activity changes, the average number of action potentials each second changes very little (Evarts 1962, 1964).

Spontaneous activity may be a poor measure of what is going on during sleep. Perhaps the response of cells to sensory input would give a more coherent picture. According to Livingstone and Hubel (1981) visual system cells in cats do show a reduction in responsiveness to visual stimuli. What is

Consciousness

Figure 9.1 Samples of EEG characteristics of the five types of sleep

1 – stage 1, non-REM
2 – stage 2
3 – stage 3
4 – stage 4
5 – stage 1, REM

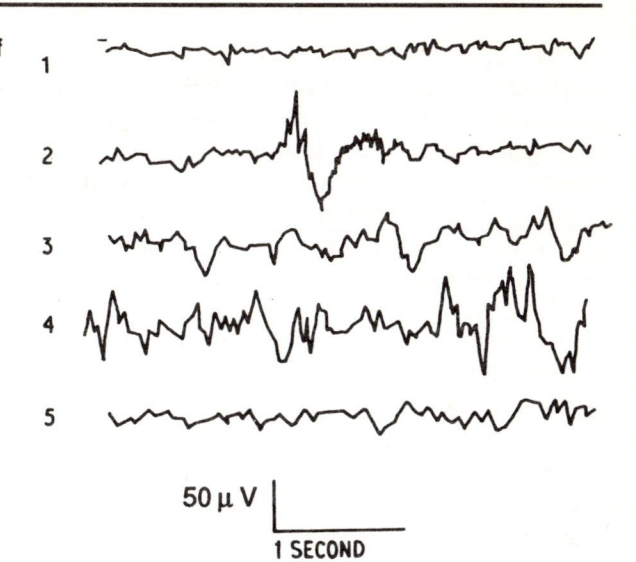

50 μV
1 SECOND

surprising is that, even when the EEG is giving all the signs of the cats being asleep, cells in the visual cortex still respond to visual input. This suggests that consciousness is not related to the presence or absence of activity in the early stages of the visual pathways. It would be interesting to repeat these studies but making recordings from areas of the 'association' cortex in which representations of objects and their properties are believed to be constructed in the brain. It is well known to electrophysiologists that anaesthetics depress responsiveness in cells at these levels of the visual system, suggesting that consciousness is more strongly related to the state of these higher order areas than to the state of primary sensory cortex, but it is naïve to assume that anaesthetics induce a state equivalent to sleep since they can also modify responses in primary sensory cortex.

Although studies of single cell activity in the cortex don't give evidence for reduced electrical activity during sleep, recordings taken from the brainstem provide a much more convincing picture. Cells in the raphe system, that lies in the midline of the medulla, the locus coeruleus, that lies in the floor of the fourth ventricle just below the cerebellum, and the mesencephalic reticular formation all reduce their firing rates during the transition from waking to sleep (Jacobs 1987; Steriade 1983). Indeed, the reduction in activity in the reticular formation is one of the best predictors of impending sleep in cats, according to Steriade (1983). Since these areas project into the forebrain this means that sleep is associated with a large reduction in a tonic input to the cortex from the brainstem. This is bound to affect the functional state of cortical cells but not necessarily in ways that are directly reflected in the numbers of action potentials they produce.

The electrical activity of nerve cells is a result of metabolic events occurring within the cells. Since much of this metabolic activity is involved in maintaining a constant potential across the cell membrane rather than in generating action potentials, the action potentials picked up by electrophysiologists don't provide a complete picture of the amount of activity going on in the cells. It is possible to infer changes in the underlying state of nerve cells from the temporal pattern of action potentials (Steriade 1983) but this is a very indirect way of learning about the state of the brain. A more direct insight into the functional state of the brain can be gained from measures of metabolic activity. As described in chapter 3 there are two ways of measuring the metabolic activity of the brain, autoradiography and emission tomography. Autoradiography is excellent for analysing the spatial distribution of activity changes in different parts of the brain but, since it involves killing the subject, can only be used with non-human animals and does not provide any information about the temporal sequence of metabolic changes. Emission tomography, on the other hand, allows only limited spatial resolution but gives excellent temporal resolution and is non-invasive, so can be used with human subjects.

Both methods show that the metabolic activity of the cerebral cortex declines during sleep (Kennedy, Gillin, Mendelson, Suda, Minaoka, Ito, Nakamura, Storch, Pettigrew, Mishkin, and Sokoloff 1982). Autoradiographic experiments using animals show that this is true of subcortical regions as well as the cortex. In addition to the reduction in spontaneous metabolic activity there is also a fall in the activity evoked in some parts of the brain by sensory stimulation. Livingstone and Hubel (1981) injected the metabolic marker 2-DG into cats while they were asleep and then exposed them to the type of visual stimuli known to be most effective in activating cells in the visual cortex of normal cats. The eye-lids were kept open to ensure adequate stimulation. In the visual cortex there was a reduction in the metabolic activity evoked in the deep layers of the cortex by this stimulation but the activity in the superficial layers did not change. This is curious because it is the superficial layers that give rise to the cortico-cortical connections that one might expect to be the basis of conscious experience, while the deep layers give rise to descending projections from the cortex to subcortical centres, including subcortical motor centres.

What controls the changes in metabolic activity in the cortex and in the neural activity in systems like the midbrain reticular formation and raphe nucleus? For many years neuroscientists have searched for a centre or system that exercised active control over sleep. Such a system would have to have three characteristics. Stimulation within it would have to provoke sleep, its destruction would have to abolish sleep, and single cell activity in the area would have to increase noticeably during the transition from waking to sleep. Although there have been many promising leads, such as Hess's (1957) report that brainstem stimulation could produce sleep in cats and Jouvet's report that raphe nucleus ablation abolishes sleep, these have tended not to stand up to closer scrutiny. For example, it has proved very difficult to replicate Hess's findings. Usually the cats only fall asleep if the stimulation is presented when they are engaged in the sort of behaviour that normally precedes sleep in cats! Jouvet's findings looked more solid but run into the problem that single unit activity in the raphe system declines rather than increases during sleep. At present it looks as if no single neural system controls sleep. As a consequence, many people working on sleep are coming to view its control in terms of interacting systems of neural areas, rather than in terms of a single executive control centre.

What of the converse of sleep, arousal? The pioneering work of Moruzzi and Magoun (1949) and Lindsley, Schreiner, Knowles, and Magoun (1950) suggested that the midbrain reticular formation had a key role. Their evidence was that stimulation evoked arousal in somnolent animals and ablation resulted in permanent somnolence. Since then it has also been shown that midbrain reticular formation activity also correlates with the level of arousal. The real issue is whether it is essential for arousal. Lindsley *et al.*'s experiments were done using single stage lesions that removed all of the midbrain reticular formation in one go. Because of the way they were done they probably also extended into the caudal hypothalamus, a region that Nauta (1946) had already implicated in the control of arousal. Subsequent experiments done using multi-stage lesions to reduce surgical trauma and restrict the ablations to the reticular formation showed that arousal would recover after reticular formation lesions (Adametz 1959). This suggests that, although the midbrain reticular formation is involved in the control of arousal, the process actually depends on the integrated activity of a number of brain systems, as is the case with sleep.

Dreaming

So far I have treated sleep as a simple loss of consciousness but, of course, it isn't so simple because most of us experience that curious state of consciousness in unconsciousness we call dreaming. In dreaming we are vividly aware of events but those events have, at best, only an oblique connection with what is happening in the outside world. One way of viewing dreaming is as consciousness disconnected from sensory input and motor output. It is, therefore, another example of a dissociation between forms of consciousness: consciousness as experience and consciousness as a cause of action. If we can determine the neural events that occur during dreaming we may be able to identify the neural events that underlie conscious experience.

The dreaming state is physiologically distinct from the rest of sleep. During visual dreaming the EEG returns to the low voltage desynchronized activity that also characterizes light sleep (see Figure 9.1) but there are other events that distinguish the two states (Jouvet 1967). The neck muscles relax completely during dreaming sleep while the eyes wander quite wildly under the closed eye-lids, the phenomenon known as rapid eye movements (REM).

Homeostatic regulation breaks down. For example, the body no longer reacts to sudden cold by increasing heat production, or to increased carbon dioxide in the inspired air by increasing respiration rate (Parmeggiani 1979). The temperature in the core of the brain usually rises quite precipitously. Single unit activity in the cerebral cortex may increase but doesn't acquire the irregular patterning that is characteristic of wakefulness. In the motor cortex the cells discharge with regular bursts, as in ordinary sleep, while in the visual cortex there are bursts of activity associated with the rapid eye movements (Evarts 1962, 1964). In the brainstem, cells in many areas, especially in the pontine reticular formation, show an increase in activity during dreaming. As is the case with the visual cortex, many of the cells in the pontine reticular formation fire in conjunction with the rapid eye movements (Morrison 1979). If larger electrodes are inserted into the pontine reticular formation, lateral geniculate nucleus, or visual cortex, large amplitude (for the brain) spikes of electrical activity can be picked up that correlate closely with rapid eye movements. These are called PGO spikes.

Significantly, nearly all of the electrophysiological correlates of dreaming sleep also occur during wakefulness, usually when the subject is highly aroused (Morrison 1979). This suggests that the relationship between a form of consciousness and the brain state during REM sleep is not accidental. Nevertheless, dreaming sleep is clearly distinguishable from the waking state in certain respects and these differences may give us clues about what is inessential for conscious experience. One thing we don't seem to need is asynchronous activity in the motor cortex. This isn't surprising since there is no co-ordinated movement during dreaming. Another thing that seems to be unnecessary is activity in the midbrain reticular formation and the raphe system. This is rather surprising, given the prominence given to the reticular formation in many accounts of the control of arousal and consciousness. It is, however, compatible with the fact that multistage lesions of the midbrain reticular formation that minimize surgical trauma do not produce a permanent loss of consciousness.

On the positive side, visual dreaming involves activity in the visual system. It would be interesting to know how far this activity actually extends into the higher order visual areas. Is the activity restricted to primary visual cortex or does it also appear in areas like the superior temporal sulcus that has the units that respond to faces? Does it get transmitted through the systems which, according to people like Mishkin, link the visual system into the memory systems of the brain? It would also be interesting to know whether the change in activity involves the superficial layers of the cortex or the deep layers in which, according to Livingstone and Hubel (1981), metabolic activity is reduced significantly during normal sleep.

At present we don't know enough about the dreaming state to know why it is associated with conscious experience. Nevertheless, its study offers a promising way of investigating the minimal conditions for that state.

Consciousness and the control of action

Introspection tells us that our thoughts, which are part of our consciousness, cause our actions. Scientifically this creates a major problem because it implies that a non-physical event, consciousness, can cause a physical one, the contraction of muscles. Needless to say, many gallons of ink have been spilt over this issue with the inevitable lack of agreement between the protagonists. Since starting off with the idea of consciousness and then trying to work out how it could control action provokes such intense reactions I propose to work in the opposite direction, to start off with the control of action and then to see what part something like consciousness would play in it, and how consciousness would emerge as a property of that control.

Until recently most explanations of action have been locked resolutely into a reflex framework. Even today people put up diagrams showing connections between the visual cortex and the motor cortex, implying a direct controlling link between one and the other, even though all of the available evidence shows that such links do not exist. The advantage of this approach is that it puts action firmly in the control of the environment and relegates consciousness to the role of a simple correlate of the brain activity, elicited by the stimuli as they evoke an action. The disadvantage is that it forces us either to deny the sponteneity of action, relative to current environmental stimuli, that even behaviourists like Skinner have always been prepared to acknowledge, or it means we have to postulate unobserved stimuli (Jeannerod 1985). It is also difficult to reconcile with the evidence that our behaviour can be affected by mental images rather than external stimuli and that we are capable of manipulating those images.

Anatomical data indicate that the control of movement must be more complicated than a simple reflex path across the cortex. As mentioned in chapter 4, if one traces the projections from the visual cortex the first thing one notices is that they fan out quite considerably. Two major projection routes can be identified, one leading down into the temporal lobe and the other up into the parietal cortex. Both of these regions project forward into the frontal cortex, which contains the motor cortex, but they do not project on to the primary motor area, area 4. Instead, they project on to the premotor area, area 6. Furthermore, these areas have other projections that could influence movement. Both project on to the basal ganglia, which form a significant part of the subcortical motor mechanisms. The temporal visual area projects, indirectly, to the amygdala and hippocampus in the limbic system, which has motor functions (Mogenson 1987) and, according to Mishkin (1982) and his colleagues, many of the effects of ablating the visual part of the temporal cortex can be produced by ablating the hippocampus and amygdala together. The parietal cortex, but not the temporal visual area, has a prominent projection to a brainstem motor mechanism, the cerebellum (Glickstein, May, and Mercier 1985).

The premotor area probably plays a significant role in the control of movement, but it is unlikely to act as a simple relay in a reflex pathway. Although the cells of area 6 often do have visual response properties they are nothing like those observed earlier in the visual pathways (Rizzolatti, Scandalara, Matelli, and Gentelucci 1981). Early in the visual pathways single units encode attributes of the visual scene, such as the colour of objects or their direction and rate of movement. At a later stage cells either have non-specific response properties or are highly selective for specific stimuli such as faces (see chapter 4). According to Rizzolatti *et al.* (1981) most of the cells in area 6 have highly specific response properties but responses are determined much more by the location of the stimuli relative to the animal, rather than the identity of the stimuli. Typically, cells in area 6 only respond when stimuli are placed near the animals' mouths or hands but they are not particularly fussy about the identity of the stimuli used. This means that the information about the identity of objects that one would consider vital to the initiation of voluntary movement is not reaching premotor cortex.

As an alternative to the reflex model some current authors suggest that movement is initiated by activity in the frontal cortex and then comes under the guidance of sensory input as it proceeds. This fits much better with the electrophysiological data on the control of movement which show that movement-related single unit activity, time locked to the onset of the movement, may appear in the frontal cortex in the absence of obvious sensory stimuli (Fuster 1973; Ono 1984). There is an analogous phenomenon that can be demonstrated in humans by averaging the EEG recorded just prior to voluntary movements. During the run up to the movement, the frontal cortex becomes progressively more negative until the movement occurs, whereupon the voltage measured from the cortex precipitately returns to normal (Walter, Cooper, Aldridge, McCallum, and Winter 1964). This electrophysiological phenomenon is known as the Contingent Negative Variation (CNV).

The neuropsychological literature re-inforces the idea that the frontal granular cortex is involved in the planning and initiation of action. Frontal lobe patients are impaired on tasks that require the spontaneous generation of actions and in the control of response strategy. For example, Milner and her colleagues (in Kolb and Whishaw 1985) have investigated the ability of frontal lobe patients to generate words and non-verbal symbols, without the aid of external cues. In the verbal generation tests the patients are asked to produce as many words as they can think of, beginning with a particular letter, and as many as they can think of, beginning with a particular letter and of a fixed length, in a five-minute period. Frontal lobe patients produce an average of thirty-five words under these conditions; controls produce about sixty. An analogous deficit appears in the symbol generation test in which the subjects had to produce as many different drawings as possible, followed by as many as they could produce using only four lines, in a five-minute period. Problems with strategic control have also been demonstrated by Milner's group, using the

Wisconsin Card-Sorting Test which I have already mentioned in chapter 6.

These findings bring out a point that has been emphasized by Luria (1973) which is that frontal lobe damage leads to a dissociation between verbal behaviour and action. Luria devised a series of ingeniously simple tests in which patients were required to carry out a simple task, like squeezing a rubber bulb, according to a set verbal rule. When this rule was reinforced with environmental stimuli the patients performed well, but when the rule and environmental stimuli were in conflict the patients did very badly. For example, in some experiments the environmental stimuli were tones of either a short or long duration. In the reinforcing condition the subjects had to make a short squeeze in response to a short tone and a long squeeze in response to a long tone. In the conflict condition the rule was reversed and the subjects had to respond to the short tone with a long squeeze and to the long tone with a short squeeze. Frontal lobe patients performed like controls on the first version but were severely impaired on the second.

It is also possible to interpret the changes in personality that follow frontal lobe damage in terms of the control of action. Two major types of change have been identified: pseudodepression and pseudopsychopathy (Kolb and Whishaw 1985). In pseudodepression the patient exhibits a generalized indifference to the world, with a loss of initiative, reduced verbal activity, and apathy. In pseudopsychopathy the patient lacks behavioural restraint, appearing immature, coarse, tactless, and sexually promiscuous. Given the severity of these changes it is surprising that disconnection of the frontal lobes was, at one time, widely used as a treatment of psychological disorders but, since the method was used to treat depression and antisocial behaviour the therapists really didn't have a lot to lose (Valenstein 1980). The depressed patients couldn't become much more apathetic and the antisocial patients couldn't become much more psychopathic but there was the possibility that the former group might become less inhibited and the latter group more so. Fortunately, psychosurgery like this has largely gone out of fashion, thanks to the advent of more effective pharmacological treatments and psychotherapeutic methods.

Having said all this, there are a number of observations that are incompatible with such a simple role for the frontal cortex. One is that frontal lobe damage has been found to produce a number of other deficits. For example, Teuber (1964) reported that the only deficit unique to a group of frontal lobe patients that he had tested was an impairment relating vestibular input to vision. Patients and control subjects were strapped into a chair and placed in a darkened room in which the only thing visible was a luminous rod which could be rotated around the gravitational vertical. The rod was displaced from the vertical by the experimenter and the subject had to adjust it back to the upright. So long as they, themselves, were vertical too frontal lobe patients had no special difficulty with this task, but when the chair into which they were strapped was rotated off the vertical as well, the frontal lobe patients had great difficulty in getting the luminous rod back to the upright position. Memory deficits have also been observed with frontal lobe patients. Generally they have no problem with learning new material but they have great difficulty with remembering the order in which events occurred. For example, if control subjects are given a series of photographs to look at and are then shown a pair of the photographs, they can usually say which one occurred first in the list. Frontal lobe patients are very bad at this task.

These additional observations raise the question of whether the frontal lobes are the site at which spontaneous behaviour is generated or whether they are simply necessary for the sorts of cognitive functions that are necessary for the normal execution of skilled actions. A further reason for doubting whether the frontal lobes are responsible for initiating action is that there are many species which we believe capable of spontaneous action but which lack clear-cut homologues of the human frontal granular cortex. Take the rat, for example. Nowhere in the neocortex is there an area that has the cellular organization characteristic of human frontal granular cortex. It is true that there are two areas, one on the medial edge of the anterior cortex and one around the anterior part of the rhinal sulcus, that have some of the same connections as frontal granular cortex (see chapter 2) but these areas in the rat have additional connections that are not present in humans. In fact the structure and connections of the medial area have a lot in common with those of an area known as the supplementary motor cortex in primates, while the rhinal sulcus area has many similarities with the area known as insular cortex in primates.

Of course, it is naïve to believe that movement initiation would depend on the frontal cortex alone in the first place. The prefrontal cortex is now known to be part of a hierarchically organized system that includes subcortical structures as well as the neocortex and the organization of action is likely to be a product of this system as a whole, rather than of any single part of it. This hierarchically organized system includes the basal ganglia which are made up of the caudate nucleus, the putamen, the globus pallidus, the amygdala, and the nucleus accumbens septi (Alexander, DeLong, and Strick 1986). Damage to the basal ganglia, or their inputs, has been identified as the cause of a number of pathologies of movement that have, as their main symptoms, disturbances of movement initiation. For example, in Parkinson's disease there is a characteristic poverty of movement (Marsden 1984), while Huntington's chorea is associated with the uncontrolled emergence of spontaneous movements. Nevertheless, we should not conclude that the basal ganglia are the site of movement initiation. Single unit recording studies (DeLong, Georgopolous, Crutcher, Mitchell, Richardson, and Alexander 1984; Evarts, Kimura, Wurtz, and Hikosaka 1984) indicate that, in reaction time tasks at least, movement initiation probably takes place outside the basal ganglia since the onset of unit activity usually follows the onset of activity in both the motor cortex and of electrical activity in the muscles involved in the movement. However, DeLong *et al.* did find some units that fired some time before the movement and they are at pains to point out that their results may be due to the use of a reaction-time paradigm. Their results may also be related to the part of the basal ganglia from which they were recording, since Rolls and his colleagues (Caan, Perrett, and Rolls 1984) have found units in the caudate nucleus that respond to sensory stimuli and which could, therefore, play a role in initiating movements to those stimuli.

Our best chance of understanding voluntary movement lies in viewing it as a product of a neural system rather than as a product of a single neural area. This has the advantage of being more realistic but has the disadvantage of making experiments more difficult. With lesions, for example, it will be difficult to distinguish between the direct effects of losing part of the system and the disruption of the other components that its loss will cause. The real problem is that researchers don't have a good idea of what a system that can spontaneously generate movement would look like. At one time it was hoped that cybernetics, the study of control systems, would provide the answer. As cyberneticists showed forty years ago, it is relatively simple to build a machine that exhibits purposive, goal-directed movement. The trick is to control its activity via a negative feedback loop, so that it is programmed to minimize the difference between its present state and some goal state. The body maintains homeostasis through such mechanisms. There is just one catch. With 'purposive' machines the goals are set by their operators and can only be changed by a decision by the operator. A guided missile cannot act as if it has decided to stop chasing the plane in front of it. It is drawn to the target like a moth to the flame. Humans, on the other hand, are capable of setting their own goals and of deciding which subgoals have to be achieved in order to reach them. It is this capacity to set goals that is most intimately linked to our concept of consciousness. Faced with a lack of a viable model it is difficult for researchers to do much more than study the single cell correlates of movement in different systems and hope that some consistent pattern will emerge. The signs are not hopeful. Our knowledge of the organization of another part of the motor system which is much simpler than the neocortex, the cerebellum, is now copious but we still lack a convincing account of what it does or how it does it. Perhaps the situation will change when the current generation of neural modellers shifts its attention from sensory and cognitive processes to the motor system.

Overview

'Whereof one cannot speak, thereof one must be silent' (Wittgenstein). If this were to be applied to consciousness this book would have been one chapter shorter since there is remarkably little of a concrete nature that can be said about it at the moment. It is significant, however, that although they don't have much to say on the subject, psychologists and psychobiologists are at least talking about it again, having banished it from their subject matter for much of this century.

Consciousness

It is clear now that there is a host of unresolved issues surrounding the topic of consciousness. One of the most important is deciding which questions are philosophical and which are empirical or theoretical matters, and not confusing the two types. For example, the relationship between consciousness and language is a philosophical one rather than an empirical one since, for most of the protagonists in the debate, it is a matter of definition. Some authors, like LeDoux (1986) and Gazzaniga (1985), feel that conscious experience has to be accessible to verbal self-report, while others, such as Oakley and Eames (1986), believe that it is possible to have non-verbal forms of consciousness. The question of whether consciousness is an 'emergent property' of the brain is also a philosophical one.

Fortunately there are also empirical issues to address, relating to the brain systems involved in consciousness. It is possible to get insights into the neural bases of consciousness in a number of ways. One is to investigate the fragmentation and deterioration of consciousness that follow particular types of brain damage. Another is to take advantage of the spontaneous variations in consciousness that we all experience when we move from wakefulness to sleep and into dreaming.

Ultimately the question we are all facing is whether consciousness can really be the product of a machine, albeit the very complex one that we call the brain. Needless to say, there are skeptics who believe that they do not feel like machines. Minsky has a simple rejoinder to that, which is to ask these skeptics whether they have ever been machines since, otherwise, they cannot speak authoritatively on what it feels like to be one. Clearly we are not like any of the man-made machines currently in existence but that doesn't preclude the possibility that there will be machines like us in the future. Quite why anybody would want to build a machine exactly like a human is another matter. Most of the time we use machines because they are not like us, rather than because they are. We want computers that can carry out the same mathematical operations again and again and again without making mistakes, something very few of us can do. We want machine tools that can make exactly the same weld in exactly the same place on every car that comes trundling down the production line, which is again beyond even the most skilled engineers. About the only reason for making a man-like machine, apart from curiosity, would be to be able to send it into hostile environments into which we ourselves wouldn't go but, if our materialist explanations of consciousness and mind are correct, that machine would be the same as a human being and so the same ethical constraints would apply. Nevertheless, serious attempts at producing such a machine are probably our best hope for understanding consciousness and the neural mechanisms that generate it.

10
Concluding remarks

In the introduction I identified a core of five issues that I believe are general to all of the current debates in psychobiology. In this chapter I intend to review the current state of play on those issues in the light of what I have said in preceding chapters. The issues of interest were: (1) the relationship between psychology and biology; (2) the value of studies on non-human animals; (3) the nature of functional specialization in the brain; (4) our response to the challenges of cognitive psychology; and (5) the need to explain behaviour in the real world.

Review of the issues

The relationship between psychology and biology

Throughout this book we have seen again and again the powerful interdependence between biology and psychology in our efforts to understand the biological bases of behaviour. In many instances it has only been the availability of good psychological theories that has made it possible to make sense of physiological data. In others, biological data have been used to set limits on the sorts of psychological theories that are tenable.

Good examples of the importance of psychological theories can be found in chapter 4, 'Perception'. One of the puzzles that has emerged from physiological studies on the visual cortex is that the same information seems to be represented in different areas, suggesting a wasteful degree of redundancy. For example, 'colour' coding cells and 'movement' sensitive cells are found both in the primary visual cortex of primates and in specialized areas in the prestriate cortex. It is only through careful analysis of the psychological bases of colour and movement perception that this problem is resolved. It turns out that the basic problem in perception is moving from the retinal image, which encodes the properties of the light reflected from the objects in the visual field, to representations of those objects and their properties. The 'colour' and 'movement' information represented in the primary visual cortex forms part of the encoding of the retinal image, whereas the activity of cells in the prestriate cortex represents the properties or attributes of the object itself. For example, the evidence we have at the moment indicates that the 'colour' coding cells in primary visual cortex are sensitive to the wavelength of the light falling on their receptive fields. Cells in the appropriate part of the prestriate cortex are, in contrast, sensitive to variations in the perceived colour of the objects in the visual field, quite independently of the predominant wavelength of light being reflected by them.

In the coming years we can also expect developments in psychological theories to direct our investigations into learning and memory. Recent developments, especially those involving network, or parallel distributed processing, theory, hold out great promise for providing a model of memory that is both sufficiently precise to make good testable predictions at the psychological level and inform the ways in which we study its neural substrates. One of the implications of this theoretical development is to blur the distinctions we normally make between memory, perception, and cognition since memory is seen as an inherent property of the systems we use to represent the world to ourselves. As a consequence, it seems fruitless to continue the search for the neural bases of memory separately from the analysis of these other cognitive functions.

The main impact of physiology has been in the fields of emotion and motivation, topics that psychologists have always traditionally considered to be the proper province of the physiologist. Physiological data have always been considered central to discussions of emotion and most theories have made great efforts to accommodate the latest physiological data. Cannon's attack on the peripheral theory of emotion espoused by James and Lange was largely based on such considerations. He argued that the properties of the autonomic nervous system were incompatible with what is required of the substrate of emotion, the evidence suggesting that its reactions were too slow and too diffuse to underpin the rapid and subtle shifts in emotional experience that we all report. Cannon and his collaborator Bard favoured a central theory instead, in which emotion was based on the activation of specified circuits in the central nervous system. Again, this position has been challenged by physiological data. As we saw in chapter 6, the current evidence indicates that the structures implicated in emotion by Cannon and Bard and later adherents of the centralist position are, in fact, either involved in the motor expression of emotion or cognitive processes essential to evaluating the emotional significance of a situation. Physiological data have also been central to the attributionist school of thought in that many theorists have felt compelled to propose a large element of cognitive appraisal in emotional experience because the evidence they had suggested that the autonomic nervous system functioned too diffusely for variations in autonomic reactions to form the basis of emotional experience.

The link between physiology and motivation is so strong in most psychologists' minds that we take it for granted that the most direct way of controlling motivation is by controlling physiological need states. As a consequence, much of the work on motivation has been devoted to determining how these physiological needs are detected and how the brain controls behavioural reactions to these states. For many years we have worked within a quite tightly constrained mechanistic model in which tissue needs trigger central mechanisms, believed to be located in the hypothalamus, that it turn generate behaviours calculated to eliminate those needs. There have been two significant developments in recent years. The first has been the discovery that the evaluation of tissue needs is much more complicated than we first thought and that it involves monitoring a large range of interacting signals. The second has been the discovery that many neural regions outside the hypothalamus are also important for motivation and that many of the properties attributed to it in the past are really those of these other structures, disrupted by hypothalamic lesions because they interrupt the connections of these areas.

Physiology has also had a negative effect in motivation, in that we have focused on 'physiological' motives at the expense of social motives. As I pointed out in chapter 5, it is rare for people in western societies to experience physiological needs that urgently, so it is unreasonable to believe that they play a major part in controlling our day-to-day behaviour. On the other hand, our social needs have become paramount since our success and wellbeing depend on our integration into a complex social organization. Although social psychologists have much to say about these other sources of motivation, physiological psychologists have been largely silent on the subject. This is probably because of the difficulty of fitting these social needs into a theoretical framework based on physiological needs. Indeed, it is only recently, with the development of systems models of motivation, that it has been possible to fit all physiological needs within a single theoretical framework.

The value of studies on non-human animals

Psychobiology is inextricably linked to the use of animal subjects but there is still considerable disagreement about the validity of the data derived from such experiments. While most people seem to be happy about letting a monkey's liver or a guinea pig's kidney stand in for their own in an experiment there is less satisfaction about letting their brains stand in for ours. If we interpret 'stand in for' in the narrowest possible sense that is a sound instinct. Clearly there must be major differences between our brains and those of guinea pigs. There must even be quite significant differences between our brains and those of other primates, since we have language and they don't. Nevertheless, there must be a way of incorporating animal data.

Different people adopt different strategies. The most optimistic carry on as if rats are small people, talking quite happily about, for example, 'frontal' cortex in the rat as if it were the same as 'frontal' cortex in humans, or about 'visual' cortex as if it were the same in all mammals. In the face of current comparative data this is a difficult position to sustain. Of those who are willing

Concluding remarks

to use animal data, the least optimistic are those who use model systems which they believe are as close to those in the human brain as possible. This group will accept data about the brains of rhesus monkeys but are disdainful of the data obtained from rats since, in their view, monkeys are a good approximation to people while rats are not. Pessimism is justified if we want to be able to study the brain of a non-human species and argue that the data we have obtained can stand as a description of what we would find if we did the same experiment on a person. There is a middle ground, which is to move from attempting to describe a particular nervous system, our own, and ask questions about the way nervous systems in general work.

Problems of cross-species extrapolation surround most of the topics discussed in previous chapters. It is now clear that there are quite major differences between species in the way that their perceptual mechanisms are organized. For example, the description of the mosaic of extrastriate visual areas described in chapter 4 is only really true of monkeys. Extrastriate visual areas are present to varying degrees in other species but it is difficult to spot the homologies between these and the areas in monkeys. The numbers of areas present vary, as do the interconnections between them. The extrastriate visual cortex in the cat, an animal widely used in studies of visual mechanisms, differs from that in monkeys in that it receives a sizeable input directly from the main thalamic visual relay, the dorsal lateral geniculate nucleus. There are some grounds for doubting whether extrapolation from monkeys to humans is entirely justified since the descriptions of the effects of damage to primary visual cortex in the two groups are hard to reconcile.

What has made progress possible is that the structures we are dealing with are analogous, even if they are not homologous. Since they carry out the same basic jobs they are likely to embody fairly consistent design principles which we can generalize from one species to another. To take a concrete example, visual systems are all likely to have mechanisms for edge detection, since this has to precede other stages in the analysis of the image. Computational models tell us that there are only certain ways of detecting edges in an image, so most visual systems are going to contain some mechanism for doing this. The same is true of motion detection. It should be possible to study these basic processes on any animal that has a visual system that is sufficiently well developed for meaningful physiological studies to be carried out.

In so far as we believe them to be based largely on primitive brain mechanisms in the limbic system and brainstem we should be on safer ground when it comes to motivation and emotion (chapters 5 and 6). The neural mechanisms involved should be the same in all mammalian species. On the other hand, there are quite serious differences between species in the way they go about satisfying bodily needs like hunger and thirst, and in the way they react to situations. Rats react to hunger by increasing their food intake while hamsters simply lose weight. Rats drink slowly, taking many minutes to restore water balance after a period of deprivation, while dogs positively gulp down water, restoring water balance almost as soon as they gain access to water. Large predators rarely show many signs of fear whereas similarly sized prey species are nervous in the extreme. Presumably these differences are reflected in differences in their brains.

When it comes to extrapolating to humans one of the major problems has been finding animal models of human problems like obesity, anorexia nervosa, or anxiety. For many years it was held that rats with ventromedial hypothalamus (VMH) lesions offered an excellent model of human obesity and there were many imaginative attempts to draw out parallels between fat rats and obese humans (Schacter 1971). This now looks less likely in the light of more recent knowledge of mechanisms underlying VMH obesity. The parallels between the lateral hypothalamus (LH) syndrome and anorexia nervosa were never sufficiently compelling to persuade people to treat the one as a model of the other. However, that does mean that we are without an animal model of this baffling disorder. When it comes to animal models of anxiety we have an embarrassment of riches, ranging from shock avoidance tasks to the extinction of instrumental responses. The problem here is choosing between them.

Both memory (chapter 7) and consciousness (chapter 9) are difficult to study in animals in the first place because of the way our concepts of them are linked with speech and language. Even if we accept that animals are capable of non-verbal memory and consciousness we have the problem that they are not directly accessible to observation and so cannot be studied directly. The experimental study of these phenomena, like that of cognition in general, has therefore had to rely on the use of inferential methods to get access to them. The groundwork for this approach was developed for human psychology in the 1950s, but its extension to animal behaviour and animal cognitive processes is much more recent. If we are interested in cognitive processes there is clearly no alternative to this approach, but we should be wary of its limitations, which stem from the fact that the interpretation of studies is highly dependent on the quality of the theory underlying the work.

There is a wide consensus among memory researchers that there is more than one type of memory process, and considerable theoretical ingenuity has gone into distinguishing various types. When I started in psychology we were all introduced to the short-term/long-term memory debate. More recently, theorists have distinguished between 'semantic' and 'episodic' memory, and the concepts of 'procedural' and 'working' memory have entered the lists. All of these types of memory are distinct, although some of the distinctions are more subtle than others. If you want to study memory in animals you obviously have to ask yourself: which type of memory? Is it reasonable to draw a distinction between 'semantic' and 'episodic' memory in the case of the rat? We can only really answer this question if the theory that draws the distinction is sufficiently precise to allow us to identify all possible examples of the two types of memory. Unfortunately for us, it is rare for theories developed on human subjects to be so precise as to allow us to make these sorts of judgements. As a consequence, much of the work on animal memory has been based more on analogy than on direct extension of theory. Inevitably, this has led to disputes between researchers. For example, as I mentioned in chapter 7, on memory, a number of researchers have tried to develop animal models of the memory deficits that follow temporal lobe damage in humans but their relevance is disputed because it is unclear how far a monkey's performance on, for example, a visual recognition task really reflects the same psychological processes as human episodic memory. One of the most important points that needs clarifying is the relationship between language and other psychological processes. In nearly all studies of human memory the materials used are verbal and the subject's behaviour is controlled by means of verbal instructions. In all studies of animal memory the materials are non-verbal and the subject's behaviour is controlled by training techniques.

The nature of functional specialization in the brain

The brain is composed of a set of subregions, cortical areas and subcortical nuclei, that can be distinguished from each other on the basis of their afferent and efferent connections, microscopic appearance, and physiological response properties. It is reasonable to assume, as generations of neurologists and physiological psychologists have done, that these elements make different contributions to psychological processes. Connectionist anatomy shows that some of these regions have direct connections with the motor system, others receive relatively direct input from the sense organs, while others stand between the sensory and motor regions. Single unit recording studies show that some areas are intimately linked to specific sensory modalities and some to movement while others have complex response properties that are neither sensory nor motor. Finally, experimental and clinical data have shown repeatedly that damage to different parts of the brain has reliable but distinctive effects on behaviour and cognitive function. Current interest hinges on two issues. The first is the relationship between these sub-areas. Do they all form functionally autonomous modules or are they interconnected so that the functions of one area depend on the integrity of another? The second concerns the most appropriate way of describing the functions of these areas. Is there a direct relationship between the psychological subprocesses identified by experimental psychologists and the functions of particular brain areas?

The existence of anatomically identifiable sub-areas is compatible with a number of models of brain organization, as I discussed in chapter 3. At one extreme we have the possibility of a fully interactive brain in which each sub-area is connected with all of the others. At the other extreme we have a fully modular system in which the number of interconnections between elements is limited. As I pointed out in chapter 3, fully interactive systems are difficult to study using many of the methods of physiological psychology. It is especially difficult to interpret the results of lesions, for example. Fully modular systems are much easier to study, but there are likely to be limits to the degree to which the CNS is organized in this way.

Anatomical and physiological studies suggest that the truth lies midway between these two extremes. It appears that the brain is organized into a number of functional subsystems within which there are numerous cross-linkages and plenty of scope for functional interactions but between which there is little cross-communication. For example, the visual areas of the cortex in primates contain two clusters of areas, one feeding into visual mechanisms in the parietal lobe and one feeding into the visual mechanisms of the temporal lobe. There are some cross linkages between these two sets of mechanisms but they are much less prominent than the linkages within the systems (see chapter 4). In other parts of the brain the clusters clearly extend across a number of levels of the nervous system, involving both cortical and subcortical structures. For example, in the chapter on motivation (chapter 5) we saw that the systems involved in the control of food intake extended from the cerebral cortex down into the brainstem, with mechanisms at all levels contributing to normal behaviour. We also saw evidence, especially from the disconnection studies by Grill and Berridge (1985), that these systems are organized interactively. The control of movement is similarly dependent on systems that extend across the different levels of the brain (chapter 9). Zones in the frontal cortex project to distinguishable zones in the basal ganglia which, in turn, project to distinguishable zones in the brainstem.

Some of the best evidence for modular organization comes from lesion studies on the cerebral cortex. Although there are considerable cross-connections between different parts of the visual cortex, ablation of areas within the secondary zone of visual areas surrounding the primary visual cortex produces surprisingly circumscribed effects (chapter 4). For example, damage to V4 produces impairments in colour perception whereas damage to V5 affects motion detection. Comparable deficits have been observed in brain-damaged humans. Some patients have been found who are incapable of seeing colour, while others have been found to be incapable of perceiving motion. Moving to the opposite end of the brain, we see that there is an extensive experimental literature showing that the effects of ablating the orbital part of the frontal cortex are dissociable from those of ablating the sulcus principalis region (chapter 9).

On the other hand, the effects of lesions made at other levels in the nervous system are much more compatible with the idea of interactive organization. I have already referred to the studies by Grill and Berridge (1985) which suggest that removing the forebrain above the level of the hypothalamus disrupts the operation of mechanisms in the lower parts of the brainstem (chapter 5). In the chapter on emotion we saw that the emotional effects of stimulating parts of the hypothalamus depend on the integrity of other areas in the midbrain. These findings are what one would expect from the level of vertical integration present in the nervous system, as revealed by anatomical studies.

Concluding remarks

It is convenient to use psychological concepts to describe the functions of different parts of the brain, largely because we don't have any alternative terms to apply, but that doesn't mean that the approach is correct. The evidence for this position is mixed at the moment. In some systems the correspondence between psychological constructs and the most appropriate way of describing the functions of particular brain areas is surprisingly good, whereas in others the fit is less impressive. This is not surprising since the quality of the fit is a function of two things, the validity of the approach and the quality of our psychological descriptions.

One way of viewing most of the work done by experimental psychologists this century is that they have been gradually refining our psychological concepts. Whereas once upon a time we had a simple concept of memory, we now distinguish between many forms of memory; short-term versus long-term storage, episodic versus semantic, and so on. Whereas we once talked of perception we now talk of depth perception, colour perception, and object recognition as psychologically distinctive processes. Thanks to the rigour with which this work has been carried out we can be confident about the validity of many of these distinctions. We can attempt to relate these subprocesses to particular brain areas, secure in the knowledge that our psychological distinctions are valid.

The fit between psychological concepts and the functions of particular neural regions is probably best in the visual system. As we saw in chapter 4, there are a number of distinctive areas in the prestriate cortex that have been characterized by their microscopic appearance, inputs, and single cell response properties. Each area appears to specialize in processing a particular attribute of the visual scene. For example, in V4 in primates the cells are colour-selective, while in V5 they are movement-selective. These physiological findings suggest that different attributes of the visual environment are being processed independently of each other, a prediction confirmed by a number of recent psychophysical studies showing, for example, that information about colour doesn't seem to activate the mechanisms involved in motion perception and that depth and colour can be attended to independently of each other.

When we move away from the visual system the position becomes altogether more problematic. Take memory, for example. There is some clinical evidence that different attributes of memory are affected differentially by brain damage. In the amnesic syndrome there is a complex pattern of memory loss in which the patients retain fairly good short-term storage but are very bad at a range of long-term memory tasks, although they can still learn a variety of skills. There is still some debate about whether the breakdown of memory follows precisely the demarcation lines drawn between memory processes by experimental psychologists (chapter 7). Furthermore, it is unlikely that any of these losses are due to destruction of the brain's memory store, since memory is probably a distributed function anyway. Instead, the best evidence we have at the moment indicates that the impairments seen in these patients are due to interference with a property of a memory store that remains otherwise intact.

Even if we cannot ascribe memory to a particular neural mechanism there is at least the possibility of describing memory dysfunctions in terms of the constructs of experimental psychology. With many other forms of brain damage the situation is much more clouded. Let us take the work on the limbic system discussed in chapters 6 and 9 as our example. In chapter 6 we looked at the work that had been done on the hippocampus since Papez first suggested that it had a role in emotion. The range of deficits produced by lesions of the hippocampus, and the range of conditions under which it is possible to activate hippocampal cells, is truly remarkable. As a consequence there have been few totally successful attempts at describing the functions of this mysterious brain region. Undoubtedly it is important for spatial ability but there are many other findings that suggest it has other functions as well, and the case for its involvement in anxiety is equally convincing. The frontal association cortex remains equally mysterious. Damage produces a number of highly characteristic deficits but again the range is so great it is difficult to identify any common thread to the results (chapters 6 and 9). We are left with the conclusion that the behavioural functions of these areas are not describable in current psychological terms.

The challenge of cognitive psychology

The rediscovery of cognitive processes in psychobiology is a welcome trend. It has influenced the way we work in four ways. The first is that people are now directly putting effort into understanding how those systems might work. The second is that people are reconsidering the functions of brain areas in the light of the possibility that they have cognitive functions. The third is the development of more realistic models of how behaviour is controlled. Finally, we have had to develop new methods for studying behaviour.

The central problem of cognitive psychology concerns the processes involved in the representation of knowledge. For many years people have been describing the properties of these representational mechanisms. Recently there have been some theoretical developments that have started to give us real insights into how these representational processes might be carried out. These models are sufficiently detailed to generate algorithms for simulating representational processes and to specify the sort of neural mechanisms that could implement them. The problem of how representation might be achieved is engrossing students of both perception and memory. Network theory is currently proving the most attractive possibility and recent years have seen some convincing demonstrations of the power of this approach to simulate a variety of cognitive activities. What worries the skeptics is that these simulations may not bear any relationship to what actually happens in the brain, since the nervous system may use entirely different mechanisms to achieve the same ends. This isn't an entirely empty criticism. After all, both people and

Concluding remarks

cars are capable of moving under their own power, but one wouldn't get many insights into human locomotion by studying a Ford Sierra. As Marr (1982) points out, a good model must not only simulate what we do, it must also simulate the way that we do it and be compatible with what is known about the neural apparatus with which we do it.

If we apply these tests, the case for network theory comes out as 'unproven' at the moment. It hasn't actually failed against any of the three criteria, but that is largely because the approach hasn't yet been tested to the full. On the first count, networks can carry out some surprisingly sophisticated cognitive operations (Rumelhart, Hinton, and Williams 1986), thus showing the potential to simulate a range of cognitive abilities. However, the range of situations in which the approach has been applied is limited and it is too soon to say whether it will fulfill its early promise. On the second count, there have been few serious attempts to test out network models against real human behaviour in the way that has been done for computational models of visual perception. For example, we know that a particular type of network can be trained to learn about family relationships but we don't know whether this model makes the same types of errors as humans do when answering questions about their families, nor do we know whether it takes the same relative (no pun intended) amounts of time to answer different questions. From what I can understand of the model it will probably fail on this second point because its parallel organization is so strong there are unlikely to be any major differences in response times for retrieving different bits of information. On the other hand, humans probably do take more time to tell you who their mother's cousin is than to tell you who their brother is, simply because they retrieve information serially. On the third count, the nervous system does have the sort of parallel organization that would allow it to function like a network and many of the effects of brain damage look very much like what you would get if a network system were damaged. It remains to be seen whether these similarities are anything other than superficial. However, it is only a matter of time before people come up with detailed models of how networks could be embodied in the CNS so that we can subject the approach to rigorous tests at this level.

Whatever the outcome of the debate on network theory, the notion of representation has affected how we view different parts of the nervous system. Take, for example, the limbic system. For years psychologists have taken it for granted that these structures are intimately bound up with emotional experience and behaviour, but alternative viewpoints have emerged recently. As we saw in chapter 6, on emotion, there is a growing body of evidence to show that many parts of the limbic system are involved in cognitive operations, representing properties of the environment, such as the time and place of salient events, rather than controlling or embodying emotion.

Representation has also affected models of how behaviour is controlled. For example, physiological psychologists have struggled for many years to build models of motivational processes based almost entirely on feedback processes,

Concluding remarks

in which the organism is enjoined to do whatever is necessary to eliminate the difference between its current bodily state and a set point for some variable within the internal environment, such as the concentration of glucose in the blood stream. These feedback models work quite well for animals that have been heavily deprived of something essential like water or food and then placed in a monotonous environment. They do not work well for non-deprived animals working in a more naturalistic environment, in which animals will eat and drink even though they have no measurable need for food and water. Models that incorporate representational processes are much more successful in accounting for behaviour under these conditions (Toates 1986).

This approach does leave a number of unanswered questions. The most important one concerns the way in which representations get translated into movements. Right from the start of this century the hard-line behaviourists criticized mentalists on the grounds that the latter couldn't explain how mental events could influence a physical entity, the body. Behavioural models that incorporate representations run straight into the same problem, or at least they appear to. From the point of view of the psychobiologist the solution to this problem is to recognize that 'representation' is, in fact, a shorthand for a process which has yet to be specified fully at the neural level. Once that has been done we will be able to talk about neural events controlling movements, with which we will be more comfortable. Nevertheless, the issue of behavioural control does raise the important point that it is not sufficient to demonstrate the existence of representational processes or even to describe how they might be implemented in the brain. We also need to specify how the mechanisms concerned interact with each other to control behaviour, a point discussed in chapter 9.

Behaviour in the real world

The problem with psychobiology, as with all other sciences, is that we are trying to make statements about what is going on in the real world on the basis of evidence derived from extremely artificial laboratory situations. In order to move between one and the other we need three things. First, we need a good, realistic description of what actually happens in the real world, as opposed to in the laboratory. Second, we need a good theory aimed at explaining what happens in the real world. Finally, we need suitable experimental paradigms for testing the predictions of our theories under controlled conditions. How far do the different areas of psychobiology I have discussed in this book stood up to these tests?

Recent work on visual perception (chapter 4) has made great strides in meeting these requirements. Scientists like Julesz (1971), working in the tradition of Gestalt psychology, have extended our descriptions of visual perception quite significantly in the past twenty years, giving us a firm foundation on which to build theories. Computational theorists like Marr (1982) and like Poggio (Poggio, Torre, and Koch 1985) have begun to fill in the second level, giving us detailed algorithms for carrying out a range of perceptual processes ranging from segregating figure and ground to determining the direction of movement of objects in the visual field. We still lack a detailed model of how these elementary properties of objects are combined into representations of the objects themselves, but progress is being made there as well. These models are sufficiently detailed to make testable predictions about the types of neural mechanisms that should mediate them and many of these predictions are supported by both neurophysiological and behavioural studies carried out under laboratory conditions, thus satisfying the third requirement.

Turning to motivation (chapter 5), this area was, for many years, much less satisfactory. This was largely because scientists moved into theory-making before obtaining an adequate description of what they were trying to explain. It is only recently, for example, that we have acquired a good working description of the variables that actually control food and water intake, and even now there are areas of uncertainty, such as the role of blood glucose level in the initiation of hunger. Much of this state of affairs can be traced to the preoccupation with homeostatic imbalances as the source of all motivation. We have now got to the stage where workers like Toates (1986) can construct systems models of motivation processes that specify the main controlling variables and the way they must interact to model natural consummatory behaviour. From the point of view of the psychobiologist this sort of model is really the first stage in a long and arduous process of giving flesh to the controllers present in it. For example, a systems model will tell you that feedback from the stomach is integrated with, say, blood glucose level to determine your immediate hunger level. What it doesn't tell you is how blood glucose and stomach distention are measured by the body, where the integration of the two signals takes place, or how the output of this integrator connects to the motor system.

There is a further, and much more serious, problem with even the most enlightened biological approaches to motivation, which is that they ignore the fact that the primary source of most human motivation lies in the social environment rather than in homeostatic imbalances arising from within the body. It is possible, in principle, to derive a systems model for social motives but this has yet to be done convincingly. We certainly know little or nothing about the neural systems that might be involved in this sort of motivation.

Workers on emotion (chapter 6) have generally been aware of the need to explain what happens in the natural environment and many of them have been especially concerned with pathological levels of emotional states, such as occur in anxiety, depression, and mania. Unfortunately, descriptive work in this area has not always been that good. Instead, many workers have concentrated on laboratory models of emotional states without a full appreciation of what really happens. In the case of pathological emotional states the models are often remote from the phenomena they are supposed to relate to. For example, in his challenging book on the septo-hippocampal system, Gray (1982) argues that behaviours that are sensitive to benzodiazepines are all good models of anxiety, since human anxiety is selectively controlled by these drugs. In the case of normal emotions these laboratory models are often highly artificial, often constraining the behaviour of the subjects to the point at which their behaviour may not be in any way representative of natural behaviour. In the absence of good descriptive work it is not surprising that theories of emotion have proved so problematic.

Our descriptions of memory processes are now very good (chapter 7). There are a number of clear-cut distinctions between memory subprocesses that can be made on the basis of reliable experimental findings. The real problem with memory is the lack of a comprehensive theory that can accommodate the data we already have. Certainly, at the present time there is no theory that is sufficiently well articulated for us to be able to extract testable predictions about its likely neural mechanisms. Not surprisingly, psychobiologists interested in memory have abandoned the idea of explaining the whole of memory in a single theory and have tended, instead, to focus on model systems of the neural processes likely to be involved. Workers like Kandel and Lynch, operating in this tradition, have made great strides in unravelling the cellular mechanisms involved in the synaptic changes believed to underpin memory (Hawkins and Kandel 1984; Teyler and DiScenna 1987). What we still lack is a model of how the cells that use these mechanisms could be put together to produce some approximation to human memory.

Our interest in the development of behaviour (chapter 8) has largely been driven by real world events such as the perceptual abnormalities seen in children raised with restricted or distorted sensory input. This has been one of the success stories of psychobiology in that clinicians have provided us with excellent descriptions of the developmental abnormalities, while the physiologists have developed detailed models of how these abnormalities might arise. When we move away from developmental abnormalities to normal development the situation is not so good. For example, although we have a good description of the neural basis of song development in song-birds the state of our knowledge surrounding the development of human language is less satisfactory. However, given the complexity of language this is scarcely surprising and I mention it here not as a criticism but to draw my readers' attention to work that remains to be done.

Consciousness (chapter 9) remains one of the most contentious areas of psychology but it is a healthy sign that people are beginning to talk about it again. Our descriptions of consciousness have not advanced much in recent years and most of us rely on our own commonsense, introspective notions when we try to evaluate theories. There are a number of provocative theories of consciousness around but, at present, none of them is sufficiently well developed to give many hints of how it is mediated by the brain.

Parting comments

In this book I have tried to do two things: to outline the main questions that psychobiology is trying to answer and to give a snapshot of the field that gives the reader an idea of how those questions are currently being answered. Undoubtedly the questions are going to be refined in the years to come and the answers that are given may change out of all recognition. On the other hand, the lessons gained from the history of psychobiology suggest that the fundamental issues will not change that much. Some sixty years after Lashley published *Brain Mechanisms of Intelligence* we are still struggling with the problem of whether it is possible to localize memory traces in the nervous system. Indeed, much of our thinking about the localization of memory is still influenced by Lashley's work itself.

One thing I have tried to avoid doing is to give a definitive account of the subject. The area is changing too rapidly, and some of the topics are too complex for proper treatment in a book of this length, for that ever to have been a reasonable ambition. My approach throughout has been to use the literature to illustrate arguments in the hope that, armed with the questions I have put into their heads, my readers can go out and tackle the rest of the literature in a similarly quizzical way. Remember that a theory is only good if it can explain your daily experiences, a theory is only as good as the last experiment that failed to refute it, and an experiment is only as good as the theory it tries to test.

References

Adametz, J.H. (1959) 'Rate of recovery of functioning in cats with rostral reticular lesions', *J. Neurosurg.*, 16, 85–97.
Alexander, G.E., DeLong, M.R., and Strick, P.L. (1986) 'Parallel organization of functionally segregated circuits linking basal ganglia and cortex', *Ann. Rev. Neurosci.*, 9, 357–81.
Allison, T. and Cicchetti, D.V. (1976) 'Sleep in mammals: ecological and constitutional correlates', *Science*, 194, 732–5.
Ashe, J.H. and Nachman, M. (1980) 'Neural mechanisms in taste aversion learning', *Progress in Psychobio. and Physiol. Psychol.*, 9, 233–62.
Barbur, J.L., Ruddock, K.H., and Waterfield, V.A. (1980) 'Human visual responses in the absence of the geniculo-calcarine projection', *Brain*, 103, 905–28.
Barlow, H.B. (1982) 'General principles: the senses considered as physical instruments', in H.B. Barlow and J.D. Mollon (eds) *The Senses*, Cambridge, Cambridge University Press, 1–33.
Barlow, H.B. (1985) 'The twelfth Bartlett memorial lecture: the role of single neurons in the psychology of perception', *Quart. J. Exp. Psychol.*, 37A, 121–45.
Bauer, J.H. and Cooper, R.M. (1964) 'The effects of posterior cortical lesions on performance of a brightness discrimination', *J. Comp. Physiol. Psychol.*, 58, 84–92.
Bellows, R.T. (1939) 'Time factors in water drinking in dogs', *Amer. J. Physiol.*, 125, 87–97.
Berger, T.W. (1984) 'Long-term potentiation of hippocampal synaptic transmission affects rate of behavioural learning', *Science*, 224, 627–30.
Bjorklund, A., Stenevi, U., Dunnett, S.B., and Gage, F.H. (1982) 'Cross- species neural grafting in a rat model of Parkinson's disease', *Nature*, 298, 652–4.
Blakemore, C. (1977) *Mechanics of the Mind*, Cambridge, Cambridge University Press.
Blakemore, C. and Cooper, G.F. (1970) 'Development of the brain depends on the visual environment', *Nature*, 228, 477–8.
Blakemore, C. and VanSluyters, R.C. (1973) 'Experimental creation of unusual neuronal properties in visual cortex of kitten', *Nature*, 246, 506–8.
Blasdel, G.G., Mitchell, D.E., Muir, D.W., and Pettigrew, J.D. (1977) 'A physiological and behavioural study in cats of the effect of early visual experience with contours of a single orientation', *J. Physiol. (Lond.)*, 265, 615–36.
Blasdel, G.G. and Salama, G. (1986) 'Voltage-sensitive dyes reveal a modular organization in monkey striate cortex', *Nature*, 321, 579–85.
Blaza, S. (1983) 'Brown adipose tissue in man: a review', *J. R. Soc. Med.*, 76, 213–16.
Blythe, I.M., Bromley, J.M., Kennard, C., and Ruddock, K.H. (1986) 'Visual discrimination of target displacement remains after damage to striate cortex in humans', *Nature*, 320, 619–21.

References

Bolhuis, J.J., Fitzgerald, R.E., Dijk, D.K., and Koolhaas, J.M. (1984) 'The corticomedial amygdala and learning in an agonistic situation in the rat', *Physiol. Behav.*, 32, 575-9.
Bures, J., Buresova, O., and Huston, J. (1976) *Techniques and Basic Experiments for the Study of Brain and Behaviour*, Amsterdam, Elsevier.
Burns, B.D. (1968) *The Uncertain Nervous System*, London, Arnold.
Caan, W., Perrett, D.I., and Rolls, E.T. (1984) 'Responses of striatal neurons in the behaving monkey. 2. Visual processing in the caudal neostriatum', *Brain Res.*, 290, 53-65.
Calvin, W.H. (1987) 'The brain as a Darwin machine', *Nature*, 330, 33-4.
Campion, J., Latto, R., and Smith, Y.M. (1983) 'Is blindsight an effect of scattered light, spared cortex, and near threshold vision?' *Behav. Brain Sci.*, 6, 422-86.
Cannon, W.B. (1927) The James-Lange theory of emotions: a critical examination and an alternative theory', *Amer. J. Psychol.*, 39, 106-24.
Cannon, W.B. (1947) *The Wisdom of the Body*, London, Kegan Paul.
Carew, T.J. and Sahley, C.L. (1986) 'Invertebrate learning and memory: from behaviour to molecules', *Ann. Rev. Neurosci.*, 9, 435-87.
Carlson, N.R. (1986) *Physiology of Behaviour*, 3rd edn, Boston, Allyn & Bacon.
Casagrande, V.A. and Diamond, I.T. (1974) 'Ablation study of the superior colliculus in the tree shrew (*Tupaia glis*)', *J. Comp. Neurol.*, 156, 207-38.
Changeaux, J.-P. (1985) *Neuronal Man: The Biology of Mind*, New York, Pantheon.
Chomsky, N. (1959) 'Review of verbal behaviour by B.F. Skinner', *Language*, 35, 26-58.
Clark, G.A., McCormick, D.A., Lavond, D.G., and Thompson, R.F. (1984) 'Effects of lesions of cerebellar nuclei on conditioned behavioural and hippocampal neuronal responses', *Brain Res.*, 291, 125-36.
Cooper, R.M., Battistella, J.A., and Rath, A.M. (1981) 'Dorsal midline thalamus, pretectum and responses to diffuse light in the rat', *Physiol. Behav.*, 26, 873-86.
Cowey, A. (1968) 'Discrimination', in L. Weiskrantz (ed.) *Analysis of Behavioural Change*, New York, Harper & Row, 189-238.
Cowey, A. (1982) 'Sensory and non-sensory visual disorders in man and monkeys', in D.E. Broadbent and L. Weiskrantz (eds) *The Neuropsychology of Cognitive Function*, London, Royal Society, 3-13.
Cowey, A., Henken, D.B., and Perry, V.H. (1982) 'Effects on visual acuity of neonatal or adult tectal ablation in rats', *Exp. Brain Res.*, 48, 149-52.
Crespi, L.P. (1942) Quantitative variation of incentive and performance in the white rat', *Amer. J. Psychol.*, 55, 467-517.
Dean, P. (1980) 'Recapitulation of a theme by Lashley? Comment on Wood's simulated lesion experiments', *Psychol. Rev.*, 87, 470-3.
Dean, P. (1982) 'Analysis of visual behaviour in monkeys with inferotemporal lesions', in D.J. Ingle, M.A. Goodale, and R.J.W. Mansfield (eds) *Analysis of Visual Behaviour*, Cambridge, Mass., MIT Press, 587-628.
DeLong, M.A., Georgopolous, A.P., Crutcher, M.D., Mitchell, S.J., Richardson, R.T., and Alexander, G.E. (1984) 'Functional organization of the basal ganglia: contributions of single-cell recording studies', in *Functions of the Basal Ganglia*, Ciba Foundation Symposium, 107, London, Pitman, 64-82.
Diamond, I.T. and Hall, W.C. (1969) 'Evolution of neocortex', *Science*, 164, 251-62.
Donchin, E. (1984) *Cognitive Psychophysiology. Event-related Potentials and the Study of Cognition*, Hillsdale, New Jersey, Erlbaum.
Donoghue, J.P. and Wise, S.P. (1982) 'The motor cortex of the rat: cytoarchitecture and microstimulation mapping', *J. Comp. Neurol.*, 212, 76-88.
Eccles, J.C. (1973) *The Understanding of the Brain*, New York, McGraw-Hill.

References

Edwards, A.E. and Hill, R.A. (1967) 'The effect of data characteristics on theoretical conclusions concerning the physiology of emotion', *Psychosom. Med.*, 29, 303–11.

Enroth-Cugell, C. and Robson, J.G. (1966) 'The contrast sensitivity of retinal ganglion cells of the cat', *J. Physiol. (Lond.)*, 187, 512–52.

Epstein, A.N. (1971) 'The lateral hypothalamic syndrome: its implications for the physiological psychology of hunger and thirst', *Progress in Physiol. Psychol.*, 4, New York, Academic Press, 263–317.

Espinoza, S.G. and Thomas, H.C. (1983) 'Retinotopic organization of striate and extrastriate visual cortex in the hooded rat', *Brain Res.*, 272, 137–44.

Evarts, E.V. (1962) 'Activity of neurons in visual cortex of the cat during sleep with low voltage fast EEG activity', *J. Neurophysiol.*, 25, 812–16.

Evarts, E.V. (1964) 'Temporal patterns of discharge of pyramidal tract neurons during sleep and waking in the monkey', *J. Neurophysiol.*, 27, 152–71.

Evarts, E.V., Kimura, M., Wurtz, R.H., and Hikosaka, O. (1984) 'Behavioural correlates of activity in basal ganglia neurons', *Trends in Neurosci.*, 7, 447–53.

Ewert, J.P. (1980) *Neuroethology*, Heidelberg, Springer-Verlag.

Farley, J. and Alkon, D.L. (1985) 'Cellular mechanisms of learning, memory, and information storage', *Ann. Rev. Neurosci.*, 36, 419–94.

Finger, S. (1978) 'Lesion momentum and behaviour', in S. Finger (ed.) *Recovery from Brain Damage: Research and Theory*, New York, Plenum, 135–64.

Fitzsimons, J.T. (1971) 'The physiology of thirst: a review of the extraneural aspects of the mechanisms of drinking', in *Progress in Physiol. Psychol.*, 4, New York, Academic Press, 119–201.

Fox, P.T., Mintun, M.A., Raichle, M.E., Miezin, F.M., Allman, J.M., and VanEssen, D.C. (1986) 'Mapping human visual cortex with positron emission tomography', *Nature*, 323, 806–9.

Friedman, M.I. and Stricker, E.M. (1976) 'The physiological psychology of hunger: a physiological perspective', *Psychol. Rev.*, 83, 409–31.

Fuster, J.M. (1973) 'Unit activity in prefrontal cortex during delayed-response performance: neuronal correlates of transient memory', *J. Neurophysiol.*, 36, 61–78.

Gabriel, M., Foster, K., Orona, E., Saltwick, S.E., and Stanton, M. (1980) 'Neuronal activity of cingulate cortex, anteroventral thalamus, in hippocampal formation and discriminative conditioning: encoding and extraction of the significance of conditional stimuli', *Progress in Psychobiol. and Physiol. Psychol.*, 9, 125–31.

Gaffan, D. (1977) 'Monkeys' recognition memory for complex pictures and the effect of fornix transection', *Quart. J. Exp. Psychol.*, 29, 505–14.

Gallistel, C.R., Shizgal, P., and Yeomans, J.S. (1981) 'A portrait of the substrate for self-stimulation', *Psychol. Rev.*, 88, 228–73.

Gazzaniga, M. (1985) *The Social Brain. Discovering the Networks of the Mind*, New York, Basic Books.

Geiselman, P.J. (1987) 'Carbohydrates do not always produce satiety: an explanation of the hunger-stimulating effects of hexoses', *Progress in Psychobiol. and Physiol. Psychol.*, 12, 1–46.

Gellman, R.S. and Miles, F.A. (1985) 'A new role for the cerebellum in conditioning', *Trends in Neurosci.*, 8, 181–2.

Geschwind, N. (1965) 'Disconnexion syndromes in animals and man. I', *Brain*, 88, 237–94.

Glickstein, M., May, J., and Mercier, B. (1985) 'Corticopontine projection in the Macaque: the distribution of labelled cortical cells after large injections of horseradish peroxidase in the pontine nuclei', *J. Comp. Neurol.*, 125, 343–59.

Goelet, P., Castellucci, V.F., Schacher, S., and Kandel, E.R. (1986) 'The long and the short of long-term memory – a molecular framework', *Nature*, 322, 419–22.

References

Goldberg, M.E. and Robinson, D.L. (1978) 'Visual system: superior colliculus', in R.B Masterton (ed.) *Handbook of Behavioural Neurobiology*, vol. 1, New York, Plenum, 119–64.

Goldman, P.S. (1974) 'An alternative to developmental plasticity: heterology of CNS structures in infants and adults', in D.G. Stein, J.J. Rosen, and N. Butters (eds) *Plasticity and Recovery of Function*, New York, Academic Press, 149–74.

Goodwin, F.K. (1984) 'The biology of depression: conceptual issues', *Adv. Biochem. Psychopharmacol.*, 39, 11–26.

Gormezano, I. and Kehoe, E.J. (1975) 'Classical conditioning: some methodological and conceptual issues', in W.K. Estes (ed.) *Conditioning and Behaviour Theory. Handbook of Learning and Cognition*, vol. 2, Hillsdale, New Jersey, Erlbaum, 143–79.

Gray, J.A. (1982) *The Neuropsychology of Anxiety: an Enquiry into the Functions of the Septo-hippocampal System*, Oxford, Oxford University Press.

Gray, R. and Johnston, D. (1987) 'Noradrenaline and β-adrenoreceptor agonists increase activity of voltage-dependent calcium channels in hippocampal neurons', *Nature*, 327, 620–2.

Gregory, R.L. (1961) 'The brain as an engineering problem', in W.H. Thorpe and O.L. Zangwill (eds) *Current Problems in Animal Behaviour*, Cambridge, Cambridge University Press, 307–30.

Grill, H.J. and Berridge, K.C. (1985) 'Taste reactivity as a measure of the neural control of palatability', *Progress in Psychobiol. and Physiol. Psychol.*, 11, 1–61.

Gross, C.G. (1973) 'Inferotemporal cortex and vision', *Progress in Physiol. Psychol.*, 5, 77–123.

Gross, C.G. and Weiskrantz, L. (1964) 'Some changes in behaviour produced by lateral frontal lesions in the macaque', in J.M. Warren and K. Akert (eds) *The Frontal Granular Cortex and Behaviour*, New York, McGraw-Hill, 74–101.

Grossman, S.P. (1963) 'Chemically induced epileptiform seizures in the cat', *Science*, 142, 409–11.

Grossman, S.P. (1967) *A Textbook of Physiological Psychology*, New York, Wiley.

Grossman, S.P. (1975) 'The role of the hypothalamus in the regulation of food and water intake', *Psychol. Rev.*, 82, 200–24.

Guillery, R.W. (1973) 'The effect of lid closure upon the growth of cells in the dorsal lateral geniculate nucleus of kittens', *J. Comp. Neurol.*, 148, 417–22.

Hawkins, R.D. and Kandel, E.R. (1984) 'Is there a cell-biological alphabet for simple forms of learning?', *Psychol. Rev.*, 91, 375-91.

Hebb, D.O. (1955) 'Drives and the CNS (conceptual nervous system)', *Psychol. Rev.*, 62, 243-54.

Hernandez-Peon, R., Scherrer, H., and Velasco, M. (1956) 'Central influences on afferent conduction in the somatic and visual pathways', *Acta Neurol. Lat.-Amer.*, 2, 8-22.

Hess, W.R. (1957) *The Functional Organization of the Diencephalon*, New York, Grune & Stratton.

Hetherington, A.W. and Ranson, S.W. (1940) 'Hypothalamic lesions and adiposity in the rat', *Anat. Rec.*, 78, 149–72.

Heywood, C.A. and Cowey, A. (1985) 'Disturbances of pattern and hue discrimination following removal of the "colour" area in primates', *Neurosci. Lett.*, 21, S11.

Hildreth, E.C. and Koch, C. (1987) 'The analysis of visual motion: from computational theory to neuronal mechanisms', *Ann. Rev. Neurosci.*, 10, 477–533.

Hirsch, H.V.B. and Leventhal, A. (1978) 'Functional modification of the developing visual system', in M. Jacobson (ed.) *Handbook of Sensory Physiology, IX, Development of Sensory Systems*, Berlin, Springer-Verlag, 279–335.

Hirsch, H.V.B. and Spinelli, D.N. (1970) 'Visual experience modifies distribution of horizontally and vertically oriented receptive fields in cats', *Science*, 168, 869–71.
Hopkins, W.F. and Johnston, D. (1984) 'Frequency-dependent noradrenergic modulation of long-term potentiation in the hippocampus', *Science*, 226, 350–1.
Horn, G. (1985) *Memory, Imprinting and the Brain. An Enquiry into Mechanisms*, Oxford, Oxford University Press.
Hubel, D.H. and Wiesel, T.N. (1959) 'Receptive fields of single neurones in the cat's striate cortex', *J. Physiol. (Lond.)*, 148, 574–91.
Hubel, D.H. and Wiesel, T.N. (1963) 'Receptive fields of cells in striate cortex of very young, visually inexperienced kittens', *J. Neurophysiol.*, 26, 994–1002.
Hubel, D.H. and Wiesel, T.N. (1970) 'The period of susceptibility to the physiological effects of unilateral eye closure in kittens', *J. Physiol. (Lond.)*, 206, 419–36.
Hubel, D.H. and Wiesel, T.N. (1977) 'Binocular cortical organization in primates, and its modifiability', *Proc. R. Soc., Series B*, 198, 1–59.
Humphreys, G.W. and Riddoch, M.J. (1987) *To See but not to See: A Case Study of Visual Agnosia*, London, Erlbaum.
Jacobs, B.L. (1987) 'Brain monoaminergic unit activity in behaving animals', *Progress in Psychobiol. and Physiol. Psychol.*, 12, 171–206.
Jacobson, M. (1978) *Developmental Neurobiology*, New York, Plenum.
James, W. (1884) 'What is an emotion?', *Mind*, 9, 188–205.
James, W. (1950) *Principles of Psychology, I*. New York, Dover.
James, W. and Lange, G.C. (1922) *The Emotions*, New York, Williams & Wilkins.
Jaynes, J. (1982) *The Origin of Consciousness in the Breakdown of the Bicameral Mind*, Harmondsworth, Penguin.
Jeannerod, M. (1985) *The Brain Machine: The Development of Neuropsychological Thought*, Cambridge, Mass., Harvard University Press.
Johnson-Laird, P.N. (1987) 'Connections and controversy', *Nature*, 300, 12–13.
Jones, E.G. and Powell, T.P.S. (1973) 'Anatomical organization of the somatosensory cortex', in A. Iggo (ed.) *Handbook of Sensory Physiology, II, Somatosensory System*, Berlin, Springer-Verlag, 579–620.
Jouvet, M. (1967) 'Neurophysiology of the states of sleep', *Physiol. Rev.*, 47, 117–77.
Julesz, B. (1971) *Foundations of Cyclopean Perception*, Chicago, University of Chicago Press.
Kaas, J.H. (1982) 'The segregation of function in the nervous system: why do sensory systems have so many subdivisions?', *Contributions to Sensory Physiol.*, 7, 201–40.
Karplus, J.P. and Kreidl, A. (1969) 'The brain and the sympathetic nerve. II. A sympathetic centre in the diencephalon', in K.H. Pribram (ed.) *Brain and Behaviour 1, Mood, States and Mind*, Harmondsworth, Penguin, 61–84.
Kasamatsu, T. (1983) 'Neuronal plasticity maintained by the central norepinephrine system in the cat visual cortex', *Progress in Psychobiol. and Physiol. Psychol.*, 10, 1–112.
Keesey, R.E. and Powley, T.L. (1986) 'The regulation of body weight', *Ann. Rev. Psychol.*, 37, 109–33.
Kennard, M.A. (1942) 'Cortical reorganization of motor function', *Arch. Neurol. Psychiat.*, 48, 227–40.
Kennedy, C., Gillin, J.C., Mendelson, W., Suda, S., Minaoka, M., Ito, M., Nakamura, R.K., Storch, F.I., Pettigrew, K., Mishkin, M., and Sokoloff, L. (1982) 'Local cerebral glucose utilization in non-rapid eye movement sleep', *Nature*, 297, 325–7.
Kesner, R.P. and DiMattia, B.V. (1987) 'Neurobiology of an attribute model of memory', *Progress in Psychobiol. and Physiol. Psychol.*, 12, 207–77.
Killackey, H., Snyder, M. and Diamond, I.T. (1971) 'Function of striate and temporal cortex in the tree shrew', *J. Comp. Physiol. Psychol.*, 74, Monogr. Suppl. 1.

References

Kilmer, W.L., McCulloch, W.S., and Blum, J. (1969) 'Embodiment of a plastic concept of the reticular formation', in L.D. Porter (ed.) *Biocybernetics of the Central Nervous System*, London, Churchill, 213–60.

Kluver, H. and Bucy, P.C. (1939) 'Preliminary analysis of the functions of the temporal lobe in monkeys', *Arch. Neurol. Psychiat.*, 42, 979–1000.

Knudsen, E.I., DuLac, S., and Esterly, S.D. (1987) 'Computational maps in the brain', *Ann. Rev. Neurosci.*, 10, 41–65.

Koffka, K. (1935) *Principles of Gestalt Psychology*, New York, Harcourt, Brace, & World.

Kohler, C., Schwartz, R., and Fuxe, K. (1979) 'Intrahippocampal injections of ibotenic acid provide histological evidence for a neurotoxic mechanism different from kainic acid', *Neurosci. Lett.*, 15, 223–8.

Kolb, B. and Whishaw, I.Q. (1985) *Fundamentals of Human Neuropsychology*, 2nd edn, New York, Freeman.

Lacey, J. (1968) 'Somatic response patterning and stress: some revisions of activation theory', in M.H. Appley and R. Trumbull (eds) *Psychological Stress*, New York, Appleton-Century-Crofts, 14–42.

Land, E.H. (1974) 'The retinex theory of colour vision', *Proc. R. Inst. Gt. Brit.*, 47, 23–58.

Land, P.W. and Simons, D.J. (1985) 'Cytochrome oxidase staining in the rat SmI barrel cortex', *J. Comp. Neurol.*, 238, 225–35.

Lashley, K.S. (1950) 'In search of the engram', *Symposia Soc. Exper. Biol.*, 4, 454–82.

Lashley, K.S. (1951) 'The problem of serial order in behaviour', in K.S. Jeffress (ed.) *Cerebral Mechanisms in Behaviour: the Hixon Symposium*, New York, Wiley, 112–36.

Lashley, K.S. (1963) *Brain Mechanisms of Intelligence*, New York, Dover.

Lavond, D.G., Steinmetz, J.E., Yokaitis, M.H., and Thompson, R.F. (1987) 'Reacquisition of classical conditioning after removal of cerebellar cortex', *Exp. Brain Res.*, 67, 569–93.

LeDoux, J.E. (1986) 'Brain, mind and language', in D.A. Oakley (ed.) *Brain and Mind*, London, Methuen, 197–216.

Legg, C.R. (1983) 'Interspecific comparisons and the hypothetico-deductive approach', in G.C.L. Davey (ed.) *Animal Models of Human Behaviour*, Chichester, Wiley, 225–45.

Legg, C.R. (1988) 'The pretectum and visual discrimination learning in the hooded rat', *Behav. Brain Res.*, 29, 27–34.

Legg, C.R. and Cowey, A. (1977) 'Effects of subcortical lesions on visual intensity discriminations in rats', *Physiol. Behav.*, 19, 635–46.

Legg, C.R. and Glickstein, M. (1984) 'Cells of origin of the cortico-pontine projections in the rat', *Soc. Neurosci. Abst.*, 10, 288.

Legg, C.R. and Turkish, S. (1983) 'Flicker sensitivity changes after subcortical visual system lesions in the rat', *Behav. Brain Res.*, 10, 311–24.

LeMagnen, J. (1985) *Hunger*, Cambridge, Cambridge University Press.

Lennenberg, E.H. (1967) *The Biological Foundations of Language*, New York, Wiley.

Lennie, P. (1980) 'Parallel visual pathways: a review', *Vision Res.*, 20, 561–94.

Lennie, P. (1981) 'The physiological basis of variations in visual latency', *Vision Res.*, 21, 815–24.

Leonard, C.M. (1969) 'The prefrontal cortex of the rat. I. Cortical projections of the mediodorsal nucleus. II. Efferent connections', *Brain Res.*, 12, 321–43.

LeVay, S., Wiesel, T.N., and Hubel, D.H. (1980) 'The development of ocular dominance columns in normal and visually deprived monkeys', *J. Comp. Neurol.*, 191, 1–51.

References

LeVere, N.P. and LeVere, T.E. (1982) 'Recovery of function after brain damage: support for the compensation theory of the behavioural deficit', *Physiol. Psychol.*, 10, 165–74.

LeVere, T.E. (1980) 'Recovery of function after brain damage. A theory of the behavioural deficit', *Physiol. Psychol.*, 8, 297–308.

Lewis, J.L., LoTurco, J.J., and Solomon, P.R. (1987) 'Lesions of the middle cerebellar peduncle disrupt acquisition and retention of the rabbit's classically conditioned nictitating membrane response', *Behav. Neurosci.*, 101, 151–7.

Lickey, M.E. and Gordon, B. (1983) *Drugs for Mental Illness. A Revolution in Psychiatry*, New York, Freeman.

Lindsley, D.B., Schreiner, L.H., Knowles, W.B., and Magoun, H.W. (1950) 'Behavioural and EEG changes following chronic brain-stem lesions in the cat', *EEG Clin. Neurophysiol.*, 2, 483–98.

Livingstone, M.S. and Hubel, D.H. (1981) 'Effects of sleep and arousal on the processing of visual information in the cat', *Nature*, 291, 554–61.

Livingstone, M.S. and Hubel, D.H. (1984) 'Anatomy and physiology of a colour system in the primate visual cortex', *J. Neurosci.*, 4, 309–56.

Low, W.C., Lewis, P.R., Bunch, S.T., Dunnett, S.B., Thomas, S.R., Iversen, S.D., Bjorklund, A., and Stenevi, U. (1982) 'Function recovery following neural transplantation of embryonic septal nuclei in adult rats with septohippocampal lesions', *Nature*, 300, 260–2.

Luria, A.R. (1973) *The Working Brain*, Harmondsworth, Penguin.

McCleary, R.A. (1966) 'Response-modulating functions of the limbic system: initiation and suppression', *Progress in Psychobiol. and Physiol. Psychol.*, 1, 209–72.

McCormick, D., Steinmetz, J.E., and Thompson, R.F. (1985) 'Lesions of the inferior olivary complex cause extinction of the classically conditioned eyeblink response', *Brain Res.*, 359, 120–30.

McFarland, D. and Houston, A. (1981) *Quantitative Ethology: The State Space Approach*, London, Pitman.

McHaffie, J.G. and Stein, B.E. (1982) 'Eye movements evoked by electrical stimulation in the superior colliculus of rats and hamsters', *Brain Res.*, 247, 243–52.

McHugh, P.R. and Moran, T.H. (1985) 'The stomach: a conception of its dynamic role in satiety', *Progress in Psychobiol. and Physiol. Psychol.*, 11, 197–232.

MacLean, P.D. (1954) 'The limbic system and hippocampal formation: studies in animals and their possible applications to man', *J. Neurosurg.*, 11, 29–44.

McNaughton, B.L. and Morris, R.G.M. (1987) 'Hippocampal synaptic enhancement and information storage within a distributed memory system', *Trends in Neurosci.*, 10, 408–15.

Mandler, G. (1975) *Mind and Emotion*, New York, Wiley.

Marr, D. (1982) *Vision*, San Francisco, Freeman.

Marsden, C.D. (1984) 'Which motor disorder in Parkinson's disease indicates the true motor function of the basal ganglia', in *Functions of the Basal Ganglia*, Ciba Foundation Symposium, 107, London, Pitman, 225–37.

Marshall, J.F. (1985) 'Neural plasticity and recovery of function after brain injury', *Int. Rev. Neurobiol.*, 26, 201–47.

Matsuzawa, T. (1985) 'Use of numbers by a chimpanzee', *Nature*, 315, 57–9.

Maunsell, J.H.R. and Newsome, W.T. (1987) 'Visual processing in monkey extrastriate cortex', *Ann. Rev. Neurosci.*, 10, 363–401.

Mayer, J. (1955) 'Regulation of energy intake and the body weight: the glucostatic and lipostatic hypothesis', *Ann. N. Y. Acad. Sci.*, 63, 15–43.

Mayes, A.R. (1988) *Varieties of Human Memory Disorder*, Cambridge, Cambridge University Press.

References

Meir, R. and Domany, E. (1987) 'Exact solution of a layered neural network model', *Phys. Rev. Lett.*, 59, 359–62.

Merzenich, M.M. and Kaas, J.H. (1980) 'Principles of organization of sensory-perceptual systems in mammals', *Progress in Psychobiol. and Physiol. Psychol.*, 9, 1–42.

Miller, N.E., Bailey, C.J., and Stevenson, J.A.F. (1950) 'Decreased hunger but increased food intake resulting from hypothalamic lesions', *Science*, 112, 256–9.

Milner, B. (1964) 'Some effects of frontal lobectomy in man', in J.M. Warren and K. Akert (eds) *The Frontal Granular Cortex and Behaviour*, New York, McGraw-Hill, 313–34.

Mishkin, M. (1964) 'Perseveration of central sets after frontal lesions in monkeys', in J.M. Warren and K. Akert (eds) *The Frontal Granular Cortex and Behaviour*, New York, McGraw-Hill, 219–41.

Mishkin, M. (1982) 'A memory system in the monkey', *Phil. Trans. R. Soc. Lond.*, 298, 85–95.

Mogenson, G.J. (1987) 'Limbic-motor integration', *Progress in Psychobiol. and Physiol. Psychol.*, 12, 117–70.

Mogenson, G.J. and Phillips, A.G. (1976) 'Motivation: a psychological construct in search of a physiological substrate', *Progress in Psychobiol. and Physiol. Psychol.*, 6, 189–243.

Mohler, C.H. and Wurtz, R.H. (1977) 'Role of striate cortex and superior colliculus in visual guidance of saccadic eye movements in monkeys', *J. Neurophysiol.*, 40, 74–94.

Mollon, J.D. (1982) 'Colour vision and colour blindness', in H.B. Barlow and J.D. Mollon (eds) *The Senses*, Cambridge, Cambridge University Press, 165–91.

Moore, B.O. and Deutsch, J.A. (1985) 'An antiemetic is antidotal to the satiety effects of cholecystokinin', *Nature*, 315, 321–2.

Morgan, C.T. (1943) *Physiological Psychology*, 1st edn, New York, McGraw-Hill.

Morris, R.G.M., Anderson, E., Lynch, G.S., and Baudry, M. (1986) 'Selective impairment of learning and blockade of long-term potentiation by an N-methyl-D-aspartate receptor antagonist, AP5', *Nature*, 319, 774–6.

Morris, R.G.M., Garrud, P., Rawlins, J.N.P., and O'Keefe, J. (1982) 'Place navigation impaired in rats with hippocampal lesions', *Nature*, 297, 681-3.

Morrison, A. (1979) 'Brainstem regulation of behaviour during sleep and wakefulness', *Progress in Psychobiol. and Physiol. Psychol.*, 8, 91–131.

Moruzzi, G. and Magoun, H.W. (1949) 'Brain stem reticular formation and activation of the EEG', *EEG Clin. Neurophysiol.*, 1, 455–73.

Nakayama, K. and Silverman, G.H. (1986) 'Serial and parallel processing of visual feature conjunctions', *Nature*, 320, 264–5.

Nauta, W.J.H. (1946) 'Hypothalamic regulation of sleep in rats', *J. Neurophysiol.*, 9, 285–316.

Nottebohm, F. (1980) 'Brain pathways for vocal learning in birds: a review of the first 10 years', *Progress in Psychobiol. and Physiol. Psychol.*, 9, 85–124.

Novin, D. and VanderWeele, D.A. (1977) 'Visceral involvement in feeding: there is more to regulation than the hypothalamus', *Progress in Psychobiol. and Physiol. Psychol.*, 7, 194–241.

Oakley, D.A. and Eames, L.C. (1986) 'The plurality of consciousness', in D.A. Oakley (ed.) *Brain and Mind*, London, Methuen, 217–51.

O'Keefe, J. and Conway, D. (1978) 'Hippocampal place units in the freely moving rat: why they fire when they fire', *Exp. Brain. Res.*, 31, 573–90.

O'Keefe, J. and Nadel, L. (1978) *The Hippocampus as a Cognitive Map*, Oxford, Oxford University Press.

References

Olds, J., Disterhoft, J.E., Segal, M., Kornblith, C.L., and Hirsh, R. (1972) 'Learning centers of rat brain mapped by measuring latencies of conditioned unit responses', *J. Neurophysiol.*, 35, 202–19.

Olds, J. and Milner, P. (1954) 'Positive reinforcement produced by electrical stimulation of septal area and other regions of rat brain', *J. Comp. Physiol. Psychol.*, 47, 419–27.

Olton, D.S. (1983) 'Memory functions and the hippocampus', in W. Siefert (ed.) *Neurobiology of the Hippocampus*, New York, Academic Press, 335–73.

Ono, T. (1984) 'Single neuron activity in dorsolateral prefrontal cortex of monkey during operant behaviour sustained by food reward', *Brain Res.*, 311, 323–32.

Panksepp, J. (1971) 'Aggression elicited by electrical stimulation of the hypothalamus in albino rats', *Physiol. Behav.*, 6, 321–9.

Panksepp, J. (1982) 'Toward a general psychobiological theory of emotions', *Behav. Brain Sci.*, 5, 407–67.

Papez, J.W. (1939) 'A proposed mechanism of emotion', *Arch. Neurol.*, 38, 725–43.

Parkin, A.J. (1987) *Memory and Amnesia: an Introduction*, Oxford, Blackwell.

Parmeggiani, P. (1979) 'Integrative aspects of hypothalamic influences on respiratory brain stem mechanisms during wakefulness and sleep', in C. VonEuler and H. Lagercrantz (eds) *Central Nervous Control Mechanisms in Breathing*, New York, Pergamon Press, 53–69.

Pasik, P. and Pasik, T. (1982) 'Visual functions in monkeys after total removal of visual cerebral cortex', *Contribs. to Sensory Physiol.*, 7, 147–200.

Patterson, G.F. (1978) 'The gestures of a gorilla: language acquisition in another pongid', *Brain Lang.*, 5, 72–97.

Pavlov, I.P. (1927) *Conditioned Reflexes*, republished (1960), New York, Dover.

Pellegrino, L.J., Pellegrino, A.S., and Cushman, A.J. (1979) *A Stereotaxic Atlas of the Rat Brain*, New York, Plenum.

Perrett, D.I., Rolls, E.T., and Caan, W. (1982) 'Visual neurones responsive to faces in the monkey temporal cortex', *Exp. Brain Res.*, 47, 329–42.

Perrett, D.I., Smith, P.A.J., Potter, D.D., Mistlin, A.J., Head, A.S., Milner, A.D., and Jeeves, M.A. (1985) 'Visual cells in the temporal cortex sensitive to face view and gaze direction', *Proc. R. Soc. Lond. Series B.*, 223, 293–17.

Petrides, M. and Milner, B. (1982) 'Deficits on subject ordered tasks after frontal- and temporal-lobe lesions in man', *Neuropsychologia*, 20, 249–62.

Pettigrew, J.D. (1974) 'The effect of visual experience on the development of stimulus specificity by kitten cortical neurones', *J. Physiol. (Lond.)*, 237, 49–74.

Phillips, C.G., Zeki, S., and Barlow, H.B. (1984) 'Localization of function in the cerebral cortex: past, present and future', *Brain*, 107, 328–61.

Poggio, T., Torre, V., and Koch, C. (1985) 'Computational vision and regularization theory', *Nature*, 317, 314–19.

Powley, T.L. (1977) 'The ventromedial hypothalamic syndrome, satiety, and a cephalic phase hypothesis', *Psychol. Rev.*, 84, 89–126.

Raichle, M.E. (1983) 'Positron emission tomography', *Ann. Rev. Neurosci.*, 6, 249–67.

Rakic, P. (1974) 'Embryonic development of the pulvinar-LP complex in man' in I.S. Cooper, M. Riklan, and P. Rakic (eds) *Pulvinar-LP Complex*, Springfield, C.C. Thomas, 3–25.

Rescorla, R.A. (1975) 'Pavlovian excitatory and inhibitory conditioning', in W.K. Estes (ed.) *Conditioning and Behaviour Theory, Handbook of Learning and Cognition*, 2, Hillsdale, New Jersey, Erlbaum, 7–35.

Rizzolatti, G., Scandalara, C., Matelli, M., and Gentelucci, M. (1981) 'Afferent properties of periarcuate neurons in macaque monkeys. II. Visual responses', *Behav. Brain Res.*, 2, 147–63.

References

Roitblat, H.L. (1982) 'The meaning of representation in animal memory', *Behav. Brain Sci.*, 5, 353–406.
Rolls, B.J. and Rolls, E.T. (1982) *Thirst*, Cambridge, Cambridge University Press.
Rolls, E.T. (1975) *The Brain and Reward*, Oxford, Pergamon.
Rolls, E.T. (1987) 'Information representation, processing and storage in the brain: analysis at the single neuron level', in J.-P. Changeaux and M. Konishi (eds) *Neural and Molecular Mechanisms of Learning*, Berlin, Springer-Verlag.
Rosvold, H.E., Mirsky, A.F., and Pribram, K.H. (1954) 'Influence of amygdalectomy on social behaviour in monkeys', *J. Comp. Physiol. Psychol.*, 47, 173–8.
Rothwell, N.J. and Stock, M.J. (1979) 'A role for brown adipose tissue in diet-induced thermogenesis', *Nature*, 281, 31–5.
Rowell, T. (1972) *Social Behaviour of Monkeys*, Harmondsworth, Penguin.
Rozin, P. (1976) 'The evolution of intelligence and access to the cognitive unconscious', *Progress in Psychobiol. and Physiol. Psychol.*, 6, 245–80.
Rumelhart, D.E., Hinton, G.E., and Williams, R.J. (1986) 'Learning representations by back-propagating errors', *Nature*, 323, 533–6.
Russek, M. (1970) 'Demonstration of the influence of an hepatic glucosensitive mechanism on food intake', *Physiol. Behav.*, 1, 1205–9.
Russell, I.S. (1978) 'Brain size and intelligence: a comparative perspective', in D.A. Oakley and H.C. Plotkin (eds) *Brain, Behaviour and Evolution*, London, Methuen, 126–53.
St James-Roberts, I. (1979) 'Neurological plasticity, recovery from brain insult, and child development', *Advances in Child Dev. and Behav.*, 14, 253–319.
Sarnat, H.B. and Netsky, M.G. (1981) *Evolution of the Nervous System*, 2nd edn, Oxford, Oxford University Press.
Satinoff, E. (1983) 'A reevaluation of the concept of the homeostatic organization of temperature regulation', in E. Satinoff and P. Teitelbaum (eds) *Handbook of Behavioural Neurobiology, vol. 6, Motivation*, New York, Plenum, 443–72.
Schacter, S. (1971) *Emotion, Obesity and Crime*, New York, Academic Press.
Schacter, S. and Singer, J.E. (1962) 'Cognitive, social and physiological determinants of emotional state', *Psychol. Rev.*, 69, 379–99.
Schiller, P.H. and Stryker, M. (1972) 'Single unit recording in superior colliculus of the alert rhesus monkey', *J. Neurophysiol.*, 35, 915–24.
Schneider, G.E. (1967) 'Contrasting visuomotor functions of tectum and cortex in the golden hamster', *Psychol. Forschung*, 31, 52–62.
Schneider, G.E. (1979) 'Is it better to have your brain lesion early? A revision of the "Kennard Principle"', *Neuropsychologia*, 17, 557–83.
Schultze, M.J. and Stein, D.G. (1975) 'Recovery of function in the albino rat following either simultaneous or seriatim lesions of the caudate nucleus', *Exper. Neurol.*, 46, 291–301.
Schwartz, R. and Coyle, J.T. (1977) 'Striatal lesions with kainic acid: neurochemical characteristics', *Brain Res.*, 127, 235–49.
Scott, W.W., Scott, C.C., and Luckhardt, A.B. (1938) 'Observations in the blood sugar level before, during and after hunger periods in humans', *Amer. J. Physiol.*, 123, 243–7.
Scoville, W.B. and Milner, B (1957) 'Loss of recent memory after bilateral hippocampal lesions', *J. Neurol., Neurosurg., Psychiat.*, 20, 11–21.
Sherk, H. and Stryker, M.P. (1976) 'Quantitative study of cortical orientation selectivity in visually inexperienced kitten', *J. Neurophysiol.*, 39, 63–70.
Sherman, S.M. (1985) 'Functional organization of the W-, X-, and Y-cell pathways in the cat: a review and hypothesis', *Progress in Psychobiol. and Physiol. Psychol.*, 11, 233–314.

References

Sherman, S.M. and Spear, P.D. (1982) 'Organization of visual pathways in normal and visually deprived cats', *Physiol. Rev.*, 62, 738–855.

Skinner, B.F. (1957) *Verbal Behaviour*, New York, Appleton-Century-Crofts.

Smith, P.J. and Gibbs, J. (1979) 'Postprandial satiety', *Progress in Psychobiol. and Physiol. Psychol.*, 8, 179–242.

Sokoloff, L., Reivich, M., Kennedy, C., DesRosiers, M.H., Patlak, C.S., Pettigrew, K.D., Sakurada, O., and Shinohara, M. (1977) 'The [14C] deoxy-glucose method for the measurement of local cerebral glucose utilization: theory, procedure and normal values in the conscious and anaesthetized albino rat', *J. Neurochem.*, 28, 897–916.

Sotelo, C. and Alvarado-Mallart, R.M. (1987) 'Embryonic and adult neurons interact to allow Purkinje cell replacement in mutant cerebellum', *Nature*, 327, 421–3.

Spear, P.D. (1979) 'Behavioural and neurophysiological consequences of visual cortex damage', *Progress in Psychobiol. and Physiol. Psychol.*, 8, 45–90.

Sperry, R.W. (1979) 'Consciousness, freewill and personal identity', in D.A. Oakley and H.C. Plotkin (eds) *Brain, Behaviour and Evolution*, London, Methuen, 219–28.

Sprague, J.M., Berlucchi, G, and Rizzolatti, G. (1973) 'The role of the superior colliculus and pretectum in vision and visually guided behaviour', in R. Jung (ed.) *Handbook of Sensory Physiology, vol. VII/3, Central Processing of Visual Information*, Part B, Berlin, Springer-Verlag, 27–111.

Steffens, A.B. (1969) 'Blood glucose and FFA levels in relation to the meal pattern in the normal rat and the ventromedial hypothalamic lesioned rat', *Physiol. Behav.*, 4, 215–25.

Stein, L. (1968) 'Chemistry of reward and punishment', in D.H. Efron (ed.) *Psychopharmacology, A Review of Progress*, Washington, US Government Printing Office, 105–23.

Stellar, E. (1954) 'The physiology of motivation', *Psychol. Rev.*, 61, 5–22.

Steriade, M. (1983) 'Cellular mechanisms of wakefulness and slow-wave sleep', in A.R. Mayes (ed.) *Sleep: Mechanisms and Functions*, London, Van Nostrand, 161–216.

Stone, J. (1983) *Parallel Processing in the Visual System: The Classification of Retinal Ganglion Cells and its Impact on the Neurobiology of Vision*, New York, Plenum.

Stricker, E.M. (1983) 'Brain neuropsychology and the control of food intake', in E. Satinoff and P. Teitelbaum (eds) *Handbook of Behavioural Neurobiology, vol. 6, Motivation*, New York, Plenum, 329–65.

Stricker, E.M. and Zigmond, M.J. (1976) 'Recovery of function after damage to central catecholamine-containing neurons: a neurochemical model for the lateral hypothalamic syndrome', *Progress in Psychobiol. and Physiol. Psychol.*, 6, 121–88.

Strongman, K.T. (1978) *The Psychology of Emotion*, New York, Wiley.

Stryker, M.P. and Sherk, H. (1975) 'Modification of cortical orientation selectivity in the cat by restricted visual experience: a reexamination', *Science*, 190, 904–6.

Teuber, H.L. (1955) 'Physiological psychology', *Ann. Rev. Psychol.*, 6, 267–96.

Teuber, H.L. (1964) 'The riddle of frontal lobe function in man', in J.M. Warren and K. Akert (eds) *The Frontal Granular Cortex and Behaviour*, New York, McGraw-Hill, 410–44.

Teyler, T.J. and DiScenna, P. (1987) 'Long-term potentiation', *Ann. Rev. Neurosci.*, 10, 131–61.

Thompson, R. (1965) 'Centrencephalic theory and interhemispheric transfer of visual habits', *Psychol. Rev.*, 72, 385–98.

Thompson, R.F. (1983) 'The engram found? Initial localization of the memory trace for a basic form of associative learning', *Progress in Psychobiol. and Physiol. Psychol.*, 10, 167–96.

Thorndike, E.L. (1913) *The Psychology of Learning (Educational Psychology II)*, New York, Teachers' College.

References

Toates, F. (1986) *Motivational Systems*, Cambridge, Cambridge University Press.
Tolman, E.C. (1932) *Purposive Behaviour in Animals and Man*, New York, Appleton-Century-Crofts.
Travers, J.B. and Norgren, R. (1983) 'Afferent projections to the oral motor nuclei in the cat', *J. Comp. Neurol.*, 220, 280–98.
Tretter, F., Cynader, M., and Singer, W. (1975) 'Modification of direction selectivity of neurons in the visual cortex of kittens', *Brain Res.*, 84, 143–9.
Tsumoto, T., Hagihara, K., Sato, H., and Hata, Y. (1987) 'NMDA receptors in the visual cortex of young kittens are more effective than those of adult cats', *Nature*, 327, 513–14.
Ullman, S. (1986) 'Artificial intelligence and the brain: computational studies of the visual system', *Ann. Rev. Neurosci.*, 9, 1–26.
Ungerleider, L.G. and Mishkin, M. (1982) 'Two cortical visual systems', in D.J. Ingle, M.A. Goodale, and R.J.W. Mansfield (eds) *Analysis of Visual Behaviour*, Cambridge, Mass., MIT Press, 549–86.
Ursin, H. (1965) 'The effect of amygdaloid lesions on flight and defense behaviour in cats', *Exp. Neurol.*, 11, 61–79.
Valenstein, E.S. (1980) 'Historical perspective', in E.S. Valenstein (ed.) *The Psychosurgery Debate: Scientific, Legal and Ethical Perspectives*, San Francisco, Freeman, 11–54.
Valverde, F. (1962) 'Reticular formation of the albino rat's brainstem. Cytoarchitecture and corticofugal connections', *J. Comp. Neurol.*, 119, 25–53.
Victor, M., Adams, R.D., and Collins, G.H. (1971) *The Werkicke-Korsakoff Syndrome*, Oxford, Blackwell.
Vinogradova, O.S. (1975) 'Functional organization of the limbic system in the process of registration of information: facts and hypotheses', in R.L. Isaacson and K.H. Pribram (eds) *The Hippocampus: 2. Neurophysiology and Behaviour*, New York, Plenum, 1–70.
VonMonakow, C. (1969) 'Diaschisis', in K.H. Pribram (ed.) *Brain and Behaviour, 1. Mood, States and Mind*, Harmondsworth, Penguin, 27–36.
Walter, W.G., Cooper, R., Aldridge, V.J., McCallum, W.C., and Winter, A.L. (1964) 'Contingent negative variation: an electric sign of sensorimotor association and expectancy in the human brain', *Nature*, 203, 380–4.
Warrington, E.K. (1982) 'Neuropsychological studies of object recognition', in D.E. Broadbent and L. Weiskrantz (eds) *The Neuropsychology and Cognitive Function*, London, Royal Society, 15–33.
Warrington, E.K. and Weiskrantz, L. (1982) 'Amnesia: a disconnection syndrome?', *Neuropsychologia*, 20, 233–48.
Weiskrantz, L. (1968) 'Treatments, inferences and brain function', in L. Weiskrantz (ed.) *Analysis of Behavioural Change*, New York, Harper & Row, 400–14.
Weiskrantz, L. (1980) 'Varieties of residual experience', *Quart. J. Exp. Psychol.*, 32, 365–86.
Weiskrantz, L. and Cowey, A. (1970) 'Filling in the scotoma: a study of residual vision after striate cortex lesions in monkeys', *Progress in Physiol. Psychol.*, 3, 327–60.
Weiskrantz, L. and Warrington, E.K. (1979) 'Conditioning in amnesic patients', *Neuropsychologia*, 17, 187–94.
Whitfield, I.C. (1979) 'The object of the sensory cortex', *Brain, Behav., Evol.*, 16, 129–54.
Wiesel, T.N. (1982) 'Postnatal development of the visual cortex and the influence of the environment', *Nature*, 299, 583–91.

Wild, H.M., Butler, S.R., Carden, D., and Kulikowski, J.J. (1985) 'Primate cortical area V4 important for colour constancy but not wavelength discrimination', *Nature*, 313, 133–5.
Wood, C.C. (1978) 'Variations on a theme by Lashley: lesion experiments on the neural model of Anderson, Silverstein, Ritz and Jones', *Psychol. Rev.*, 85, 582–91.
Wood, C.C. (1980) 'Interpretation of real and simulated lesion experiments', *Psychol. Rev.*, 87, 474–6.
Woodruff, G. and Premack, D. (1981) 'Primative mathematical concepts in the chimpanzee: proportionality and numerosity', *Nature*, 293, 568–70.
Woodruff-Pak, D.S., Lavond, D.G., and Thompson, R.F. (1985) 'Trace conditioning: abolished by cerebellar nuclear lesions but not lateral cerebellar cortex aspirations', *Brain Res.*, 348, 249–60.
Woody, C.D. (1986) 'Understanding to cellular basis of memory and learning', *Ann. Rev. Psychol.*, 37, 433–93.
Yeo, C.H., Hardiman, M.J., and Glickstein, M. (1985) 'Classical conditioning of the nictitating membrane response in the rabbit. II. Lesions of the cerebellar cortex', *Exp. Brain Res.*, 60, 99–113.
Yeo, C.H., Hardiman, M.J., and Glickstein, M. (1986a) 'Classical conditioning of the nictitating membrane response of the rabbit. IV. Lesions of the inferior olive', *Exp. Brain Res.*, 63, 81–92.
Yeo, C.H., Hardiman, M.J., and Glickstein, M. (1986b) 'Middle cerebellar peduncle lesions impair classical conditioning of the eye-blink response', *Neurosci. Lett.*, Suppl. 26, S559.
Zeigler, H.P. (1983) 'The trigeminal system and ingestive behaviour', in E. Satinoff and P. Teitelbaum (eds) *Handbook of Behavioural Neurobiology, vol. 6, Motivation*, New York, Plenum, 265–327.
Zeigler, H.P., Jacquin, M.F., and Miller, M.G. (1985) 'Trigeminal orosensation and ingestive behaviour in the rat', *Progress in Psychobiol. and Physiol. Psychol.*, 11, 63–196.
Zeki, S. (1983a) 'Colour coding in the cerebral cortex: the reaction of cells in monkey visual cortex to wavelength and colours', *Neurosci.*, 9, 741–66.
Zeki, S. (1983b) 'Colour coding in the cerebral cortex: the responses of wavelength-selective and colour-coded cells in the monkey visual cortex to changes in wavelength composition', *Neurosci.*, 9, 767–82.
Zihl, J. (1980) '"Blindsight": improvement of visually guided eye movements by systematic practice in patients with cerebral blindness', *Neuropsychologia*, 18, 71–7.
Zihl, J. and VonCramon, D. (1985) 'Visual field recovery from scotoma in patients with post-geniculate damage. A review of 55 cases', *Brain*, 108, 335–65.
Zilles, K. and Wree, A. (1985) 'Cortex: areal and laminar structure', in G. Paxinos (ed.) *The Rat Nervous System, vol.1, Forebrain and Midbrain*, Sydney, Academic Press, 375–415.

Author index

Adametz, J.H. 181
Adams, R.D. 130
Aldridge, V.J. 184
Alexander, G.E. 186
Alkon, D.L. 140
Allison, T. 178
Alvardo-Mallart, R.M. 168
Ashe, J.H. and Nachman, M. 119

Bailey, C.J. 98
Barbur, J.L. 65
Barlow, H.B. 9, 54, 77
Battistella, J.A. 67
Bauer, J.H. 67, 128
Bellows, R.T. 91
Berger, T.W. 142
Berridge, K.C. 90, 102, 107, 195
Bjorklund, A. 168
Blakemore, C. 154–6, 172
Blasdel, G.G. 156
Blaza, S. 96
Blum 173
Blythe, I.M. 65
Bromley, J.M. 65
Bucy, P.C. 113, 118
Bunch, S.T. 168
Bures, J. 35, 36
Buresova, O. 35, 36
Burns, B.D. 54
Butler, S.R. 75

Caan, W. 77, 187
Calvin, W.H. 175
Campion, 65
Cannon, W.B. 6, 7, 105, 107, 124, 190
Carden 75
Carew, T.J. 140, 141
Carlson, N.R. 36, 41, 109

Casagrande, 66
Castellucci, V.F. 141
Changeaux, J.-P 149
Chomsky, N. 158
Cichetti, D.V. 178
Clark, G.A. 136
Collins, G.H. 136
Conway, D. 35, 53
Cooper, G.F. 154
Cooper, R. 184
Cooper, R.M. 67
Cowey, A. 30, 37, 66, 67, 75, 78, 128, 164
Cowey, A. 164
Coyle, J.T. 41
Crespi, L.P. 5
Crutcher, M.D. 186
Cushman, A.J. 41
Cynader, M. 155

Dean, P. 10, 36, 38, 42, 43, 78
DeLong, M.A. 186
Deutsch, J.A. 93
Diamond, I.T. 28, 65, 66, 73
DiMattia, B.V. 32, 117, 119, 135, 138, 176
DiScenna, P. 141, 201
Domany, E. 131
Donchin, E. 52
Donoghue, J.P. 50, 51
DuLac, S. 80
Dunnett, S.B. 168

Eames, L.C. 188
Eccles, J.C. 171
Edwards, A.E. 108
Enroth-Cugell, C. 15, 64
Epstein, A.N. 98, 101

Author index

Espinoza, S.G. 27
Esterly, S.D. 80
Evarts, E.V. 178, 182, 186
Ewert, J.P. 36

Farley, J. 140
Finger, S. 164, 175
Fitzsimons, J.T. 84–6
Foster K. 112, 137
Friedman, M.I. 84, 87–9, 101
Fuster, J.M. 184
Fuxe, K. 40

Gabriel, M. 112, 137
Gaffan, D. 117, 131
Gage, F.H. 120
Gallistel, C.R. 123
Garrud, P. 115
Gazzaniga, M. 12, 18, 48, 174–8, 188
Geiselman, P.J. 90
Gellman, R.S. 133
Genetlucci, M. 184
Georgopolous, A.P. 186
Geschwind, N. 48
Gibbs, J. 49, 92, 93
Gillin, J.C. 180
Glickstein, M. 27, 122, 133, 134, 183
Goelet, P. 141
Goldberg, M.E. 28, 66, 67
Goldman, P.S. 163
Goodwin, F.K. 111
Gordon, B. 110
Gormezano, I. 134
Gray, J.A. 113, 114, 116, 117, 201
Gray, R. 143
Gregory, R.L. 42, 43
Grill, H.J. 90, 102, 107, 195
Gross, C.G. 10, 63, 77, 121
Grossman, S.P. 83, 98, 105, 107, 112, 113, 118
Guillery, R.W. 152, 153

Hall, W.C. 28
Hardiman, M.J. 133, 134
Hawkins, R.D. 4, 29, 140, 141, 201
Head, A.S. 77
Hebb, D.O. 103
Henken, D.B. 164
Hernandez-Peon, R. 8
Hess, W.R. 107
Hetherington, A.W. 19
Heywood, C.A. 30, 75

Hikosaka, O. 186
Hildreth, E.C. 74
Hirsch, H.V.B. 150, 154, 156
Hirsh, R. 35
Hopkins, W.F. 143
Horn, G. 159, 160
Houston, A. 97
Hubel, D.H. 14, 27, 31, 76, 150, 151, 154, 155, 178, 180, 182
Humphreys, G.W. 78
Huston, J. 35

Ito, M. 180
Iversen, S.D. 168

Jacobs, B.L. 111, 179
Jacobson, M. 10, 149
James, W. 3, 6, 105, 109, 124, 125, 162, 190
Jaynes, J. 172
Jeannerod, M. 3, 11, 183
Jeeves, M. 77
Johnson-Laird, P.N. 145
Johnston, D. 143
Jouvet, M. 180, 181
Julesz, B. 199

Kaas, J.H. 28, 79
Kandel, E.R. 4, 29, 140, 141, 143, 201
Karplus, J.P. 109
Kasamatsu, T. 157
Keesey, R.E. 83
Kehoe, E.J. 134
Kennard, C. 65
Kennard, M.A. 163
Kennedy, C. 53, 180
Kesner, R.P. 32, 117, 119, 138, 139, 176
Killackey, H. 65
Kilmer, W.L. 173
Kimura, M. 186
Kluver, H. 113, 118
Knowles, W.B. 181
Knudsen, E.I. 80
Koch, C. 60, 74
Koffka, K. 4
Kohler, C. 40, 41
Kolb, B.I.Q. 8–10, 58, 79, 120, 128, 177, 184, 185
Kornblith, C.L. 35
Kreidl, A. 109
Kulikowski, J.J. 75

217

Author index

Lacey, J. 108
Land, E.H. 74–6
Land, P.W. 27
Lange 105, 109, 190
Lashley, K.S. 5, 10, 71, 127, 129, 202
Latto, R. 65
Lavond, D.G. 132, 133, 136
LeDoux, J.E. 188
Legg, C.R. 27, 30, 67, 122
LeMagnen, J. 51, 83, 86–8, 90, 91, 94, 95, 98–100
Lennenberg, E.H. 158
Lennie, P. 54, 70, 71
Leonard, C.M. 28
LeVay, S. 151
Leventhal, A. 150, 156
LeVere, N.P. 128, 129, 166
LeVere, T.E. 128, 129, 166
Lewis, J.L. 133
Lewis, P.R. 158
Lickey, M.E. 110
Lindsley, D.B. 181
Livingstone, M.S. 27, 31, 76, 180, 182
LoTurco, J.J. 133
Low, W.C. 168
Luckhardt, A.B. 86
Luria, A.R. 38, 58, 79, 185
Lynch, G.S. 201

McCallum, W.C. 184
McCleary, R.A. 18, 112, 113
McCormick, D. 134, 136
McCulloch, W.S. 173
McFarland, D. 97
McHaffie, J.G. 29
McHugh, P.R. 49, 92, 93
MacLean, P.D. 108
McNaughton, B.L. 7, 19, 146
Magoun, H.W. 108, 181
Mandler, G. 105, 124
Marr, D. 60, 62, 63, 198, 199
Marsden, C.D. 186
Marshall, J.F. 166–9
Matelli, M. 184
Matsuzawa, T. 176
Maunsell, J.H.R. 27, 30, 64, 72, 73, 76
May, J. 27
Mayer, J. 87
Mayes, A.R. 130
Meir, R.E. 131
Mendelson, W. 180
Mercier, B.E. 27
Merzenich, M.M. 79

Miller, N.E. 98–100
Milner, A.D. 77
Milner, B. 116, 121, 129, 131, 184
Milner, P. 109
Minaoka 180
Mishkin, M. 79, 117, 121, 131, 132, 180, 182, 183
Mistlin, A.J. 77
Mitchell, D.E. 156
Mitchell, S.J. 186
Mogenson, G.J. 98, 113, 119, 183
Mohler, C.H. 47, 66
Mollon, J.D. 13
Moore, B.O. 93
Morgan, C.T. 7
Morris, R.G.M. 7, 19, 115, 131, 139, 142, 143, 146, 176
Morrison, A. 182
Moruzzi, G.H.W. 108, 181
Muir, D.R. 156
Machman, M. 119

Nadel, L. 19, 52, 113, 115
Nakamura, R.K. 180
Nakayama, K. 30
Nauta, W.J.H. 181
Netsky, M.G. 23
Newsome, W.T. 27, 30, 64, 72, 73, 76
Norgren, R. 174
Nottebohm, F. 160
Novin, D. 88

Oakley, D.A. 178, 188
O'Keefe, J. 19, 35, 52, 53, 113, 115
Olds, J. 35, 52, 53, 109, 136
Olton, D.S. 7, 19, 32, 116, 117, 138
Orona, E. 112

Panksepp, J. 109–11, 123, 125
Papez, J.W. 6, 7, 11, 18, 105, 107, 108, 112, 113, 118, 120, 124, 197
Parkin, A.J. 32, 113, 116, 130, 131
Parmeggiani, P. 182
Pasik, P. 65
Pasik, T. 65
Patlak, C.S. 53
Patterson, G.F. 158
Pavlov, I.P. 4, 5, 129, 134
Pellegrino, A.S. 41
Pellegrino, L.J. 41
Perrett, D.I. 77, 187
Perry, V.H. 164
Petrides, M. 121

Author index

Pettigrew, J.D. 154–7
Pettigrew, K. 53, 180
Phillips, C.G. 9, 98
Poggio, T. 60, 200
Potter, D.D. 77
Powley, T.L. 19, 83, 89, 98
Premack, D. 176

Raichle, M.E. 30, 35, 52, 53
Rakic, P. 28
Ranson, S.W. 19, 200
Rath, A.M. 67
Rawlins, J.N.P. 115
Reivich, M. 53
Rescorla, R.A. 129, 135
Richardson, R.T. 186
Riddoch, M.J. 78
Rizzolatti, G. 184
Robinson, D.L. 28, 66, 67
Robson, J.G. 15, 64
Roitblat, H.L. 144
Rolls, B.J. 84–6, 91, 92
Rolls, E.T. 49, 51, 77–9, 84–6, 91, 92, 110, 123, 124, 146, 187
Rosvold, H.E. 119
Rothwell, N.J. 95, 96
Rowell, T. 176
Rozin, P. 37
Ruddock, K.H. 65
Rumelhart, D.E. 145, 198
Russek, M. 88
Russell, I.S. 23, 24

Sahley, C.L. 140, 141
Sakurada, O. 53
Saltwick, S.E. 112
Sarnat, H.B. 23
Satinoff, E. 103
Scandalara, C. 184
Schacher, S.F. 141
Schacter, S. 105, 112, 124, 125, 193
Scherrer, H. 8
Schiller, P.H. 50, 51
Schneider, G.E. 43, 163
Schreiner, L.H. 181
Schultze, M.J. 165
Schwartz, R. 40, 41
Scott, C.C. 86
Scott, W.W. 86
Scoville, W.B. 116, 129, 131
Segal, M. 35
Sherk, H. 35, 155, 156
Sherman, S.M. 64, 70, 71, 150

Shinohara, M. 53
Shizgal, P. 123
Silverman, G.H. 30
Simons, D.J. 27
Singer, J.E. 105, 112, 125
Singer, W. 155
Skinner, B.F. 83, 158, 183
Smith, P.A.J. 77
Smith, P.J. 49, 92, 93
Smith, Y.M. 65
Snyder, M. 65
Sokoloff, L. 53, 180
Solomon, P.R. 133
Sotelo, C. 168
Spear, P.D. 150, 165–7
Sperry, R.W. 171
Spinelli, D.N. 154
Sprague, J.M. 66, 67
Stanton, M. 112, 137
Steffens, A.B. 86
Stein, B.E. 29
Stein, D.G. 165
Stein, L. 110
Steinmetz 133, 134
Stellar, E. 7, 19, 82, 83, 91, 97, 98
Stenevi, U. 168
Steriade, M. 179, 180
Stevenson, J.A.F. 98
Stock, M.J. 95, 96
Stone, J. 64
Storch, F.I. 180
Stricker, E.M. 51, 84, 87–9, 98, 101, 169
Strongman, K.T. 105, 106, 108
Stryker, M.P. 35, 50, 51, 155, 156
Suda, S. 180

Teuber, H.L. 43, 122, 185
Teyler, T.J. 141, 201
Thomas, H.C. 27
Thomas, S.R. 168
Thompson, R. 173
Thompson, R.F. 56, 116, 132–7, 139
Thorndike, E.L. 4, 7
Toates, F. 95, 103, 199, 200
Tolman, E.C. 5
Torre, V. 60
Travers, J.B. 174
Tretter, F. 155
Tsumoto, T. 157

Ullman, S. 60
Ungerleider, L.G. 79

Author index

Ursin, H. 118

Valenstein, E.S. 22, 108, 120, 185
Valverde, F. 174
VanDerWeele, D.A. 88
VanSluyters, R.C. 155
Velasco, M. 8
Victor, M. 130
Vinogradova, O.S. 115
VonCramon, D. 65, 165

Walter, W.G. 184
Warrington, E.K. 32, 79, 116–18, 126
Weiskrantz, L. 10, 17, 32, 42, 43, 65, 66, 116–18, 121, 126, 128
Whishaw, I.Q. 8–10, 79, 120, 128, 177, 184, 185
Whitfield, I.C. 31, 79

Wiesel, T.N. 14, 150–5
Wild, H.M. 75
Winter, A.L. 184
Wise, S.P. 50, 51, 54
Wood, C.C. 44, 45, 47
Woodruff, G. 176
Woodruff-Pak 132
Woody, C.D. 135, 136
Wree, A. 40
Wurtz, R.H. 47, 66, 186
Yeo, C.H. 133, 134, 139, 146
Yeomans, J.S. 123
Yokaitis, M.H. 133
Zeigler, H.P. 98, 100, 101
Zeki, S. 9, 74–6
Zigmond, M.J. 51, 98, 169
Zihl, J. 65, 165
Zilles, K. 40

Subject index

2-deoxy-glucose 53
6-OHDA 157, 167

accessory optic system 63
agnosias 132
Alzheimer's disease 162
amnesic syndrome 196
amphetamine 110
Amygdala 108, 113, 131; epileptiform activity 118
analogy 26
anorexia nervosa 193
anxiety 193, 200
aperture effect 73
archistriatum 160
arousal 8, 108, 112
associative learning 44
attack 118; affective 109, 123; predatory 110, 123
attention 8
auditory 79
autonomic nervous system 6, 108, 119, 176, 190; sympathetic 6
avoidance learning 112, 113
axon sparing lesions 41

basal ganglia 168, 183, 186, 195
basal nucleus of Meynert 132, 143
behaviourism 3, 11, 20, 103, 126, 144, 158, 183, 199
binocularity 150
blindsight 65
blood glucose 51, 55, 199
blood salt 55
brainstem 26

caudate nucleus 139, 165
cellular dehydration 51

central motive state 7
cerebellum 132, 135, 179, 183
chlorpromazine 110
cholecystokinin 92, 93
cognitive map 19, 138
collateral sprouting 168
columns 31
commissurotomy 174–6
common ancestor 26
complex cell 31
computerized axial tomography 41
conditioning: classical 4, 11, 20, 56, 126, 127, 129, 132, 134, 140, 142; instrumental 11, 66, 114, 126, 127
consciousness 12, 126, 193
contingent negative variation 184
corpus callosum 48, 177
cortex 40, 41, 129; association 10, 58, 179; auditory 31, 80; barrel 27; Broca's area 17, 18, 164; cerebral 6, 8, 9, 17, 20, 26, 107, 127, 173, 180; cingulate 6, 107, 108, 112, 137, 138; frontal 9, 10, 17, 22, 28, 40, 108, 120, 163, 183, 184, 191, 195; inferotemporal 38; middle temporal area 72, 73; motor 5, 9, 28, 40, 50, 135, 163, 183, 186; parietal 40, 58, 77, 79, 80, 183; premotor 184; prestriate 30, 58, 72, 74, 75, 77, 79, 80, 189; primary visual 17, 26, 58, 64, 66, 67, 71–4, 75, 79, 80, 150, 155, 164, 189; secondary visual 64; sensory 179; somatosensory 28, 79; superior temporal sulcus 77; temporal 58, 77–80, 113, 129, 183; visual 5, 14, 26–8, 40, 43, 47, 64–6, 154, 166, 169, 182, 183, 191, 192, 195
cytochrome oxidase 26, 76

Subject index

cytochrome oxidase blobs 27, 31, 76, 155

delayed response task 120, 121, 163
deneravation supersensitivity 169
depression 16, 200; antidepressants 110, 111
deprivation, alternating 153; monocular 150, 157
Descartes 3, 4
diaschisis 165
difference of Gaussians 61, 63
disconnection 48, 55
dominance hierarchy 119
double dissociation 43, 44
dreaming 181

electroencephalogram 11, 52, 178, 184
emergent properties 171
emotion 6, 105, 190, 195, 200; anger 118; anxiety 111; approach 111; cognitive approach 106; fear 111, 118; human 109; panic 111; rage 111; secondary 111
equipotentiality 127
event related potentials 52
evolution 23; common ancestor 23, 25; common features 25; convergent 25, 30, 31; divergent 24
extinction 114, 134
eye-movements, saccadic 29, 66

feature detection 14
fornix 6

gestalt 4, 5

habituation 140
hippocampus 6, 18, 32, 33, 56, 107, 108, 113, 131, 132, 135, 138, 141, 167, 197
homeostasis 103, 182, 187, 200
homology 25, 26, 30
hunger 49, 192
Huntington's chorea 186
hyperstriatum 159, 160
hypoglossal nerve 160
hypothalamus 7, 51, 87, 97, 102, 107, 109, 111, 119, 181, 191, 195; antero-ventral 100; lateral 20, 83, 88, 97, 98, 101, 102, 110, 123, 193; lesions 2; mammillary bodies 6, 107, 131; medial forebrain bundle 110; nigro-striatal bundle 110; stimulation 109; suprachiasmatic nucleus 63; ventromedial 19, 40; ventromedial nucleus 83, 97–100, 109, 123, 193

imprinting 149, 159
internal environment 84

Korsakoff syndrome 131.

language 17, 48, 49, 56, 149, 162, 172, 176, 201
latent-learning 5
lesion 34–6, 39
lesion momentum 164
limbic system 7, 11, 12, 107, 124, 131, 192, 197, 198
localization of function 8, 9, 12
locus coeruleus 110
long-term potentiation 141

mania 200
mass action 127
memory 10, 32, 37, 38, 113, 114, 116, 185, 193, 196; Alzheimer's disease 130; Amnesic syndrome 130; anterograde amnesia 130; episodic 117, 194; Korsakoff syndrome 130; procedural 117; recognition 117, 194; reference 117; representation 144; retrograde amnesia 130; semantic 117; short term 20, 121; visual 10; working 19, 33, 117
mentalism 199
metabolic activity 53–5, 180
metabolic correlates 35
microelectrodes 50, 53
mid-brain reticular formation 108, 124, 179–81
monoamine oxidase inhibitors 110
monocular segment 153
motivation 6, 7, 190, 200; angiotensin 86; arterio-venous difference 87; blood glucose 86, 94, 99; brown adipose tissue 96; cellular dehydration 85; control systems 95; diabetes 87, 99; dietary induced thermogenesis 96; dietary variety 95; drinking 51, 83, 84, 91; drives 7, 104; eating 51, 83, 84, 86, 195; extracellular thirst 86; glucose availability 87, 99, 100; glucose utilization 87; insulin 86, 89, 99,

Subject index

101; intestine 92; liver 88; meal size 94; oral metering 93, 94; osmolarity 84; palatability 90, 100; pancreas 99; renin 86; secondary drives 103; stomach 92; temperature regulation 103; time-sharing 97; two-centre theory 19, 82, 91, 97

N-methyl-d-aspartate 142
neophobia 119
networks 78, 131, 145, 190, 197, 198
neurotransmitter 10, 11, 140; acetylcholine 132, 143, 167, 168; catecholamine 51, 110; dopamine 110; indoleamine 110; noradrenaline 110, 143, 157, 160; serotonin 110, 141
nictitating membrane response 132, 142
nuclear magnetic resonance 41

obesity 193
object recognition 10
ocular dominance 31, 150, 157
ocular dominance columns 152
optic tract 63
orientation selectivity 31, 150, 154

pain 120
Parallel Distributed Processing 145
Parkinson's disease 186
perception 38, 196, 200; aperture effect 72; colour 13, 30, 57, 74, 75; computational approach 59; edge 192; edge detection 60; grandmother cell 77, 78; motion 74, 192; retinex theory 74; spatial frequency analysis 15; visual 13, 14, 37, 38, 64
periaqueductal grey 109
phylogenetic scale 16
place learning 114
plasticity 148
positron emission tomography 53, 55
pretectum 63, 66, 67
protein 141, 159; synthesis 159
pseudodepression 185
pseudopsychopathy 185
psychosurgery 22, 185; prefrontal leucotomy 22, 120
punishment 109, 114

radial arm maze 32, 115, 138, 168
Raphe nuclei 111, 179, 180
rapid eye-movements 181

receptive field 31, 68, 72, 154
recording 35, 36, 51
reflex 3, 6, 176, 183; cephalic phase 89, 90
regeneration 167
reinforcement 4, 5, 7, 16, 32, 110, 114, 158; intracranial self-stimulation 110, 123; partial 114
representation 197
response perseveration 121
reticular formation 135, 173, 174, 182
retina 13; ganglion cell 59, 64, 69; off-centre ganglion cell 62; on-centre ganglion cell 62; W-cells 64, 68–70; X-cells 64, 68–71; Y-cells 64, 68, 70, 71
reward 109

satiation 51
Scotoma 66
scotoma 65
sensitive period 160
sensitization 140
septum 114, 168
serial lesion effect 164
single unit recording 13, 35, 52, 54, 136
sleep 178
somatosensory 79, 80
song learning 149, 160
spasticity 163
spatial ability 121, 176
spatial frequency 68
spatial orientation 10
speech 9, 10, 17
split-brain 49
squint 153, 157
stereotaxic technique 41, 50
stimulation 34–6; chemical 49; electrical 49
stimulus-response 4, 5, 7, 144
stomach 49, 51
substantia nigra 168
superior colliculus 28, 43, 47, 50, 63, 66, 67, 102, 135, 163
symbol generation test 184
symbolic communication 158
synapse 10, 11
system substitution 167

testosterone 161
thalamus 40, 41, 107; anterior 131; anterior nucleus 107; dorsal lateral geniculate body 63, 64, 80, 192;

223

Subject index

dorsal lateral geniculate nucleus 64; dorsomedial nucleus 28; lateral geniculate body 27, 151; lateral posterior nucleus 164; posterior nucleus 136; ventral lateral geniculate body 63, 107
thirst 192
tranquilisers, major 110; minor 114; valium 114
transplanation 168
tricyclics 110

trigeminal nerve 101, 174
trigger-features 14

ventral tegmental area 110
ventricles 8
verbal generation test 184
vertical integration 12
vicariation 166

zero crossing 60, 63